How to Live by Grace

Also by Wojciech Giertych, O.P.,
from EWTN Publishing:

The Mystery of Divine Love

The Spark of Faith

HOW TO LIVE
⸺ BY ⸺
GRACE

Divine Fruitfulness in Human Action

BY WOJCIECH GIERTYCH, O.P.
THEOLOGIAN OF THE PAPAL HOUSEHOLD

TRANSLATED BY
JUSTYNA KRUKOWSKA

EWTN Publishing, Inc.
Irondale, Alabama

Copyright © 2025 by Wojciech Giertych

Printed in the United States of America. All rights reserved.

Cover design by LUCAS Art & Design, Jenison, MI.

Cover image: *Sermon on the Mountain* (1896), by Karoly Ferenczy, WikiArt, public domain.

Excerpt from *I Want to See God: A Practical Synthesis of Carmelite Spirituality* by Pere Marie-Eugène, O.C.D. © 1953 The FIDES Publishers Association. Used with permission of the publisher, Christian Classics™, an imprint of Ave Maria Press®, Inc., Notre Dame, Indiana 46556; www.avemariapress.com.

Unless otherwise noted, Scripture references are taken from the Catholic Edition of the Revised Standard Version of the Bible, copyright 1965, 1966 by the Division of Christian Education of the National Council of the Churches of Christ in the United States of America. Used by permission. All rights reserved.

Excerpts from the English translation of the *Catechism of the Catholic Church* for use in the United States of America copyright © 1994, United States Catholic Conference, Inc.—Libreria Editrice Vaticana. English translation of the *Catechism of the Catholic Church: Modifications from the Editio Typica* copyright © 1997, United States Conference of Catholic Bishops—Libreria Editrice Vaticana.

No part of this book may be reproduced, stored in a retrieval system, or transmitted in any form, or by any means, electronic, mechanical, photocopying, or otherwise, without the prior written permission of the publisher, except by a reviewer, who may quote brief passages in a review.

EWTN Publishing, Inc.
5817 Old Leeds Road, Irondale, AL 35210
Distributed by Sophia Institute Press, Box 5284, Manchester, NH 03108.

paperback ISBN 978-1-68278-413-6
ebook ISBN 978-1-68278-414-3

Library of Congress Control Number: 2024952374

First printing

To my students

Contents

Preface to the English Edition ix

Introduction 1

1. The Complementarity of Nature and Grace
   in the Christian Life 7

2. God, Who Bestows Happiness 41

3. The Fecundity of God in Human Acts 55

4. The Moral Qualification of Human Acts 95

5. Liberating Freedom 145

6. Let Us Drink, to Conscience First,
   and to the Pope Afterward! 157

7. Conscience or Superego? 177

8. Integrating the Emotions into Moral Life 189

9. Faith Holds on to the Holy Spirit, Who Then Leads 241

10. Tire Valve, Template, or Yeast? 303

    About the Author 321

Preface to the English Edition

Long before Pope Francis remarked that theology should not be just worked out at a desk but should be contextual,[1] I was convinced that teaching the principles of moral theology has to serve life — in particular, the spiritual life. This is because — as voices calling for renewal in the post–Vatican II period have made it clear — the old separation of ethical reflection from the spiritual life has to be dropped. A purely academic reflection on theoretical moral quandaries and on principles that are necessary to resolve them is insufficient. The challenges of life have to be tackled within a true relationship with the living God, and therefore, moral teaching, which is a form of preaching, has to dispose toward the grace of the Holy Spirit and has to show how that grace may be used in practice.

Even though Pope Francis calls us to listen to what is happening on the streets, in life "out there," the prime context of my theological thinking is not the encounter of theology with developments in science, with social and political dramas, or with bioethical issues that need to be dealt with in the light of ethical principles. For me, year after year, it was the faces of my students in class that made my theological research and teaching contextual. Those students came from a world often marked by brokenness; they were young, at a stage of life when they needed formation, so as to attain Christian maturity. Some, seeing the chaos of an unstable society, were tempted to lock themselves into a rigid protective shell. In time, they discovered that

---

[1] Apostolic letter *Ad theologiam promovendam* (November 1, 2023).

they needed to be formed interiorly and that salvation is not in external rules but in the grace of God, which shapes the heart, personal liberty, and the creativity of charity.

I began my teaching in Kraków, addressing young men who were preparing for the priesthood in the Dominican Order. This was after the election of Pope St. John Paul II and the collapse of communism, and the Church was very popular in Poland. The seminaries were flooded with men who were wondering what to do with their lives, and the priesthood seemed a respected option. But in their years of formation, their motivations had to be clarified, the scars of the *homo sovieticus* had to be dealt with, and personal liberty had to be formed, so that their choices would be authentic and mature. In time, many of these men left the order, hopefully grateful for the years that helped them to grow in faith and maturity. And those who remained Dominicans are now serving the Church.

Since 1994, I have been teaching in Rome, in the Angelicum, where I have students from all over the world, but primarily from the United States, Africa, and Asia. Among them are seminarians, religious sisters, and young laypeople, in their early twenties. They also are at the stage in life when they need to structure themselves, forming their thinking, convictions, decisions, and feelings in accordance with a real relationship with God, maintained and nourished daily.

It was for them that I prepared my course on fundamental moral theology, offering much of what I had seen was necessary in Poland. Over the years, I have published several books on various aspects of my teaching, writing them all in my own language, Polish. Now I begin working on their translation into English.

This book, which represents the core of my course, is not, therefore, an academic work addressed to colleagues involved in research and university teaching. It is intended for students who are shaping their lives and for pastors and chaplains who are helping them in their pilgrimage of faith.

I based my theological synthesis primarily on the works of saints, including two Doctors of the Church: St. Thérèse of Lisieux and St. Thomas Aquinas. I also profited from St. John Paul II, in particular his encyclical *Veritatis splendor*, and from the writings of a French Carmelite, Bl. Marie-Eugène of the Child Jesus. Several theologians who have shown a renewed reading of Aquinas have been particularly helpful — among them, Fr. Servais Pinckaers, O.P., Daniel Westberg, and Fr. Marie-Joseph Le Guillou O.P.; the psychologists Anna A. Terruwe and Conrad Baars; and my professors from the Angelicum: Fr. Dalmazio Mongillo, O.P., Fr. Fabio Giardini, O.P., Fr. Quintín Turiel, O.P., and Fr. Brian Mullady, O.P.

In preparing my course, I have not always bothered to note the sources of my teaching. We learn wisdom from the giants who have preceded us, and often in class we repeat their teaching. An attentive reader of my book will probably recognize the places where I am repeating what I had read somewhere, presenting in a shorter form the substance of the teaching of my masters. I may therefore be accused of plagiarism; I have tried to mention my sources in footnotes, however, although not consistently. I have no shame here because I am not trying to be original. My intent has been to make Catholic teaching about the spiritual and moral life available to my students. The sources are various, but the synthesis, the tying together of what I have to say, and its presentation are my own.

This book has had two editions in Poland, in 2006 and in 2014. I thank Fr. Michał Paluch, O.P., the former rector of the Angelicum, who, for a long time, has been urging me to translate my books into English, and I sincerely thank Justyna Krukowska, who translated this book into English. I also thank EWTN and Devin Jones, Taylor Wilson, and Nora Malone, who have consented to publish the work and have suggested further editorial revisions.

Fr. Wojciech Giertych, O.P.
The Vatican, June 29, 2024
Solemnity of Sts. Peter and Paul

Introduction

FECUNDITY IS A COMMON THEME in the Bible, starting with the book of Genesis. On the third day of Creation, God says, "Let the earth put forth ... fruit trees bearing fruit in which is their seed, each according to its kind" (Gen. 1:11). When God blesses the first couple, he says to them, "Be fruitful and multiply" (Gen. 1:28). The psalmist, in turn, praises the husband who is "like a tree planted by streams of water, that yields its fruit in its season" (Ps. 1:3). God, Who is the Giver of life, loves life. He could make the whole richness of life and nature appear at once, in a single moment. In His wisdom, however, He has determined that the things that are good, the things that will be filled with His power, must come to fruition slowly and must be accompanied by patient anticipation and the generous gift of people, so that they will be like the bread offered at the altar, the "fruit of the earth and the work of human hands." God clearly rejoices when goodness is born, passing through the human gift and the human capacity to embrace the gift from on high. Jesus often mentions this truth: "As the branch cannot bear fruit by itself ... neither can you, unless you abide in me.... He who abides in me, and I in him, he it is that bears much fruit, for apart from me you can do nothing.... By this my Father is glorified, that you bear much fruit" (John 15:4–5, 8).

The presence of grace within human effort is a mystery. It can neither be measured nor described with the accuracy of sociological or psychological research. A theological inquiry that takes the revealed truths of faith as its starting point, however, may seek to describe how openness to the prevailing presence of grace manifests itself within human actions. It may seek to demonstrate how, through the power of grace, man can be liberated from threefold repression: emotional repression, in which trapped feelings do not gravitate toward their objects; intellectual repression, in which the enslaved mind, closed in its limited perspective, does not reach out toward the fullness of truth; and the most dangerous one: spiritual repression, in which grace, blocked from within, is not allowed to transform the human ethos. A theological discourse, centered on grace coming to fruition within the creatively acting individual, is helpful only when it shows the paths and the wide dimensions of personal liberation. Thus, the term *moral theology* is to be jealously reserved for the kind of discourse that has as its main object the God of promise and revelation, Who manifests Himself within sanctified human actions. This distinguishes moral theology from ethics, be it philosophical ethics, which looks at moral actions in the light of reason, or theological ethics, which also looks primarily at moral actions, occasionally illuminating them with the light of revelation.

The chapters of this book are tied together by a theological reading of St. Thomas Aquinas's *Summa theologiae*, based on the conviction that Aquinas divides his work into three parts, on the assumption that there are three ways in which God is in things.[2] Analogous predication allows us to affirm that God exists in one way as the Creator, present in creation and sustaining it in being; in another way, He is present through grace as He sanctifies people; and in a third way, He is present in Christ, in Whom humanity and divinity are mysteriously joined in a unique Hypostatic Union, which is continued in the sacraments of the Church. This distinction allows us to view the second part of the *Summa theologiae* through the eyes of a theologian and to perceive in it, above all, a description of the fecundity of grace that manifests itself in the mature, upright, independently generous man who, open to supernatural assistance, becomes the image and icon of God. Such an approach saves the

---

[2] *Ad Col.*, chap. 2, lect. 2, no. 97: "God is in things in three ways. One way is common, that is, by his power, presence and essence. He is present in another way in the saints, that is, by grace. The third way is found only in Christ, and he is present here by union." *Commentary on the Letters of St. Paul to the Colossians*, trans. F. R. Larcher, B. Mortensen, and D. Keating (Lander, WY: Aquinas Institute for the Study of Sacred Doctrine, 2012).

reading of Aquinas's moral theology from a narrow perspective limited to a purely philosophical analysis of the moral act and its psychology.

Another factor that heavily influenced this way of reading Aquinas's theology is the recognition that, over the centuries, something has gone wrong with the interpretation of the nature of the will. Aquinas's remarks, which often seem to be incomprehensible, become clear once the instinctive understanding of the will is purged from accretions from later centuries.

The modern understanding of the will is radically different from Aquinas's optimistic perspective. The decisive moment in European thought separating our times from the Middle Ages was the fourteenth century, when, under the influence of William of Ockham, a transformation in the understanding of the nature of the will took place. Instead of perceiving it as a spiritual power, endowed by the Creator with an orientation toward the good, requiring the support of reason, with which it cooperates, and capable of receiving the supernatural input of grace, the will was understood to be an autonomous power, inherently independent, completely divorced from the external influences of either reason or grace generating virtue, and as being in a rival position in respect to God, Who, being more powerful, imposes on it from without His own will, expressed in an arbitrary law. (This understanding of the will and freedom, originating in the late Middle Ages, has profoundly marked the Polish understanding of liberty, always seen as a "freedom from," fighting against the power of the king or the domination of the partitioners, rather than a "freedom for," promoting personal responsibility and integrity.) The error regarding the nature of the will set it in necessary and eternal conflict with the moral law, which henceforth appears as the enemy of the freedom of the will. The difference between Luther and the cardinal Cajetan, which consequently became the difference between Protestantism and Catholicism, and even between the modern mentality and the great Catholic tradition, lies precisely here, in Ockham's erroneous theory. According to Cajetan — who followed Aquinas — divine causality works through human causality. God, Who is the Creator of the human will, may act within human freedom in such a way that He does not destroy it but strengthens it even further. According to Luther, divine and human causality necessarily compete. That is why, in the Lutheran worldview, there is no room for the fruitfulness of grace within human action, no room for infused virtues or for mortal sin, which kills grace, because, at best, grace can envelop man from the outside, without penetrating the source of his actions. Modern Catholicism defended the role of grace within life, but unfortunately, the theory of the dual ultimate finality relegated the supernatural life to the realm of the extraordinary. Catholic moral theology was also affected by Ockham's unfortunate legacy. This resulted in an emphasis on the role of obligation in moral teaching, which led to excessive legalism, a casuistic approach to morality, and a distrust of the acting person's reason; and finally, it brought about a rift between a minimalistic moral theology and a separate, somewhat esoteric theology of spirituality. In consequence, conventional moral teaching did not bring out the role of grace in life. Pelagian overtones generated rigorism, sometimes even neurotic reactions, and subsequently undermined confidence in Catholic moral teaching.

Since moral theology can be best defined as the teaching about God present within human action, I see it as an expression of evangelical preaching. My lectures on fundamental moral theology delivered in Kraków and in Rome have resulted in four books that discuss the basic inner workings of responsible and spiritually transformed action.[3] I always try to take as my starting point not the philosophical view, rooted in the natural law, but the fact that the Christian has been endowed with grace. This theological view does not negate reason and its arguments, but it absorbs them into the description of what God accomplishes in man. My students' reactions confirm my conviction that in living out the life of faith, we need more than just touching experiences or captivating stories. A careful formation of the mind within the Faith is necessary, so that we can know exactly what we believe and what are the practical consequences of openness to God's power. Only then can we have genuine convictions and, based on them, consistently make decisions about ourselves and others.

---

[3] This volume, as well as *Rachunek sumienia teologii moralnej* (Kraków: Wydawnictwo M, 2004); *Bóg źródłem prawa: Ewangelia, Izrael, Natura, Islam* (Kraków: Wydawnictwo M, 2008); *Odtruwanie Łaski* (Kraków: Wydawnictwo M, 2011).

This book, in its second revised edition, discusses the essential psychological and moral components of sanctified behavior. Naturally, it is addressed to people of faith, to those who have already received the grace of faith in Baptism. This grace is sometimes ignored and undeveloped. It is nestled in the depths of the soul, like a forgotten hidden computer app. Perhaps it would be worthwhile to retrieve this grace and see what it can accomplish in our lives?

Wojciech Giertych, O.P.
The Vatican, April 27, 2014
Canonization day of St. John Paul II

1

The Complementarity of Nature and Grace in the Christian Life

"Don't worry about me, don't worry about me, I'm gonna cope just fine!" These lyrics of a popular Polish song reflect the attitude of being upset, a momentary impulse of angered love, and a declaration of self-sufficiency aimed to elicit pity and ultimately reconciliation. Under the guise of slighted pride, the opposite claim can be detected: we are not made for solitude, we need each other, but first we must duly focus our efforts on our common pilgrimage through this world. Harmonizing two hearts is not always easy, and it frequently involves surviving challenging times, moments of affirmation of one's autonomy, of rifts, and of reconciliation.

The same is true of man's struggle with God. We cannot get through life without God, although that may seem feasible at times. If the uproar and clamor of those who separate themselves from God in the name of independence, like the outburst of a child going through a defiant phase, are present in the culture of modern times, are they not an echo of a cry coming from deep within, a cry for love, for divine help, and for abundant grace where sin has abounded (Rom. 5:20)? Isn't it a sign that we are unable to cope with the difficult harmonizing of our nature with God's love, which appears incomprehensible, unintelligible, and baffling in its ways, just as the love of parents often appears incomprehensible to children? The problem, of course, is primarily existential. It concerns man's humble learning of the ways of God. It also has its theoretical dimension, presenting a real challenge to the theologizing mind that strives to name God's mysteries. How can God's love meet man? What are the laws of the interaction of God's grace with man's freedom, with his nature, and with his natural, worldly aspirations?

The proper designation of man's relationship to the gift of God's grace — or, to put it another way, of nature to supernature — has puzzled theologians for centuries. This problem was raised in the twentieth century in a particularly poignant way by Cardinal Henri de Lubac,[4] who noticed a shift in emphasis that started in the late Middle Ages and ultimately produced a disquieting theological climate found neither in the Church Fathers nor in the great medieval theologians. This is the climate in which, on one hand, autonomous ethics is born and the entire discourse on grace is viewed as completely superfluous and incompatible with what goes on in human life, and on the other hand, a deep pessimism emerges, convinced about universal corruption and the insufficiency of nature itself, along with an agnosticism regarding the possibility of deriving any binding moral guidelines from rational reflection on human nature. Is human nature so self-sufficient that it can teach man, or is it so corrupt that it cannot illumine anything? Does human nature necessarily require the salvific intervention of God, Who grants revelation for the cognitive realm, and the grace of redemption for the realm of volition? If, indeed, the contribution of the supernatural is necessary for the weak nature, then what is the essence of this supernatural contribution? Where does the interface between nature and grace take place, and where is the boundary between natural and Christian ethics?

The English Jesuit John Mahoney, in his review of the history and challenges of Catholic moral theology,[5] expresses dissatisfaction with the natural law theory, which became the standard reference point in the pronouncements of the Magisterium in modern times. Whether it was defending the indissolubility of marriage, criticizing communism, condemning duels, or rejecting contraception, natural law was invariably invoked, implying that human reason, although subject to error, has the capacity to recognize the

---

[4] Henri de Lubac, *Surnaturel: Études historiques* (Paris: Aubier, 1946); *Le mystère du surnaturel* (Paris: Aubier, 1965); *Augustinisme et théologie moderne* (Paris: Aubier, 1965); *O naturze i łasce* (Kraków: Znak, 1986).

[5] John Mahoney, *The Making of Moral Theology: A Study of the Roman Catholic Tradition* (Oxford: Clarendon Press, 1987).

right path of moral conduct. As the world seemed to heed the Word of God less and less, the Church's Magisterium still hoped that the world would be willing to accept rational conclusions deduced from the metaphysical intuition of human nature. Consequently, strong emphasis was placed on the natural law. But what is this nature that can instruct? Is the Church's Magisterium necessary for drawing moral conclusions from an examination of nature? Mahoney reminds us that post-Tridentine theology undertook speculations on "pure nature" abstracted from its elevation in Adam, its fall in Original Sin, and its redemption in Christ. This theoretical view of nature was juxtaposed with grace. Following Rahner's theology, Mahoney describes the concept of "pure nature" as a *Restbegriff*, a residual notion, developed by completely expunging the supernatural components from nature to find its "purely" natural foundation. Convinced that nature conceived in this way underlies Aquinas's theory of natural law, Mahoney grapples with unsettling questions: Does not such an advanced speculation on nature reach too far beyond human experience? And on the other hand, if we conclude that nature can provide light for human morality, does this not mean that the whole purpose of revelation boils down to supporting cognition, which is accessible without revelation anyway? As he points out, "Revelation as such has nothing in matters of moral behavior to add to the best of human thinking, but such human moral thinking is by no means always or invariably at its best."[6] Mahoney is surprised by the resistance of many Catholics against the accepting of the conclusion that there is nothing specifically distinctive about Christian ethics when compared with the best humanistic ethics. He does not see that ethics is merely an instruction addressed to reason, which it can only persuade, while, in the Christian life, something even more profound takes place: a cooperation with God, dwelling in the human soul, Who enlightens reason, stimulates the will, and not only cleanses from sin but also works within human freedom, empowering it to multiply God's goodness. In the Church, there is room for another conversation, theological and not just ethical, that strives to describe and point toward God's action in the human soul. Mahoney senses, however, that something is missing if one equates

---

[6] Mahoney, *Moral Theology*, 109.

Christian morality with humanistic morality; hence, he proposes that we are in need of "an enriched view of morality rather than ... an impoverished view of religion."[7] It seems that he lacks the courage to say outright that this enriched view of morality can be born only of the mysterious action of God, which, by the power of grace, accompanies the Church's preaching, and that theological discourse can fully sensitize the believer to this operation of grace. He attributes the increasing prevalence of the substitute theme of the human person and human dignity in theology to a disaffection with the concepts of nature and natural law. He also argues that instead of systematically separating the order of nature and supernature, theology should encapsulate God's single design toward humanity, one that is both creative and salvific.

Mahoney's book was written before the publication of the encyclical *Veritatis splendor*, in which St. John Paul II draws heavily on the theology of St. Thomas Aquinas, referencing both his teaching on the natural law and his teaching on the new law, the law of grace, still insufficiently explored. De Lubac's contesting of the theory of "pure nature" and of dual — natural and supernatural — finality as they appeared in post-Tridentine theology prompted a new exploration of the understanding of the relationship between nature and supernature in the teachings of St. Thomas himself, and it is from this body of renewed Thomistic studies[8] that the encyclical *Veritatis splendor* draws. This does not mean, however, that the mindset formed by the radical separation of nature and supernature immediately disappeared. It persists and colors expectations concerning the Church's moral teachings, and it generates difficulties. Therefore, the proper designation of nature and grace and their mutual correlation warrant a clarification.

Unexpectedly, at the end of the twentieth century in the United States, a theologian emerged who was able to articulate with great eloquence what was at stake here. Lawrence Feingold is a marble sculptor by profession. After

---

[7] Mahoney, *Moral Theology*, 110.
[8] See Marie-Joseph Le Guillou, "Surnaturel," in *Le témoignage de Dieu* (Saint-Maur: Parole et Silence, 1996), 83–103; Georges Cottier, "Le désir naturel de voir Dieu," in *Quand un homme témoigne de Dieu. Colloque IV: Père Marie-Joseph Le Guillou, Montmartre, 1998* (Saint-Maur: Parole et Silence, 1998), 19–46.

receiving Baptism in the Anglican church and then converting to Catholicism with his wife in 1988, he became a prominent theologian. His fundamental study of the natural desire to see God[9] is likened by reviewers to the works of Aquinas's great commentators, such as Cardinal Thomas Cajetan, O.P., Francesco Silvestri, O.P., Domingo de Soto, O.P., Bartholomew Medina, O.P., Domingo Báñez, O.P., and Francisco Suárez, S.J. Having examined the positions of these distinguished theologians of the Renaissance and Baroque eras, Feingold showed the value of the precise teachings of St. Thomas Aquinas and his many followers and critiqued the solution proposed by Cardinal de Lubac. This great theological debate, rightly started by de Lubac, with echoes that influenced the teachings of Vatican II and the subsequent Magisterium of the Church, allows not just for a more faithful reading of the teachings of Aquinas but, more importantly, for amending the description of a genuinely Christian morality. Acknowledging God's fundamental design — which includes human nature, intrinsically meaningful and having its own finality, recognized by the natural law but not enclosed in this nature, since it both precedes creation and encompasses a perspective deeper and further than nature itself — forces a development of a description of an ethos raised to a higher, supernatural level. In this description, the pride of place must be given to grace, bestowed on man by virtue of the Redemption and enabling communion with the personal God already here and now.

The fact that God reveals Himself as our ultimate end and that we can accept Him as such does not create serious difficulties. Experiences of the spiritual life show that this is possible. Difficulties arise as we try to penetrate this reality rationally. What do we mean when we say that God is the ultimate end of man? Can we speak of a finality written into human nature and into the nature of all created things? The problem is not only philosophical but also theological. The orientation "toward God" is not only the consequence of the human structure but also a specific gift of grace. What, then, is the relationship of natural finality to grace? To clarify the gift of the supernatural life, do we have to invent the concept of "pure nature," of a nature that exists

---

[9] Lawrence Feingold, *The Natural Desire to See God according to St. Thomas Aquinas and His Interpreters* (Naples, FL: Sapientia Press, 2010).

apart from the supernatural order? If that is the case, does it not follow that we could be completely happy without the gift of grace? If we come to such a conclusion, this will elevate the supernatural life to the extraordinary and miraculous sphere, and it will mean that we can live out our lives completely divorced from and indifferent to the realm of grace. Can we not say that the majority of people in the world, or the atheists at least, live their lives without engaging with the grace of God, and it seems that somehow they manage rather well in living without God?

Finality in nature?

One of these challenging issues is the question of finality in nature. Metaphysical reflection perceives a basic dependency of all beings on the mind of the Creator. In each existing thing, we perceive a certain logic that is an echo of the creative mind of God. This claim is, of course, a metaphysical rather than a biological assertion. When we observe the cyclical nature of the seasons and its fruitful consequences for agriculture, we can arrive at the intuition that there is finality in nature, but we are not demonstrating this intuition. This intuition is of a different order from biological knowledge. It can be grasped only by the mind. The intuition of finality is a basic premise in thinking about ourselves and our place in the universe. Admittedly, we know that there are people who reject this intuition, which they are unwilling to follow. The mind can become contaminated, and it may suffer from intellectual repression that cripples or rather discourages it from addressing the most fundamental questions.

St. Thomas Aquinas, starting with this metaphysical intuition of finality, would say that the way in which particular beings express their inherent finality depends on their nature. The stone expresses its finality executively; it just is. It does not think about anything; it does nothing; it just is, and by being, it praises its Creator. The animal, being a higher species, fulfills its finality not only by being an animal but also by living out the inclinations of its animal nature. The bird, moved by sensitive cognition and appetite, is acting upon this finality when it builds its nest and when it bears and educates its offspring. Man, since he is a rational animal, directs himself to his end in a rational way, by undertaking conscious choices that direct him to his ultimate end. The finality of man is rational, as it flows from his rational human nature.

Modern philosophy is unwilling to study the question of the finality of beings. If we accept the thesis that there is finality in beings, we have to accept that, at the base of this finality, there must be some Mind. A philosophy that accepts finality must be theistic by its very nature. Natural sciences do not study finality; they study phenomena and collect measurable information about them. They do not ask the deepest question that children ask: "What is it?" To respond fully to the question about a thing, we must examine its final cause. What end does this thing serve? What is the meaning given to this thing by the one who created or made it? We will not answer the question about what a new machine is without specifying its end. Similarly, we will not explain the essence of man, or specific elements of his structure — e.g., his spiritual powers or his sexuality — without addressing the question of finality. What is the deepest finality that the Creator wrote into human nature?

If we claim that there is finality in the world, we conclude that the world is sensible, that there is a wise Mind that cares for this world. If we deny the existence of finality in things, it follows that the world is absurd. Leszek Kołakowski rightly pointed out that we can then describe this world, but the world is deaf — *surdus*: the world is not listening to what we say.[10] The word *absurd* comes from this deafness of the world, which is not listening to our words. Similarly, what we can say about the world is an illusion, and the word *illusion* comes from *ludus* — a "game." We are playing a game, describing some things, but the world is ignoring our game and remains indifferent to our words. A world without finality is a world that is lost in complete pointlessness and absurdity. And man is then a speck of dust, thrown into a cosmos with no meaning, no sense, no values, and no end. Kołakowski notes that there have been few atheist philosophers who, like Jean-Paul Sartre and Friedrich Nietzsche, have had the courage to contemplate the icy emptiness of a world with no Absolute, no sense!

---

[10] Leszek Kołakowski, *Religion: If There Is No God ... On God, the Devil, Sin and Other Worries of the So-Called Philosophy of Religion* (Glasgow: Fontana, 1982), 211–212.

By teaching us that the world is created by God, revelation tells us that the world makes sense, that it has a final end, and that we, men endowed with spiritual faculties, can arrive at this end, which transcends this world. In the life of God, given freely, we can find our plenitude and our end. God is the ultimate end of all beings because He created them all and because all beings are dependent on Him. But only rational beings — angels and men — can be united to God by knowing and loving Him. "He chose us in him before the foundation of the world … in love to be his sons through Jesus Christ" (Eph. 1:4–5).

Is the orientation "toward God" a natural phenomenon, or is it a particular gift of grace?

Philosophical analysis shows that there is a natural innate inclination in man's being to know God, resulting from the structure of the spiritual faculties, which are able to pose ultimate questions and which tend toward goodness. Beyond this natural innate inclination of the spiritual powers, and because of it, occasionally a consciously adopted natural desire to see God arises in man.[11] Man, then, can reach out beyond this world. Already St. Augustine noticed this in his famous "Fecisti nos ad Te!" — "You have made us for Yourself, O Lord, and our heart is restless until it rests in You."[12] This consciously adopted natural desire to see God is written into the spiritual faculties of man. We are simply curious about God. We want to know the cause and the end of our existence. Where did we come from? Why did we appear on earth? Where are we going? Who, or what mind, created us? Through our philosophical questioning, we can arrive at the conclusion that there is an Absolute, a Prime Mover, and an Ultimate End.

From the conclusion that God exists, we then move to the natural desire to see God. Since God exists, we want to see Him; we want to know His essence. The natural human intellect is open to the totality of reality. Our curiosity will not be satisfied by a mere part. Only God can satisfy the openness of the human intellect. Similarly, the will, with its spiritual appetite for

---

[11] Feingold, *Natural Desire*.
[12] *Confessions*, bk. I, chap. 1.

goodness, is open to the limitless horizon of goodness shown by the intellect. Nothing can satisfy the spiritual faculties apart from God Himself, Who is supreme Truth and supreme Goodness. It is not enough to say that man is a rational animal. In man there is something angelic; there is an aspiration for the ultimate, for the divine reality. We are not like fruit that has to be stored in a refrigerator or in a jar so that it does not rot. When man is closed even in the limits of the great cosmos, that closing causes him to rot — because in man there is a reaching out, outside this world, outside the cosmos, to the Cause of that cosmos.

Man's reaching out toward God Himself is also a searching for happiness. We perceive a basic contradiction between the actual state of our spirit and its capacity, and so we have the natural desire to see God. Since man's spiritual faculties reach beyond the cosmos toward the Creator, this final, most fundamental desire necessarily expresses the search for the fullness of happiness. Can this desire be fulfilled in a natural way, or is inevitable frustration written into nature — and into human but not animal nature? Aristotle thought that supreme happiness consists in contemplating supreme truth, but only the philosopher has the time and the means to do this. Who among us can satisfy the hunger for supreme truth to such a degree that we can find happiness in it? As we perceive through philosophy the fundamental importance of the natural desire to see God, we conclude that supreme happiness can only be elitist. Only profound thinkers have access to this supreme happiness. This is ultimately a rather sad conclusion. Antiquity knew the story of the fox that wanted to eat the grapes, but they were too high, so the fox said to himself that they were probably sour anyway, and he walked away sad. Our human nature has the ability to uncover the natural desire to see God, but we do not find in our nature the means of attaining that desire. The aspiration of the spirit by itself leaves us sad.

The claim that the natural desire to see God may appear in man is a philosophical thesis, not a theological one (although we can make use of it in a theological context, as we penetrate the revealed truths of faith). Philosophy of religion perceives in man the openness to God, and sociology of religion or cultural anthropology confirms this conclusion, as they study the phenomenon of religion. If the natural desire to see God is not satisfied by meeting the God of revelation, Who grants us grace, then that desire will express itself in multiple and deformed ways. In bookshops we can find many books about ghosts, prophecies, forms of mysticism from the Far East, and the supposedly salutary value of psychological training or yoga. All these books witness the curiosity, the dissatisfaction, the reaching out to something more, to something that will provide peace and happiness. The arguments, however, that Aquinas presents to defend the existence of the natural desire to see God are neither psychological nor sociological but are metaphysical. This desire, consciously adopted, is a consequence of the structure of the human intellect, which is open to ultimate cognition. The intellect is curious; it wants to know the deepest causes and reasons. The natural desire to see God is not — as Ludwig Feuerbach would make us believe — a fruit of alienation. It does not arise in us only because of education and social pressure. It is a product of the nature of our intellect. That is why Aquinas says that this natural desire to see God exists not only among people living on earth, but also in angels, both good and evil. It exists in Hell, where, in the soul that is closed in by pride and rejects the gift of grace, it is the source of suffering. The thesis about the existence of man's natural desire to see God is a philosophical conclusion that points out that we came out of God's hands with a built-in orientation toward Him.

The philosophical observation about the curiosity of man who seeks God does not, however, exhaust the truth about man. The philosophical conclusion meets with the theological truth. In theology, we begin not with a rational reflection but with the revealed mystery that can never be fully exhausted. In theology, we look from the top, from the perspective of the heart of the Father, which was manifested to us and which we can approach, thanks to the gift of faith. The natural orientation toward God does not in itself tell us anything about the fullness of the divine gift. What could the pagan Aristotle have known about divine gifts? Revelation, however, tells us the truth about God, Who wants for us the supernatural life. "He has showed you, O man, what is good; and what does the Lord require of you but to do justice, and to love kindness, and to walk humbly with your God?" (Mic. 6:8). Conversation with God through cognition and love is possible only by a special divine gift. We are elevated by God Himself to a higher, better mode of existence, in a way pleasing to Him, in which we can encounter Him. The fecundity of the supernatural life takes place through human nature, and so also through the natural desire to see God, but it is not the fruit of these natural human faculties and this natural desire. There is no natural means of moving from the level of nature to supernature. We cannot by our own means elevate ourselves from the natural level and from natural curiosity to the level of friendly interaction with the living God. This is possible exclusively through the gift of grace. That is why it is impossible to convince another person about faith. Faith is a divine gift. In responding by our love to the divine call, cooperating with the grace that we have received, we can contribute to the development of grace in us (or we can poison the life of grace in us), but we cannot by our own efforts grant ourselves or anybody else the supernatural life of God. Church teaching is very clear on this point. The Second Council of Orange of 529 stated:

> If anyone says that mercy is divinely conferred upon us when, without God's grace, we believe, will, desire, strive, labour, pray, keep watch, endeavour, request, seek, knock, but does not confess that it is through the infusion and the inspiration of the Holy Spirit that we believe, will or are able to do these things, as is required ... he contradicts the apostle who says: "What have you that you did not receive?" [1 Cor. 4:7] and also "By the grace of God I am what I am" [1 Cor. 15:10].[13]

This means that the whole sequence of verbs that express our striving for God (believe, desire, strive, work, pray, watch ...) describes a reality that is supernatural through grace. In our nature alone, there is no capacity that would allow for an appropriate "as necessary" approaching of God. This teaching was repeated by the Council of Trent, in canon 3 of the *Decree on Justification*:

> If anyone says that without the prevenient inspiration of the Holy Spirit and without his help, man can believe, hope and love or be

---

[13] *The Christian Faith: In the Doctrinal Documents of the Catholic Church*, ed. J. Neuner and J. Dupuis (New York: Alba House, 1982), no. 1918.

repentant as is required, so the grace of justification be bestowed upon him — *anathema sit* [let him be accursed].[14]

Just as in the Second Council of Orange, we have here the expression "as necessary" (*sicut oportet*). Finally, the same First Vatican Council of 1870, which, on the one hand, decreed that "God, the beginning and end of all things, can be known with certainty through the natural light of human reason,"[15] added that

> God in his infinite goodness has ordained men to a supernatural end, viz., to share in the good things of God, which utterly exceed the intelligence of the human mind.[16]

We have, therefore, two seemingly contradictory statements. On the one hand, there is in man a natural orientation toward God. With his philosophical mind, man is able (although with difficulty) to arrive at the conclusion that God exists, that He is man's natural end, and that man can, in his reason, perceive the existence of a natural desire to see God. At the same time, God has destined us to Himself as to a supernatural end — that is, to a friendly engaging with Him, and the entry into this relationship requires the gift of grace, without which engaging with God is impossible. There is no natural desire of supernature. When we desire the living God and move toward Him, that, in itself, is the fruit of grace working within us. The decree of Vatican I is quite clear. It is important that we accept God as our end, and not only as our natural end but as our supernatural end. It is important that we desire, search for, and love God, as the One Who, in a mysterious way, has revealed Himself to us and manifested His divine life in His loving paternal arms. It is important that the striving for God takes place as a result of the interior movement of grace, and not merely because of a purely philosophical curiosity. There is an essential difference between searching for the Absolute — the ultimate truth and the ultimate reason that justifies the order in the world (a search of which Aristotle was capable) — and engaging with God in faith and

---

[14] *The Christian Faith*, no. 1953.
[15] *The Christian Faith*, no. 113.
[16] *The Christian Faith*, no. 114.

love through the power of grace (which even an uneducated man, having no capacity for philosophy can experience). The supernatural life is not just the fulfillment of a natural curiosity; it is an entry into a reality of a completely different order from the order of nature. It is this engaging with God in grace that God desires for us all. God "desires all men to be saved" (1 Tim. 2:4).

The search based on the natural desire to see the Absolute and the engaging with God in faith are not the same. God is calling us to a participation in His inner life, and to the reception of this participation as our supernatural end. This perspective is fundamentally mysterious, and if it is to be received, it needs to be received as such, as a mystery of the revealed love of God. However, that orientation toward God through grace finds its foundation, so to speak, in the natural desire to see God. The possibility of the encounter of grace and nature and the transformation of human nature by grace are explained in Thomistic theology through the metaphysical category of obediential potency. This potency denotes the susceptibility of the human being to the workings of grace. Just as, in a piece of wood, there is a susceptibility to be changed into a statue if a sculptor takes the wood into his hands, so, in man, there is a disposition to be transformed by the power of grace. This susceptibility is different from a natural potency. It is in the nature of wood to decay, whereas, to become a statue, it needs the hand of a higher being — that is, the sculptor. Additionally, obediential potency denotes not only a lack of resistance toward the higher being but also a positive given. We do not make statues out of liquids or gases; statues can be made of wood, although a piece of wood left to itself will never change into a statue. The entire created reality is dependent on God, but only man, not any animal, is *capax gratiae* because man in his spiritual structure has the aptitude to be changed by grace. This transformation is completely the work of God, but it takes place through the human faculties. God's grace does not deform or warp us by directing us toward something that would be against our nature, although the gift of grace reaches much further and deeper than the possibilities of nature alone. God shows us "what no eye has seen, nor ear heard, nor the heart of man conceived" (1 Cor. 2:9), but between the deepest inclinations of nature and the gift of God, there is not and cannot be a fundamental contradiction (although while growing in the life of God, we frequently see a painful resistance of nature, unused to the gift of grace and rebelling against it).

Henri de Lubac pointed out a certain distortion that appeared on this issue in modern Catholic theology, in which the natural order was sharply set against the supernatural order. De Lubac claimed that the father of this error was the fifteenth-century author Denis the Carthusian. Referring to the theory of two truths taught by the disciples of Avicenna, against which Aquinas fought, Denis the Carthusian introduced the theory of a double ultimate finality. Man supposedly has a natural ultimate end, a consequence of a "pure nature" that is absolutely self-sufficient and not oriented toward God, and above this natural finality God has oriented man to a second ultimate end that is supernatural. Denis the Carthusian was aware that his theory is not found in the works of Aquinas, but, according to de Lubac, half a century later, Cardinal Thomas de Vio Cajetan, a great commentator on Aquinas, accepted this theory as supposedly coming from Aquinas. Cajetan studied in Padua, the center of humanism and philosophy. The idea of a "pure nature" was well received by the Renaissance humanists who studied the natural religion. The ideas of "pure nature" and of double ultimate finality were then followed by multiple theologians.[17] This theory was popular up to the twentieth century. There is no mention of the theory of dual ultimate finality in the writings of Aquinas. He writes about two kinds of happiness — imperfect happiness and perfect happiness — but he makes no mention of dual ultimate finality. It is obvious to a theologian that there can be only one ultimate end, which is union with God, loved above all. We can, however, restrict our view to a purely philosophical reflection and focus only on nature, its inner structure and finality.

---

[17] Feingold claims that de Lubac's interpretation did not do justice to Denis the Carthusian or Cajetan. He says that Denis did not think of nature as self-sufficient and closed in, but he merely did not understand how there could be a natural desire of an object that transcends the order of nature (*Natural Desire*, 78–79). Cajetan, in turn, did not make himself very clear when discussing the supernatural orientation toward the God of revelation when he commented on Aquinas's teaching on cognition stemming from natural curiosity (*Natural Desire*, 167–182). We should not, then, blame Cajetan excessively for further theological distortions.

The theory of a dual ultimate finality, built upon the concept of "pure nature" closed in on itself, boils down to the statement that God first created man, giving him a nature that is capable of satisfying its inclinations, and then God redirected that nature, leading it in a superior, supernatural direction. This theory does not necessarily reject supernatural reality. It can be reconciled with faith, but it implies that the supernatural order belongs to the realm of the extraordinary and the miraculous, external to nature. Ever since, nature and supernature were perceived as functioning in a parallel way, and the fact that there is a natural desire to see God in human nature and a natural disposition to receive grace was overlooked. Theologians thought that they were waging a holy war in defense of orthodoxy by denying the existence of a natural, consciously cultivated desire to see God and by defending a pure nature closed in on itself. In fact, they were losing ground to naturalism, making concessions for a world that was less and less interested in the supernatural ultimate end. The idea of a self-sufficient "pure nature" became more and more demanding. Once the idea was accepted, it became sufficient, complete, coherent, and independent of any higher order.

It seems that the theory of "pure nature" in theology is one of the reasons behind eighteenth-century deism and then atheism. Many of the ideas that the philosophers of the eighteenth century are accused of were held by theologians earlier, beginning from the sixteenth century.[18] When the natural order was set against the supernatural order, and the autonomous "pure nature" was stressed, the supernatural order began to be understood as an addition or an ornament, whereas what is natural began to live its own

---

[18] Feingold thinks that, following de Lubac, we are wrong to draw deism and atheism from the theory of "pure nature." Modern thought is born out of a contempt for nature and from negating the cognitive powers of reason, seemingly unable to grasp the essence of natural things, natural law, and the existence of God, rather than out of a neo-Thomistic affirmation of the coherence of the natural order and the cognitive powers of reason. This mutilation of natural reason is rooted in fourteenth-century nominalism, in the Reformation, and in the Jansenist distrust of corrupt nature rather than in an imprecise reception of the teachings of St. Thomas. *Natural Desire*, 134.

life. If man has a natural ultimate end within the temporal order, why should he bother with some supernatural end? It suffices that man succeeds in this world — and the life of grace, the engaging with God, may be good for the chosen souls, for religious, but not for regular people! Furthermore, when modern moral theology that was built upon the Decalogue became minimalist, and, in response to its shortcomings, an extra theological discipline called spiritual theology was later created, this confirmed the conviction that the supernatural order is somehow extraordinary and, as such, optional and redundant in the moral life.

The questions raised by de Lubac resonated deeply in the works of Vatican II.[19] They prompted reflection on the deeper meaning of terms that, until that point, were taken for granted. The Council did not use the concept of "pure nature." Instead, it strongly emphasized the universal call to holiness and rejected the splitting of man through a seemingly dual ultimate finality and the dividing of people into two categories: the elites and those who were to be spiritually unprivileged. The Council used the term *supernaturalis* sparingly and ignored the theory of two orders, although it did not reject this distinction. The Council viewed man in the context of one divine order — the *ordo divinum*, which includes both the creation of man and his salvation. The Council's theological anthropology flows from gazing at Christ. The face of the Risen One, which has been given to us,[20] is the primary reference point for theological anthropology.

> It has pleased God to unite all things, both natural and supernatural [*tam naturalia quam supernaturalia*], in Christ Jesus "so that in all things He may have the first place" (Col. 1:18). This destination [of man to God], however, not only does not deprive the temporal order of its independence, its proper goals, laws, supports, and significance for human welfare but rather perfects the temporal order in its own

---

[19] Étienne Michelin, *Vatican II et le "Surnaturel": Enquête préliminaire 1959–1962* (Venasque: Éditions du Carmel, 1993).

[20] See the excellent introduction to the theology of Vatican II: Marie-Joseph Le Guillou, *Le visage du Ressuscité* (Saint-Maurice, Switzerland: Éditions Saint-Augustin, 1996).

intrinsic strength and worth and puts it on a level with man's whole vocation upon earth.[21]

Sanctity is not an extraordinary (i.e., rare) gift, to which only a few chosen souls have access. Sanctity is the work of grace, and all members of the Church are called to it.[22] The supreme heights of sanctity are possible for all Christians through the development of the graces given in Baptism, and it happens in the context of the natural order. (This truth is emphasized in the Church's many canonizations.) We need not treat the supernatural order as something extra and optional, like the extra deck in a London bus. It is incorrect to treat grace as a reality that is parallel to nature or even its rival. God, Who is the Creator of nature and the Giver of grace, works through grace not beside nature but within it. The reception of God as our Lord and as the end of our lives takes place within the human life, within its actual social context, within our psyches and natural inclinations. The interface between nature and supernature is the human soul, where God plants His love. The Christian conscience, sensitive to the gift of divine love, becomes the locus of reception of grace and the center from which it radiates. The Holy Spirit, dwelling in the human soul, does not take anything away, nor is He jealous when He directs us to the Savior and, through Him, to the heart of the Father.

That God has so fallen in love with man that He unites Himself with man, reveals Himself to him, and directs him to Himself, in no way entails a questioning of the dignity of human nature. It does mean, however, that the orientation toward God that able philosophical minds can perceive within human nature is elevated and transfigured by the gift of grace. Thanks to the movements of grace, the striving for God as the beloved Father becomes the reality of life not only of metaphysicians searching for the Absolute but also of all humble souls willing to receive from the hands of God His gratuitously given gift. The natural desire for the vision of God, written into the metaphysical structure of the human mind, is undoubtedly the most important and

---

[21] Second Vatican Council, Decree on the Apostolate of the Laity *Apostolicam actuositatem* (November 18, 1965), no. 7.
[22] Second Vatican Council, Dogmatic Constitution on the Church *Lumen gentium* (November 21, 1964), nos. 39–42.

most noble of natural human desires, but it is not necessarily experienced as such. It is frequently ignored and not consciously cultivated, unless some special circumstances suddenly remind us of God and intrigue our minds. The grace of the Holy Spirit, however, which germinates with faith in the human soul, transforms that natural desire for God. It purifies the desire of the pride of self-sufficiency and makes engaging with God through faith the major axis of human life. The natural desire to see God is inefficacious of itself, because nature cannot fulfill it (and if man tells himself that by his own efforts he can attain supreme happiness, he is sinning by pride), but what is impossible by our own efforts becomes possible through the helpful hand of God. When God imparts Himself to us, He is known and loved as the revealed end of our lives, and the three Persons of God enter into a personal relationship with us. Communion with God, which flows from grace, does not replace the natural desire to see God; rather, transforms it and grants it an appropriate dynamism and vigor.

Placing the interface between grace and nature at the very heart of human personality means that the Church's sanctifying mission in the world is carried out primarily through the conscience formed by the theological virtues of faith, hope, and charity. This entails the primacy of the personal conscience over social relations. Guided by this insight, the Council calls for abandoning the excessive emphasis on the Church's political role in favor of solicitude for what happens in the human heart. (The visible structure of the Church is necessary primarily for the administration of the sacraments, through which grace is dispensed, and for the open proclamation of the Word of God, which nourishes the inner life. The Church is not just a hidden mystical reality. She is a Body, united with Christ the Head, and the People of God.) But it is more important for the Church to watch the workings of grace in hearts and to support its growth than to get involved in politics or pursue civil safeguards intended to defend the rights of the Church. If God lives in our hearts and is loved, who can harm us? The theology of the spiritual life, therefore, takes pride of place in the Church's reflection, since it is the life of grace that is the essence of the life of the Church. Naturally, this does not mean averting the eyes from the matters of this world. The temporal world has its own dignity and its own needs, and when Christians give their hearts to the Holy Spirit, this triggers sacrificial responsibility and entails social ramifications. The transformation of the world, however, is achieved primarily through the transformation of individuals who are open to grace.

To sum up, then, it must be said that, although there is an inclination toward God in man's natural spiritual powers, enabling a consciously cultivated natural desire to see God, which expresses the deepest human cognitive curiosity, this desire is incapable of granting true fulfillment. What man is able to do with his life on his own is incomparable to the gift that God gives and to the promised happiness that becomes the lot of those who accept and cooperate with the gift of grace in their hearts. This gift of grace finds fertile ground in human nature, but in God's design it also precedes nature and reaches beyond it, toward the Divine Persons, toward the living and yet mysterious Holy Trinity, and not merely toward the Absolute that justifies the existence of created reality. God, granting us His life and engaging with us in a friendly way, desires that, by the power of grace, the best of nature should flourish in us. As, in the risen face of Christ, the divinity appears in all the splendor of His human personality, so the gift of grace radiates in the nature of a sanctified man. This radiation of God's goodness in man is God's greatest gift to man and, consequently, the Church's greatest gift to the world. To accept and assimilate this gift, man must be personally oriented in faith and love, and therefore in grace, toward the God Who gives Himself.

Can the prospect of merely natural happiness be enough for man?

We saw, based on philosophical observation, the possibility of a natural desire in man for the vision of God. If it is natural, is it not possible for man to find a satiation of this desire by himself, relying solely upon the vital forces of his nature, without the help of divine grace? Should not our human nature be self-sufficient, enabling us to participate in a natural happiness within the scope of this world? Can we not point to philosophers or representatives of various natural religions who find some satisfaction for their curiosity about the Absolute? And does not this satisfaction grant them the happiness that is supremely possible in this world, which for them is quite sufficient? Why should we pine for something greater, or humble ourselves to receive a gift from the hands of God, if we can somehow manage in this world on our own? Is it necessarily true that without being oriented toward God by grace, man will become a wreck?

In responding to these doubts, we must stress that it is true that, through philosophy and natural religion, man reaches out toward the Absolute only to the best of his abilities. This natural search for God in the case of man deprived of the grace of faith will appear as a natural ultimate end and the supremely possible happiness. Within this natural finality, man can achieve some happiness, to the best of his ability and by the standards of this world. But this happiness that is proportionate to the natural powers of man cannot be compared to the Beatific Vision of God, which has been promised to us in revelation.

The mystery of the heart of the Father revealed by Christ, the mystery that is open through the reception of the gift of grace, completely transcends the horizon of natural happiness. It is not our task to console those whose eyes have not been opened by saying that in the darkness of disbelief they can also find some crumbs. Our task consists in sharing the perspective that was shown to us when Christ healed the eyes of our souls! Let those who find it interesting analyze a purely natural happiness. For the one who has received the light of faith, this is not a very profitable occupation, and it is, in fact, ridiculous. The fact that the believer accepts the outstretched arm of God does not mean that he suffers from a despicable humiliation, unworthy of man. The animal attains the end that is appropriate to its nature through the powers of that nature, but man, who is called to rest in the heart of God, cannot rely solely upon his nature, and so he accepts the outstretched friendly hand of God. This, however, is not a proof of a degradation of man in comparison with the animal but is, in fact, a proof of the great elevation of man.[23] That which is impossible for human nature becomes possible due to the help of a Friend. If man could, with his

---

[23] Thomas Aquinas, *Summa Theologiae* (*ST*), Ia-IIae, q. 5, art. 5, ad 2: "A nature which can attain the perfect good, although it needs outside help, is of a higher condition than that which can attain without such recourse only a lesser good" (trans. T. Gilby, vol. 16, [London: Blackfriars, 1969]).

natural strength, take final happiness in his hands, there would be no room in this self-sufficiency for the love of God. God told us a great deal about Himself, that He is a loving God, Who desires love, when He showed us a supernatural happiness in which we grow through humble faith and love. And God told us also a great deal about ourselves when He revealed the truth that He directs us to His heart.

Is God not "forced" to grant us grace?

In an attempt to fathom speculatively the relationship of nature to grace, theologians have faced the difficult problem of the gratuity of grace. If we say, as we have said, that man is ordained by God to participate in the happiness of God, does it not follow that God *has to* grant us His grace? Since God created human nature as ordained toward the supernatural life, does it not follow that He would be unjust if He did not give His grace? And if God is "forced," does it not mean that grace is a necessity and not a gratuitous gift of God? How can we reconcile God's being "forced" with the free pleasure of God, Who gives His gifts as He wills?

These and similar problems arise when the languages of the discourse are mixed. If we take nature metaphysically, it follows that grace is absolutely gratuitous. There is nothing in nature that would force supernature. Grace is a pure gift of God. Whereas when we view theologically the actual state of man who is called out of love to participate in the love of God, we see that grace is necessary for man. God is somehow "forced," but He is forced by His own love, which for Him is binding. God is faithful to His own promises, and He leads people in various ways toward sanctity. The ways in which people are led to an experience of faith and the ways in which they respond to divine movements are as diverse as the people themselves. God, in the richness of His love, has multiple ways of knocking at the hearts of men. Not all of God's ways are known to us. We know that the Father has expressed the plenitude of His Word in Christ and that through His sacrifice He is giving us life. That is why we preach Christ. This does not mean that we exclude more mysterious ways of the fecundity of the grace of Christ in the hearts of men. That is why the Church accepts as her own the statement contained in the confession of faith of the Gallic priest Lucidus, from 473:

> I confess that depending upon the order of time, some have been saved by the law of grace, others according to the law of Moses, and others according to the law of nature, which God has written in the hearts of all men, but all in the hope of the coming of Christ, and nobody since the beginning of time has been absolved of the original fault in any other way, but through the intercession of the sacred blood.[24]

Salvation is achieved only by the power of Christ's grace. The reception of this grace produces an inner transformation of the heart. When man entrusts himself to God, and, by virtue of this trust, complements all his actions with the supernatural love that he has mysteriously received, his actions are significantly transformed. The love flowing from the heart of the Holy Trinity is "reincarnated" within human generosity. This is obviously not an automatic occurrence. It requires a spiritual disposition, an actual effort to apply creatively the gift of grace we have received here and now, at this particular moment, and to treat our neighbor with greater kindness, gentleness, and love embraced for God's sake and for His good pleasure. The confession of faith of Lucidus of Gaul, made at a time when the geographical and historical awareness we have today was lacking, essentially contains the teachings of Vatican II on the workings of grace outside the visible structure of the Church.

God's grace will always remain a mystery. We have no right, therefore, to erect walls to try to block God's action. Seventeenth-century Jansenism implanted in the thinking of Catholics the prideful notion that God's grace is precious and thus bound to be very rare. From there, it is easy to slip into restricting the workings of grace with our philosophizing — and into condemning enemies. Meanwhile, the ancient Church rejoiced in any manifestation of grace that was recognized outside of Christianity. Before a missionary went to preach the gospel to the pagans, the Holy Spirit anticipated his preaching, mysteriously opening hearts to the grace of faith. The fact that the working of grace can sometimes be mysterious and impossible to measure or control does not mean that it is nonexistent. We can rejoice when we recognize the

---

[24] *Enchiridion Symbolorum*, no. 341.

manifestations of grace in people's hearts, but we cannot strongly condemn those in whom this working has not yet blossomed with radiance.

In his discourse on grace, Cardinal Charles Journet, the leading architect of the ecclesiology of Vatican II, quoted the texts of psalms sung during pilgrimages to the shrine of the idol Vishnu in India. These non-Christian chants, composed in the eighteenth century, included the following passage:

> How can our minds grasp him of whose light the sun and moon are but a reflection?... This God of love can be reached only by love.... We have fashioned a Vishnu of stone, but the stone is not Vishnu; adoration is given to Vishnu, and the stone remains in the stone figure.... It is your glory, O God, to be called the Savior of sinners.... The saints call you the Lord of those who despair; and when I heard it, my heart took courage.[25]

As part of the services, during which the Hindus would douse the idol with perfume, could not a faith-filled and confident entrustment to God have been born in their hearts? Is there not a secret stream of grace there, the grace of Christ, directing them to the heart of the heavenly Father? Cardinal Journet observes:

> Among these pilgrims there are, doubtless, some who dwell mainly on the words of the hymns and who perform the traditional rites and sacrifices simply as a matter of custom, and others who pay little attention to the meaning of the hymns and whose main concern is with the idolatrous practices. The former, unlike the latter, belong spiritually to Christ and the Church.[26]

The operation of grace directing hearts toward the supernatural goal that is God is mysterious and, as such, beyond measure. We can only be delighted when we perceive this action of God. This, of course, does not exonerate the Church from her duty to proclaim the gospel to the whole world. Neither

---

[25] Charles Journet, *The Meaning of Grace* (New York: P.J. Kenedy and Sons, 1960), 119.
[26] Journet, *The Meaning of Grace*, 119–120.

does it mean that in those in whom the action of grace is not enhanced by the light of God's Word and the sacraments, it would not be at risk of going unnoticed or being distorted. Nor does it mean that we can adopt a position diametrically opposed to the Jansenist claim, assuming that the fullness of grace is given automatically and equally to all people.

When we consider the issue theoretically, undoubtedly the distinction between nature and supernature — that is, the structure of the human being given to man by virtue of creation, and the gift of Christ's revelation and grace — is the most significant. This means that there is an essential division between those who have not received the grace of Christ and those who, by God's good pleasure, have received it, if only in a mysterious way. Salvation is impossible without grace, and the path of supernatural life cannot be taken by the power of natural effort. But since grace cannot be measured, it is impossible to take a "census" of God's people — as King David awkwardly tried to do (1 Chron. 21:1) — since that would constitute an attempt at strictly defining the limits of God's generosity. Far more important for the spiritual life, however, is another division: between those who received and responded to inner stirrings from God and those who, having received grace, did not respond to it or, like the rich young man in the Gospel, responded only up to a certain point — and lacked the magnanimity for further growth in spiritual life. The gift of grace, given out of God's goodness, demands a personal response. God bestows on people not only human nature, which is given to all alike, but also grace, which allows for personal communion with God. This grace, accepted and embraced by man, allows God to enjoy a trusting communion with man. God is the Father and not just the Creator. He is Creator precisely because He is Father, and, as Father, He desires contact with the man who trusts Him, who grasps His hand and responds with love to His love, who expects the promised gift, and who does not only strain himself through cold calculations regarding the philosophical enigma about the source and meaning of life.

Is "pure nature" still possible?

In theology, we deal with what really takes place or has taken place. We know from revelation that we have been chosen by God and are destined for holiness, which is not so much a moral correctness but rather a participation in the holiness of God Himself. This means that the divine will of showering us with grace has been revealed to us, but we do not know how this takes place and whether it happens in the case of each individual. We know, of course, that we can place an obstruction before God and refuse the given grace; we can kill it within us through mortal sin; or we can fail to develop it. Whatever the case, even in rejecting grace, man, as he exists in the real world, is somehow correlated with supernature. In rejecting the gift of grace, man does not place himself in a completely pure situation, in a nature distilled from grace. If then, we study man only in the light of reason and not faith, and we try to perceive his nature with its inner structure and inclinations, which allow us to formulate the natural law, it is always an analysis of the real man, the man whom God desires to save, as we know by faith.

When the hypothetical concept of "pure nature" was devised, it was used as an attempt to answer the question about what man would be like if he were not ordained toward the supernatural life, if he had not committed Original Sin, and if he had no interest in the question of God. This theory attempts to construct man as if through a surgical incision, ignoring his being ordered to God. Such an intellectual exercise does not tell us anything about the real man, but instead it gravitates apologetically toward the prejudices of unbelievers, and by adapting to their doubts, it tries to show man himself without reference to grace.

A certain fallacy is clear in this apologetic maneuver, a manipulation, an assumption made so as supposedly to come closer to the listener, who, for some reason, is closed to the revealed truth, in the hope that purely natural arguments will convince him. If we adopt as our departure point the hypothetically autonomous "pure nature," we abandon the theological truth about man. Such a procedure makes the teaching about natural law incomprehensible. The reflection on the natural law that we have from Aquinas, and that the Church follows, does not refer to man trapped in "pure nature" who is not ordered toward God; it refers to the real man, who is in need of grace. In order to engage in a relationship with God, Adam needed grace no less before the Fall than he did after it, although man after

Original Sin needs to apply that grace to more numerous, wounded aspects of his personality.[27]

The hypothesis of the autonomous "pure nature" leads also to the false suggestion that revelation serves only for the reparation of that which has been distorted by sin in the supernatural life. This is a reduction of revelation to the postlapsarian situation of man with the suggestion that "pure nature" itself does not need to be instructed by God. We lose, then, the perspective of the original project of God from before the world was made (Eph. 1:4–5), the perspective of introducing man into a relationship with God as adopted children, brothers of sisters of the Firstborn out of many (Rom. 8:29).

We could therefore conclude that the hypothesis of "pure nature" is unnecessary and that it falsifies the theological picture of man. It does not tell us anything about man as he is, or as he was, but only as he could have been, had God hypothetically not wanted to ordain him to Himself. The Magisterium of the Church, however, in raising this hypothetical question, does introduce the category of "pure nature." Pius XII's 1950 encyclical *Humani generis*, laments that some theologians

> destroy the gratuity of the supernatural order, since God, they say, cannot create intellectual beings without ordering and calling them to the beatific vision.[28]

It does not follow from this that God does, in fact, create many men who are not ordained in some way to participate in His life. The text of the encyclical brings in the suggestion of a "pure nature" only to stress the gratuity of grace. God's grace is in no way owed to man. It is not a consequence of nature; it is a complete novelty in respect to nature. Although, by virtue of creation, the human nature contains within it the paradox of a limited and dependent being marked by an openness to something more, there is no natural desire in nature for the supernatural. Nature itself cannot define, desire, or embrace supernature. The desire for grace emerging in the human

---

[27] "Man does not need grace more after sin than before it, but he needs it for more things." *ST*, I, q. 95, art. 4, ad 1, trans. E. Hill, vol. 13 (1964).

[28] Pope Pius XII, encyclical *Humani generis* (August 12, 1950), no. 26.

heart is always first God's gift, as the Second Synod of Orange put it. The possibility of the existence of people unaffected by grace, suggested by Pius XII, raises the question of their status. Such a speculative question can be posed; indeed, any question can be posed. This does not mean that we have the resources to provide a complete answer to each and every hypothetical question. What we proclaim in theology with certitude is grounded in the revealed Word of God. Ultimately, then, it is better to proclaim and delve with theological insight into what we know, that is, into those mysteries that have been revealed to us and, through the assistance of the Holy Spirit, have been clarified throughout Church history, leaving those questions to which revelation has not given us a thorough explanation either with no answer or with a vague answer.[29]

Pius XII's proposition about the possibility of man's existence in "pure nature," without being elevated to the supernatural order, is not in itself absurd and must therefore be accepted. It points to the fundamental goodness of the natural order as such. It shows that there is no intrinsic fundamental inconsistency within human nature, even when it achieves only the imperfect happiness proper to its nature. Moreover, this proposition employs philosophy to recognize the right place of man within the hierarchy of being. We must not conclude from this, however, as Feingold points out,[30] that it is just as fitting for God to elevate man to grace as it is not to elevate him. On the contrary, man's supernatural elevation to grace most fully corresponds to the merciful nature of God, Who then reveals His generosity as it pleases Him. Likewise, it corresponds to natural human aspirations, in which a natural curiosity about God can be born, but it also elevates man much further and

---

[29] St. Paul mentions pagans who follow nature and are obedient to their conscience, although they have no revealed law (Rom. 2:14–16). It is not clear, however, whether and to what degree hidden grace is at work within them. We do know that "without faith it is impossible to please [God]. For whoever would draw near to God must believe that he exists and that he rewards those who seek him" (Heb. 11:6). Thus, those who were not baptized but believe that God exists and entrust themselves to Him are already living in grace. We do not know how many have not received the grace.

[30] Feingold, *Natural Desire*, 425, 437–438.

higher than a response to that curiosity, toward the living God Himself, and what is more, it is God's response to our weakness, marked by sin, that we can confidently show to God.

The nonexclusion of the theoretical possibility of a "pure nature" capable only of incomplete happiness provides the necessary context for reflection on the gratuity of grace. Being endowed with grace by God always constitutes a unique election of man, and the believer must persist in grateful receptivity to this unique and mysterious guidance by God, without inventing any justification for this divine choice. Human arguments explaining God's choices are not only invariably wrong, but they also destroy the openness to God's incomprehensible mystery realized in this very concrete human life.[31] God's covenant with man is realized through the gift of grace and through further particular choices. This happens in the case of the Chosen People, in the case of a priestly or religious vocation, and in the case of the marriage covenant elevated by God to the level of a sacrament, as well as in many other ways. It is precisely to safeguard the gratuitousness of grace and God's free pleasure in such choices that the Church's Magisterium allows the idea of the possibility of a state of "pure nature" not ordered to a supernatural relationship with God. Of course, a grateful awareness of God's special gift of grace requires constant purification, safeguarding us against a presumptuous haughtiness, but this is a different issue. And the bestowal of grace itself is, in relation to nature, a new gift, and, as such, it allows for the idea that there may also be people created by God who do not receive this gift.[32] Thus, the claim of a

---

[31] Reflecting on the diversity of God's gifts, whether in nature or with regard to the grace that believers receive, or in the election of Israel, St. Thomas quoted the words of St. Augustine, whose advice was that we refrain from cheap philosophizing if we do not wish to go astray: "Do not seek to determine why he draws one and not another to himself if you wish to avoid error." *Super Ioannem*, tr. 26; *ST*, I, q. 23, art. 5, ad 3; Ia-IIae, q. 98, art. 4 (trans. D. Bourke and A. Littledale, vol. 29, 1969).

[32] The possibility of the existence of a "pure nature" not endowed with grace opens the discussion about the status of "expendable" embryos and miscarried fetuses. They are undoubtedly human beings entitled to human dignity. However, the absence of Baptism and, moreover, the lack of development of the spiritual powers of reason and will allow the idea that supernatural

nature not ordered to grace is not a purely hypothetical supposition, and it has its place in theological reflection on grace.

We should not assume, however, that this "pure nature" is so completely self-sufficient that it can compete with grace and that when it is nevertheless endowed with it, it can treat this fact as indifferent and meaningless — in other words, that nature can just as easily dispense with grace, considering it superfluous. The fact that certain individuals may do just that and reject grace, claiming to be content with the natural perspective alone does not mean that they are not greatly diminishing themselves, not to mention that they show themselves to be ungrateful toward God's gift. If they previously received the grace of faith, even if only at the moment of Baptism, then, by rejecting grace, they do not position themselves back in "pure nature." At that point, their nature is endowed and then is offended by the gift. One who receives the gift and then rejects it is not in the same position as one who never received the gift.

The relationship of grace to nature

While insisting on the superiority of the theological perspective, which draws on revelation and recognizes a deeper perspective in man, we should not deny the value of a purely philosophical approach to man. We can look at human nature apart from the order of grace, and this philosophical view will perceive man's structure and the natural inclination of his spiritual powers toward plenitude. Philosophy seeks to comprehend with natural reason that which can be understood, and it is able arrive at truth, although it may be incomplete. The philosophical mind, when it seeks to comprehend the

---

life has not begun in them, and therefore the just and merciful God grants them a status that corresponds to their still immature and "pure" nature. St. John Paul II, in his encyclical *Evangelium Vitae*, wrote the following words to mothers who had had an abortion: "To the same Father and his mercy you can with sure hope entrust your child" (99). In the official Latin version, these words replaced the earlier version: "You will come to understand that nothing is definitely lost and you will be able to ask forgiveness from your child, who is now living in the Lord." The Holy Father retracted his earlier version because there are no grounds for a firm belief that children who die before birth enjoy eternal life.

human person metaphysically, perceives the intrinsic meaningfulness of the human being. Philosophical anthropology, unlike any descriptive science of man, delves into the logic, coherence, and inner purposefulness of man and all that encompasses him. The philosophy of man recognizes his composition of body and soul, his psychic structure, his social reference, and his sexual differentiation. The philosophy of God, or natural theology, on the other hand, penetrates into what can be known about the Absolute on the basis of natural curiosity and the perspicacity of the mind. It actualizes the natural, emergent desire to see God, and its answer can point to such a satisfaction of that desire as nature, and natural religiosity, often mixed with serious errors, can offer. Philosophical ethics, on the other hand, starting from the analysis of the natural metaphysical inclinations present in the human being, draws the conclusions of natural law, which are a rational construct teaching moral principles, justified by human nature itself. These rich, multifaceted philosophical explorations are not easy, but they are possible. They are rooted exclusively in reason. Adopting a broader theological horizon within which nature is situated provides, for a believer, a corrective context and a deeper inspiration, but philosophical reflection as such is still rooted in reason. The fact that the philosophical reasoning is conducted reliably and that its conclusions are grounded not in revelation but in reason does not mean that these conclusions will automatically be persuasive to others. It is not surprising that many people do not accept the arguments of natural law, and even if their minds are metaphysically trained, and therefore capable of accepting the entire rational argument, they may end up shrugging their shoulders and saying, "I'm not interested in that" or "I think my nature is different."

Recognizing the inner coherence of human nature, which is possible through philosophical reflection, is useful for theological reflection as well. When we take the revealed mysteries as our starting point, we may attempt to describe the fecundity of grace, which is realized within nature and not apart from it. A proper grasp of the essence of human nature and its operations allows for a more comprehensive description of the expansion of grace within the ethos, as long as, through faith, the revealed truth of grace is recognized and this truth is not subordinated to the data of the sole philosophical reason. In theology, the revealed mysteries of faith are not sifted through purely rational criteria. We accept the truth of faith about the presence and fecundity of the supernatural life within the human ethos because it was revealed to us. Faith here is not some fundamentalist "add-on" that mistrusts reason and despises nature. Grace presupposes nature and respects it, but it also elevates it to a higher level. Therefore, a theological synthesis must respect nature, which, although wounded by sin, is nevertheless not so completely corrupt that it cannot be a teacher, and it must respect grace. That is why Aquinas discusses the natural law but also gives a privileged place to the new law, the evangelical law of grace, which expresses the initiation into the inner life of God and openness to the guidance of the Holy Spirit. Similarly, the moral teaching of the Church must encompass both dimensions. It cannot be limited to an ethical discourse that rationally justifies the rules of conduct deduced from nature. It must strive for something greater. It must show the believer's participation in the inner life of God through a theological discourse undertaken in faith, in unity with the mysterious workings of grace, while providing instruction on the workings of God in the soul, on the laws of the development of the life of God, and on the possibilities of using the talent of grace to the fullest or of haplessly squandering it.

God's showering of grace upon man in no way wounds the nature of man. Grace is not a a heavy suit of armor imposed upon man from without. Grace fits nature. When God showers us with His love, He works within the natural human faculties, eliciting their natural beauty. The man who is sanctified by God becomes ever more natural, more human, more fascinating in his personality by fully responding to the interior movements of grace. If we observe artificiality or stiffness in someone, or an attitude of unrelentingly fierce religiosity and a zealous growing aggressiveness in his religion, this is a clear sign that the person's religious life is faulty and not a path to sanctity. True sanctity is gracious; it has a fascinating beauty, naturalness, and simplicity.

This does not mean, however, that openness to the workings of grace in the soul comes smoothly or without resistance. Man does not feel grace, but he can recognize whether he is guided by faith and acts upon it or whether the perspective of faith is ignored or even consciously rejected. Grace, precisely because it is not nature, is always new and even surprising to nature.

In the practice of the spiritual life, the supernatural order is met with opposition from our personality. There is only a certain level of the life of God that human nature can endure. Just as a virus causes fever in a body that is defending itself, supernatural life sometimes provokes opposition in the soul, in the psyche, and in the body. It is normal that the paths of the spiritual life are marked by struggles and crises. As God conquers the soul, the ungodly surfaces in man. Temptations arise during prayer. After years of seeming devotion to God, new difficulties suddenly arise, exposing hidden obstacles to God within the soul. It is God Himself Who then provokes the soul, as if tearing open the wounds of the psyche, in order to show where the ungodly was merely humanly sealed, blocking the fire of the Holy Spirit. In His desire for man to be completely transformed by grace, God Himself performs painful purifications, and expects trustful and passive submission to this action. When the masters of the spiritual life speak of "wrestling with nature" or "fighting the old man," they are not challenging the metaphysical goodness of human nature. They are merely highlighting the necessity of putting God's action first.

Theology uses the Latin term *assumptio*, which refers to the Assumption of Our Lady. It denotes an elevation or a taking up of her body and soul from above. We can apply this term to the life of grace in every one of us. If we truly enjoy true a relationship with God through faith and love, this means that we are lifted up by God and our whole personality, taken up by God, is gradually transformed. Such a person acquires a spiritual beauty that is somehow recognizable. People of faith can recognize the fruits of grace in others. The individual will be truly holy only when all of him is taken up by God, when his whole nature yields to the beneficial influence of supernature. The eternal happiness that is promised to us begins here on earth, when we live out the spirituality of the Beatitudes and when, open to grace, we let God take us up and transform us. Only when the entire personality, including the emotions and the body, is transformed by grace may a spiritual paternity or maternity develop in a person; this consists in contributing, through sacrifices and a charming personality, to the generation of the divine life in others. If we mistakenly imagine our anticipated beatitude, whether earthly or eternal, as an eternal rest, then our hope has to be purified. For happiness flows from action, from a union with God that is fruitful, in which there is active love and not a lazy inaction. The saints did not hope that in Heaven they would rest after the difficulties of this world, but they delighted in the thought that charity, passing through their generous personality and transformed already in this world by grace, would become even more fruitful in Heaven and that, by their love in Heaven, they would contribute to the growth of love in this world.

Since the grace of Christ is given to us, since we live now in the plenitude of time, it follows that the Church addresses the redeemed man, and not the fictitious man living in the state of "pure nature." The moral teaching of the Church is transmitted in faith, so it considers the fact that the preached word is simultaneously accompanied by the hidden working of the Holy Spirit, steering to eternity. This raises to a higher, supernatural level the perspective that is facing us. That is why St. John Paul II could declare:

> It would be a very serious error to conclude ... that the Church's teaching is essentially only an "ideal" which must then be adapted, proportioned, graduated to the so-called concrete possibilities of man. [...] Of *which* man are we speaking? Of man *dominated* by lust or of man *redeemed by Christ*? [...] God's command is of course proportioned to man's capabilities; but to the capabilities of the man to whom the Holy Spirit has been given; of the man who, though he has fallen into sin, can always obtain pardon and enjoy the presence of the Holy Spirit.[33]

The perspective of the Church in her moral teaching is always within a supernatural context. God not only revealed Himself as the end of man, but He also leads us to Himself by His grace, within the context of human life and dilemmas. The protests that the moral teaching of the Church elicits have their source partially in the forgetting of the spiritual dimension of the Church's teaching, not only by those who listen — which, naturally, must be forgiven — but also by those who teach in the name of the Church. Apologetics, which hangs on to the "natural" horizon and is focused only on what the

---

[33] Pope John Paul II, encyclical *Veritatis splendor* (August 6, 1993), no. 103.

"natural man" is capable of accepting rationally, distorts the moral teaching. A conscious acceptance of the supernatural end as it has been revealed by the loving God does not necessarily have to estrange the contemporary listener. It is exactly the opposite: Such a teaching is intriguing through its mystery, and the witness of faith attracts the faith of others toward the mystery of God. A response to humanity's going astray is not an impoverished religion reduced to morality but a moral teaching enriched by grace. A religion reduced to a purely ethical moralization is off-putting. But a moral teaching expressed in faith and openness to the assistance and decisive presence of the Holy Spirit opens hearts to His sanctifying influence.

There are no limits in surrendering to God. There is no threshold beyond which it is impossible to grow. St. Paul says, "All who are led by the Spirit of God are sons of God" (Rom. 8:14), and these words reveal the highest horizon of continuous, absolutely dispositional submission in faith to the guidance of God Himself. St. Maximilian Kolbe, throughout his life, sought to fathom Mary's bond with the Holy Spirit. In the last text he wrote, on February 17, 1941, just before his arrest, he pointed out the mysterious implication inherent in Mary's naming of herself in Lourdes: "I am the Immaculate Conception." Mary did not use the term "immaculately conceived," as in earlier apparitions, but "Immaculate Conception." This designation, as St. Maximilian writes, denotes the proper name of the Holy Spirit![34] The Holy Spirit is the One Who brings forth goodness in the Church in an immaculate way. Our actions are frequently impure, tainted by ambition, subordinated to our own ideologies. Mary, being wholly immaculate in her availability to the movements of the Holy Spirit, shows the supreme transformation of nature by supernature, the consummate acceptance of the revealed God as her ultimate happiness.

---

[34] The same intuition was also shared by the French mystic Marthe Robin. See H. M. Manteau-Bonamy, O.P., *Hors de la Femme point de salut?* (Paris: Mame, 1991), 49.

2

God, Who Bestows Happiness

Revelation of the Father's heart

WE CAN APPROACH THE QUESTION of man's ultimate happiness with confidence, without hesitation, because we know that the answer to this question has been given to us. God, in His goodness, has revealed Himself and His heart to us. In his open heart, Jesus has shown the heart of the Father, which longs for us. In theological reflections, we start from God, from the truths that He has revealed to us.

We know that the question of happiness has fascinated many people. All people desire happiness and wonder where this happiness can be found. Unlike modern thinkers, ancient philosophers put the search for happiness at the center of their ethical deliberations. They proposed different answers to this question. For the Stoics, happiness lay in virtue; for Aristotle, the pinnacle of happiness was the contemplation of truth. The Epicureans gave a more down-to-earth answer, suggesting pleasure as the way to satisfy the hunger for happiness. It was these metaphysical pursuits of the philosophers, rather than sentimental ones, that St. Augustine was invoking when he uttered his famous confession to God: "You have made us for Yourself, and our hearts are restless until they rest in You."[35] In theology, we don't need to tread those tormented paths of human thought again. The answer has been given to us. God has given Himself to us, and we can look at our lives from the summit, taking the open arms of our Heavenly Father as our starting point. Just as, in

---

[35] *Confessions*, bk. I, chap. 1.

exploring a city, we first look at a map that shows us the whole outline of the city before we focus on the details, so in looking at human life, we can start from the merciful God, Who appears not only as the Creator and source of moral order but also as the loving Father Who longingly awaits us.

Accepting God, Who can bestow the fullness of happiness as our ultimate goal, does not warrant suspicion. Ever since the dominant role in ethical thought was attributed to obligation, doubt has been cast on the honesty of putting the desire for happiness first. It was held that prioritizing the hunger for happiness may increase selfishness and mar our image of God. But when obligation was placed above happiness, the truth that God is a Father was forgotten. God was viewed as a sovereign and a judge, and the fact that He is a Father Who knows our deepest needs was overshadowed. Meanwhile, God's Word reveals to us in various ways the perspective of union with the Father Who awaits us, a union in which the Holy Trinity as a whole is involved. The Father tells each one of us, just as He tells His Son, "Son, … all that is mine is yours" (Luke 15:31). Our home is in Heaven, and living in the hope of a full union with God at the end of time and at our death belongs to the core of Christian life. We look forward to the resurrection of our bodies. We cry out, "Thy kingdom come" (Matt 6:10). We know that when the eye of the soul is directed toward God, the "whole body will be full of light" (Matt. 6:22). Christ is the Head of the Church, "from whom the whole body, joined and knit together … makes bodily growth and upbuilds itself in love" (Eph. 4:16). The point is that we should not be like immature people, "tossed to and fro and carried about with every wind of doctrine" (Eph. 4:14), but should "attain to the unity of the faith and of the knowledge of the Son of God, to mature manhood, to the measure of the stature of the fullness of Christ" (Eph. 4:13). Moved by the Holy Spirit, we find in Christ the path leading to the Father along with our dignity as children of God, children adopted by God. "All who are led by the Spirit of God are sons of God. For you did not receive the spirit of slavery to fall back into fear, but you have received the spirit of sonship. When we cry, 'Abba! Father!' it is the Spirit himself bearing witness with our spirit that we are children of God, and if children, then heirs, heirs of God and fellow heirs with Christ" (Rom. 8:14–17). Union with the Holy Trinity and knowing the Divine Persons from within their mutual relations is completely beyond our natural abilities, and yet, at the beginning of the Sermon on the Mount, the Lord Jesus teaches us that our beatitude lies precisely in seeing God, possessing the kingdom of Heaven, having mercy shown to us, and being called the sons of God (see Matt. 5:3–12). The desire for happiness, which is the deepest longing of the human heart, is satisfied by the gratuitously given gift of God.

How does this happen on a practical level? How does God's gift permeate our daily lives?

The life of man is the vision of God

While St. Irenaeus of Lyons's statement "The glory of God is man fully alive" is very well known, the second part of that sentence is rarely quoted: "Moreover, man's life is the vision of God." St. Irenaeus adds, "If God's revelation through creation has already obtained life for all the beings that dwell on earth, how much more will the Word's manifestation of the Father obtain life for those who see God."[36] The vision of God is not an indifferent matter, nor is it far off. It is fundamental to our hope. The Lord Jesus prayed, "And this is eternal life, that they know thee the only true God, and Jesus Christ whom thou hast sent" (John 17:3). Meanwhile, St. John leads our hope beyond being the children of God toward the vision of God Himself: "We are God's children now; it does not yet appear what we shall be, but we know that when he appears we shall be like him, for we shall see him as he is" (1 John 3:2).[37]

God alone can give Himself to us so that we can see, know, and love Him. We cannot force God to give Himself to us; we can only touch His Heart through showing Him our misery, our lowliness, and our need for His

---

[36] Quoted in *Catechism of the Catholic Church* (*CCC*), no. 294.
[37] The belief that beatitude in Heaven consists in the vision of God was officially confirmed in Pope Benedict XII's constitution *Benedictus Deus* of 1336. There, we read, "These souls have seen and see the divine essence with an intuitive vision and even face to face, without the mediation of any creature by way of object of vision; rather the divine essence immediately manifests itself to them, plainly, clearly and openly, and in this vision they enjoy the divine essence. Moreover, by this vision and enjoyment the souls of those who have already died are truly blessed and have eternal life and rest." *The Christian Faith*, no. 2305.

grace, but His gift is completely free, given out of love for us, His beloved. Our spiritual life consists in placing complete trust and hope in none other than God Himself. The closer we are to God, the less we put our trust in anything that is not God. There is some grandeur in this supernatural hope! We expect our happiness from the hands of God alone! No lesser created being, no angel, no saint, no earthly reality, no human being, no money, no honor, no political power, no ideology can satisfy the hunger for happiness that is within us. Only God Himself can fulfill us completely, and our confidence, bordering on impudence, allows us to expect happiness from no one but God Himself!

No goods lesser than God can give us supreme happiness, tempting as they may sometimes seem. The supernatural perspective sometimes gets blurred in our human consciousness, and then other suggestions emerge, somehow closer and more concrete, but they cannot satisfy us fully. Once tried, they always leave us with a feeling of distaste and dissatisfaction. They are still not what we are looking for! The human mind and will tend toward the universal, toward that which transcends the world of the senses. Our senses are important in life, and they provide necessary sensations, but happiness is not about satisfying the senses. If we could take a drug that would give us a sense of satisfaction from our work, but without actually doing the work, would such artificial gratification give us happiness? Supreme happiness cannot be found in sensations. Man's greatness lies in the fact that he longs for that which transcends all sensation and imagination; he longs for God, Who lets Himself be known and loved.

In this reaching out to God, should primacy be given to loving God or to knowing Him? This question has bothered Christians for centuries, so there is a double track in Christian thought. The Franciscan tradition focuses on the primacy of love. The Thomist tradition insists on the primacy of cognition. This contradiction is only seeming, depending on the approach to the problem. If we look at the issue from the point of view of our spiritual faculties, we will place cognition at the central point. The will is always dependent on cognition. To love, we have to know what we love. The object of the movement of the will is the object shown by the intellect to the will, to which the will is attracted, and not just the experience of the desire within the will. It follows that happiness is more in the intellect than in the will. Only when the intellect has focused upon that which is known can the will rest in the object of happiness. That is why St. Augustine defined happiness as the joy of truth. The intuition of truth, and truth that concerns the most important matters, is most attractive to man. In the search for truth, there is something similar to mountain climbing. Why do people climb mountains? Simply because the mountains are out there, and they attract us by their beauty. Similarly, truth has a beauty that fascinates the human mind. The cognition of truth, a truth that fascinates and that we want to share, causes an increase of love. Friendship is true and deep only when it is based upon values that have been mutually discovered, when we can catch our neighbor by the sleeve and say: "Look!" Love does not consist in the looking into each other's eyes, but in looking together in the same, important direction.[38]

In the Beatific Vision of God, the activation of the intellect and the will are simultaneous. In Heaven there will be no faith and hope, because they will no longer be needed. Only charity will remain. We will see and love God. If we look at the question of happiness in the ontological order, we ascribe a primacy to the intellect over the will — that is, to cognition over loving. In the moral order, however, there is a primacy of loving over cognition. Did not the sin of Adam consist exactly in the placing of knowing above loving? The biblical image shows us Adam living in a trustful, childlike intimacy with God up to the moment when, under the temptation of the evil one, he conducts an experiment. Adam wants to test God; he wants to see if what God says is in accord with reality. In reducing God to the level of an object of cognition, Adam elevates his intellect above love, and then he falls out of the union of love. That is why, in our earthly life, there is a primacy of loving over cognition.

In Heaven, the vision of God is pure and direct, and it will immediately turn into love. Here on earth, love is more important, and it presupposes faith and hope, which predispose toward love. God has tied our meeting with Him with faith and not with cognition, so as to preserve the quality of

---

[38] Cf. "Love does not consist in gazing at each other, but in looking outward together in the same direction," attributed to Antoine de Saint-Exupéry.

our love. If we were to meet God through knowledge, this would generate pride, and the worst type of pride — that is, intellectual, demonic pride. That is why it is much more important that we have faith and love of God than theological or religious knowledge. There is something specifically ugly in the attitude of a theologian of doubtful quality who is proud of his knowledge and at the same time who makes fun of the faith of simple people. True faith, which is a humility of the intellect, opens up the exchange of love with God. And this exchange will never end in the life to come. This means that charity, which is lived out on earth, gives us already a participation in the reality of Heaven. Charity is the only reality of Heaven that can be lived out here on earth.

Since the participation in the love of God commences here, the happiness that God gives to us accompanies us in our earthly life. We do not experience yet the seeing of God face-to-face, but we may experience today the promises contained in the Beatitudes, which open the Sermon on the Mount. The Sermon on the Mount, which grants us a Christian moral perspective, analogous to the Old Testament perspective given on Mount Sinai, begins with Christ's response to the question of happiness. The promised happiness is paradoxical and contrary to our disordered reflexes. It is possible only through divine grace. The *Catechism of the Catholic Church* points out that "the Beatitudes depict the countenance of Jesus Christ and portray his charity" (CCC 1717), and *Veritatis splendor* tells us that they are "a sort of self-portrait of Christ" (no. 16). This does not mean that we are faced with a perspective experienced uniquely by Christ. The Beatitudes play a role in our lives. They "sustain hope in the midst of tribulations; they proclaim the blessings and the rewards already secured, however dimly, for Christ's disciples" (CCC 1717). The grace of Christ flows as a hidden stream in human hearts and elicits a resonance in them that is more attractive than purely rational argumentation. It is true that "such beatitude surpasses the understanding and powers of man. It comes from an entirely free gift of God: whence it is called supernatural" (CCC 1722). This does not mean that the Beatitudes involve a distant and impossible reality. It is due to the power of divine grace, which is given now, that the Beatitudes are attractive, because what is impossible in human terms becomes divinely possible. Humanly speaking, it is not possible always and everywhere to be in favor of being poor in spirit, of meekness, of peace and purity of heart. Life situations are sometimes very complicated. But when we live in faith and trust in the accompanying power of Christ, we can perceive a spiritual beauty and supreme value in introducing peace where there is hatred, in the poor counting only upon the power of God in the hope of the victory of the kingdom of Heaven, in patiently suffering persecution for justice, in silent generous love that changes the face of the earth. One who has personally experienced that "it is more blessed to give than to receive" (Acts 20:35) can recognize the truth of the Beatitudes and accept with joy that they "confront us with decisive choices concerning earthly goods; they purify our hearts in order to teach us to love God above all things" (*CCC* 1728).

The practical consequences of being focused on God

The recognition that we find supreme happiness in God entails an appropriate reorientation of life, so that God can be sought and loved above all. Since the gift of happiness in God surpasses completely all human capacities and imagination, we are not able, on the basis of our natural dispositions, to aspire to participate in the inner life of God, nor can we meet God. This, however, is possible thanks to the gift of grace, which contains the theological virtues of faith, hope, and charity. Faith is a divinely given disposition that enables contact with God. Even though we cannot give ourselves faith — we receive it from God — the development of that faith depends on our efforts. As we express faith, we surrender to God, relying on His power, His promises, and the truth He has revealed. We can liken faith to a faucet that must be pressed continuously rather than simply turned on in order for water to come out of it. When we express our faith, when we surrender ourselves to God, an encounter with Him takes place, and, in a mysterious manner, God gives Himself. When we cease exercising faith, He has no access to us. God is goodness itself and wants to give Himself, but that giving is dependent on our practice of faith. Consequently, the first and foremost matter in the spiritual life is to establish in our lives the central place of contemplative prayer, through which we express our faith.

The masters of the spiritual life exhort beginners to ensure the regularity and quality of their union with God. The first step in the spiritual life is the growth of yearning for God. That is why beginners are encouraged to commit to a regular practice of personal prayer. It is not the length of the prayer that is decisive but its regularity. If someone cares daily to devote half an hour to be in silence with God, this will soon bear fruit. It is important that the delicate plant of the spiritual life be fortified, that an authentic, mutual conversation with the living God takes place. The experience of sinfulness or even the memory of past sins does not have to be an obstacle. We are weak like children, and that is why we need this engaging with God. The introduction of a personal rhythm of prayer, however brief, is demanding but brings order into life. It is important that in this there is a conscious desire for God, which is expressed in the regularity of the practice of prayer and in the great desire for the plenitude of the gift of God. The manner of prayer and its length must be adapted to the vocation; it is lived out differently by a person living a cloistered life and by a busy layperson. Each person is free to develop a permanent rhythm of prayer and tend to its quality as he sees fit and according to his circumstances. It is not essential that a particular program be fulfilled. The establishment of a personal, friendly relationship with God is essential, and that forms a basic axis of the spiritual and moral life.

In prayer, when we go beyond sensual experiences, beyond thinking about God toward surrendering to Him in faith, a true encounter with Him takes place, and this is crucial for the supernatural character of our lives. In the Christian life, it is not the struggle with sin, the struggle to acquire moral virtues, that is to be in the first place but the solicitude for the primacy of the relationship with God — and this takes place through the practical exercise of the three virtues that God has implanted in our soul: faith, hope, and charity. Thinking about our personal sinfulness may overshadow the spiritual life when the feeling of guilt caused by sin leads to a concentration on self and on frenzied attempts to purify oneself from the filth. In such an attitude, we forget that it is not we who purify ourselves; it is God, Who, in His grace, liberates us from evil and enables us to love. That is why we should resolve to practice a trustful orientation toward God, despite, or perhaps even because of, our weaknesses. St. Thérèse of Lisieux affirms, "What pleases him [the Good Lord] is that he sees me loving my littleness and my poverty, the blind hope that I have in his mercy."[39] Faith does not give a vision of God, but when it is practiced, hope and charity follow, and through them a contact with God is experienced. This union with God already here on earth opens us to further graces. If we give ourselves to God, then supernatural divine charity becomes the ultimate norm of conduct, and divine fecundity will be manifested in our actions. The whole difficulty consists in relying on God in any problems we experience, as He is known in the darkness of faith.

Receiving God as the One to Whom we aspire and surrender grants an essential axis to our entire lives. Thus, we do not fall into a pointless, confused nihilism. By living in God, we are fully rooted and certain as to where we come from and where we are going. Of course, we are distracted by many events, we have responsibilities toward our loved ones, we live fully engaged in this world, but our focus may be elsewhere, on God, beyond these temporal things. Many forces may move us, from human curiosity, to emotions, to purely biological needs; these are important and necessary, but they do not merit the dignity of the ultimate finality. They are like the branches of a Christmas tree that extend outward. In the tree, what is most important is the trunk, which is oriented upward. Likewise, in the spiritual life, the orientation toward God is most important, since it allows a gradual ordering of all other desires and all secondary goals in life around the fundamental axis that is directed toward God.

If the end is truly ultimate, it may only be one. The gospel calls us to receive the unique end that is life in God consciously as a gift from God, Who discloses Himself, as a sovereign end that subordinates to itself all the other intermediary ends. Man either has God as his ultimate end, or he has himself as his ultimate end, his own self-deification, which appears in various incarnations. If we make an idol out of riches, money, power, or honors, we place ourselves above God. This is the essence of sin — that, in a given

---

[39] Letter 197, to Céline, Les Archives du Carmel, https://archives.carmel delisieux.fr/en/correspondance/lt-197-a-soeur-marie-du-sacre-coeur-17 -septembre-1896/, accessed May 21, 2024.

moment, ultimate fulfillment is sought in something other than God, and in this way, the source of divine life is cut off.

Putting God in the first place in life does not happen immediately. Often it seems as if God is first, but as soon as difficulties appear, it turns out that the heart turns to something else. There are also absurd actions in life, there are inconsistencies, in which it turns out that the ultimate rule of life is not the search for God but an immature inclination. That is why the spiritual life requires purifications that place the focus on God and grant it a primary place. The development of the spiritual life aids psychic and spiritual integration, which, in turn, grants harmony to life around its fundamental axis. That we observe contradictions and inconsistencies in human actions — not only in schizophrenics — but this does not mean that there is no fundamental end. It simply means that the divine image is clouded or is not elicited in that person.

In the spiritual and moral life, the focus on God needs to be purified, so that the intuition of God, the intuition that shows wherein lies the greatest, most important truth, will become dominant in life. It is not surprising that Aquinas begins the "moral section" of the *Summa Theologiae* by posing the question about man's final end and that St. John Paul II titled his encyclical about the fundamentals of Christian morals *Veritatis splendor* — the splendor of truth. If moral theology searches for the signs of God in the image that is the mature person, then the starting point will be an education toward purposeful action, in view of the supreme, consciously chosen end, which captivates by its truth. The purification of the focus on God that is consciously chosen as an end liberates from immature willing and contributes toward a development of conscious willing. If God is recognized as an end, this means that the meeting with God is not limited to a merely passive looking at Him. A supposed contemplative prayer, limited to being dissolved in God, generates egoism. God is our ultimate end. This means that the focus on God is through all three theological virtues. In faith, the revealed mystery is received. In hope, God and His mysterious direction of life are accepted as the source of supreme happiness. In charity, there is the giving of oneself to God through a conscious and practical undertaking of the gift of self. In practice, these three theological virtues fuse into one focus on God.

In this direction toward God, sin does not have to be an obstacle. We should not think that crystal purity is needed before we can approach God. Our Lord promises the Samaritan woman who had lived with six men "a spring of water welling up to eternal life" (John 4:14). The spring of grace is important. We should not be too bothered that the water flows over hard rocks or through mud. What matters is the living water, which, in time, will wash out the mud and cut down the rough edges of the stones. We may have the feeling that our life looks like crawling through the mud of sin, but if our nose sticks out of the mud, if our focus is on God in faith and trustful charity, God will, in time, free us from sin, and the spring of grace will wash out the sin. This purification takes place during our entire lives, with the interplay of our own efforts and the workings of the Holy Spirit. The third part of the *Catechism*, devoted to life in Christ, ends with a reminder of what St. Teresa of Avila said as a child: "I want to see God!" The tenth commandment, showing the need of the purification of all earthly desires, aims at giving this most fundamental desire the pride of place in lives. " 'I want to see God' expresses the true desire of man. Thirst for God is quenched by the water of eternal life (cf. John 4:14)" (*CCC* 2557).

The practical recognition of God as the ultimate end of life's pilgrimage brings about an essential change in that life. Grace, which is given by God, bears fruit in entire life. We do good, and God is present in that good in a mysterious way. So all human action acquires a supernatural dimension and expresses the love of God in a concrete manner, which is clear for the believer. Human nature seems completely encompassed by the action of God. When describing this reality, the Fathers of the Church compared it to playing a musical instrument. God, playing the guitar that is man, brings out a beautiful melody. This comparison is picturesque but faulty, because God does not use us as passive instruments. The action of the grace of the Holy Spirit passes through the human faculties, through the intellect and the will, through talents and mature initiatives. In the Christian life, what is important is openness to this supernatural transformation of human action. In spiritual theology, theologians studied the works of the mystics to see how God becomes increasingly present in the life of prayer. Just as important, and perhaps even more so, is investigating how the grace of the Holy Spirit is present in action. It is only then that that action is truly divine — that it is truly apostolic and truly contributes to the building up of the Church.

The granting of a supernatural dimension to action, and the entry into the reality of beatitude that God offers, requires cooperation and a personal effort. God created man free, and He has not given up His agenda of liberty for man. The gift of beatitude comes from God, but God expects our cooperation in the development of grace. We can compare this to a child learning a skill, such as riding a bicycle. The adult shows the child how to ride the bicycle and then the child asks to do it alone. Maturity requires independent initiative, and the child is happy when he can experience his independence, when he has his own achievements.

God created man without man, but He will not save man without his cooperation in the assimilation of grace. That is why the gift of self in a personal independent generosity that flows from grace is necessary for spiritual growth, so that man may be transformed from within through the power of God. In the language of theology, that cooperation with grace is called *merit*. We cannot merit grace itself, since it is freely given, but we can grow in the life of grace when we follow up God's call with a personal response. As we freely and consciously undertake good acts, not only out of utility or pleasure but in view of goodness itself, the image of God within us will grow.

Fr. Józef Bocheński captured this aptly when he compared happiness to the toil of a worker at a machine. A worker's attention is focused on the work that he is doing and not on the heat that is the by-product of the generated energy. Similarly, happiness is not something that should be pursued as such. Happiness comes when the attention is focused outside the personal experiences, toward the goodness that is worth undertaking. When we search for God, for the goodness that He shows us, and when we give ourselves totally to that goodness, we discover that "it is more blessed to give than to receive." Growth of the life of grace, then, takes place through the generous undertaking of goodness, with the sole motive that is the love of God. It is not, therefore, only the hunger for happiness that lies at the basis of the moral life. At the basis is the openness to truth and goodness and, even more — openness to God, and this pursuit of God elicits happiness. Christian life consists in a constant calling out to God, in creatively answering the call of His grace, which leads to happiness. If a life is truly lived with God, it is permeated with a reaching out toward happiness, toward eschatology, and toward the final union with God. In daily life, freely giving oneself to God may become increasingly intense, expressing more and more trust and love, and there is no limit to the love that can be offered to God.

3

The Fecundity of God in Human Acts

IN THE SERMON ON THE Mount, Jesus exhorts us to act in such a way "that [men] may see your good works and give glory to your Father who is in heaven" (Matt. 5:16). This is not an externally imposed injunction, which would be terrifying in itself on account of its impossibility. Rather, it is a harbinger of God's presence within human actions, a presence that can be so transparent that this epiphany elicits the desire to praise God. When there is openness to grace, it happens that "God is at work in you, both to will and to work for his good pleasure" (Phil. 2:13). Since "all who are led by the Spirit of God are sons of God" (Rom. 8:14), the one who lives in an attitude of a childlike trust in God is strengthened from within by the Holy Spirit with His power and His divine fruitfulness.

According to St. Thomas Aquinas, the most certain manifestation of the grace of the Holy Spirit in a person is disclosed when faith makes its power felt through love (see Gal. 5:6). This observation does not have to be viewed as describing some impossible situation. We know this from experience. When we meet someone who trusts in God and who, despite difficulties and his own personal limitations, is able to make sacrifices, we find this attitude fascinating. The person who knows how to give of himself in a creative, unique, and generous way elicits appreciation. In this attitude, there is something of God, a certain radiation of divine grace. With His creative power, God sustains the world in its existence, but divine goodness is an additional gift, which passes through human gestures and human ingenuity. This further action of God, which passes through the richness of the human gift, warrants more than simply the designation of its being a divine effect. There is something more to it, a certain fecundity as it passes through the human gift, through a free and creative contribution of a person who puts himself at God's disposal with courage and generosity. It is as if God needed the richness of a human personality and creativity so that His goodness could become fully visible. It would be unworthy of God and man if that additional goodness of God's grace were to go passively through man. God does not treat us as inanimate puppets. The radiance of His grace calls for our mature personality and our free, personally given gift.

The question that arises, then, for theology is that of this mysterious presence of God within human generosity. How is it that God is present in our actions? How does human freedom meet with God's power and mercy? A moral theology that is fully theology, rather than a philosophical ethics or a theological ethics, above all seeks God not merely in His vestigial presence in created beings but the living God, Who shows His mercy within human agency. Moral theology aspires to teach which inner dispositions need to be adopted so that God may be allowed to enter, so to speak, inside the seemingly most trivial human actions. It describes the inner liberation that, by the power of grace, frees from spiritual repression and from the inner bondage that blocks the flourishing of goodness in man. In theological reflection on morality, what matters is not so much describing what man does to God but what God does to man. How is it that God brings out the best in each of us, and how does He enable it to become the key feature of our lives? A theological elucidation of the inner mechanisms of human action will strive to aim further than just providing an ethical analysis of acts. A theologian sensitive to the accompanying presence of God will direct his attention toward that transformation of man in which the personality, the depth of the soul, and each act are fully subordinate to the movements of the Holy Spirit.

"For freedom Christ has set us free" (Gal. 5:1)

Contrary to reservations expressed by people outside the Church, she is not afraid of freedom. It is true that, since the age of the Enlightenment, the standard of freedom has been raised against the Church, to which she responded with strong words of admonishment. That does not mean, however, that the Church has ever renounced the freedom heralded by St. Paul and even Christ Himself. The perspective of freedom is one of the essential elements of Christian hope. The Church prays for freedom and is concerned that people will acquire freedom. Should we conclude, then, that the Church wants only freedom for herself and can struggle for it ferociously in times of threat, but as soon as her political influence grows, she abandons the defense of freedom and solicitude for it?

Church teaching on liberty may seem to be a contradiction in terms when there is a switch from one conceptual register to another. A politician whose perspective is merely temporal will speak about freedom in a different way from the Church, which is grounded in revelation. When St. John Paul II concludes that "freedom itself needs to be set free. It is Christ who sets it free,"[40] the issue of freedom is immediately placed within a theological context, one that is even mysterious. A mystery can never be exhausted or locked in a simple formula. If Christ does something with our freedom that may be described as a liberation toward a deeper freedom, this means that we can attempt to access this reality exclusively within faith. Understandably, liberty is a justified subject matter of philosophical or social reflection, but here it is a different perspective that is at issue: the freedom that is the fruit of the salvific action of God. In theology, we are dealing with God, Who effects through grace a significant transformation of our lives. Hence, from within faith, we can pose theological questions. How does God liberate our freedom? What does this mean? How do the workings of God's grace meet our freedom? If God enters our freedom with His grace, does this not somehow limit our freedom? What kind of purification of concepts must happen, in the light of revelation and theological tradition, so that the mystery, remaining a mystery, may become more digestible to us and, even more importantly, so that we may be able to partake in the promised reality?

The term *freedom* means more than being liberated from external pressure. When the *Catechism of the Catholic Church* teaches that "by deviating from the moral law man violates his own freedom, becomes imprisoned within himself" (CCC 1740), we feel instinctively that the word *freedom* is

---

[40] *Veritatis splendor* 86.

used appropriately here. Man may harm himself through sin and addiction, and, as a result, he becomes less free. St. Paul, who was, after all, familiar with slavery in the ancient world, writes about a much worse kind of slavery — the internal slavery, in which we can recognize our spiritual afflictions: "For I know that nothing good dwells within me, that is, in my flesh. I can will what is right, but I cannot do it. For I do not do the good I want, but the evil I do not want is what I do.... Wretched man that I am! Who will deliver me from this body of death?" (Rom. 7:18–19, 24). Union with Christ brings freedom, enables it to overcome bad inclinations and bestows a special dignity upon man. "In him we have communion with the 'truth that makes us free' (cf. John 8:32). The Holy Spirit has been given to us and, as the Apostle teaches, 'Where the Spirit of the Lord is, there is freedom' (2 Cor. 3:17). Already we glory in the 'liberty of the children of God' (Rom. 8:21)" (CCC 1741). Christianity instructs mankind that we have been invited to share in the life and love of the Holy Trinity, and that God expects our free response. This perspective undoubtedly elevates man's dignity in an extraordinary way. A particular manifestation of this dignity was the emergence of consecrated life in the early Church. In the world of ancient Rome, where adult children had no rights until the death of their parents, a young Christian woman might renounce the marriage her parents had planned for her and declare that her bridegroom was Christ! There were teenage girls in the second century who, defending their virginity "for the kingdom of Heaven," accepted martyrdom. Holy virgin martyrs such as Agatha, Lucy, Cecilia, and Agnes thus stood up not only for the truths of salvation but also for the dignity and rights of women.

Is it to be inferred from these biblical proclamations and wonderful examples of fortitude that a person is not free until the transformation by the grace of the Holy Spirit has been accomplished in him? So, if a person is ensnared by sin, and the sanctifying work of God's grace has not begun, he must remain in sin, because he is enslaved, because such is his unsanctified nature? If this were so, there would be no room for moral responsibility in a person not living in grace. Is such a person free enough to be accountable for evil deeds, or is he perhaps so tossed around by the forces of evil, against which he is powerless without the help of grace, that he bears no moral responsibility for those deeds? Revelation, while showing the prospect of man's emancipation in Christ, does not at the same time negate the original freedom, not revoked by sin. "Do not say, 'Because of the Lord I left the right way'"; for he will not do what he hates.... It was he who created man in the beginning, and he left him in the power of his own inclination.... He has placed before you fire and water: stretch out your hand for whichever you wish" (Sir. 15:11, 14, 16).

Proclaiming the perspective of grace, that is, showing in theology the truth about God present in the actions of a sanctified individual, we need to introduce appropriate distinctions so that, on the one hand, we will not preach a joyful, flowery passivism and, on the other hand, we will not fall into a pessimistic assessment of wounded human nature. Both extremes involve the danger of distorting spiritual life. The truth must remain in the middle. Aquinas sees the image of God in a mature man, guided by his own reason and free choice. In penetrating the character of God's fecundity, which manifests itself in the mature generosity of an individual sanctified by grace, it is necessary to consider his natural characteristics. A person, receiving the grace and happiness announced by God, is not like a wooden block upon which supernatural gifts would rain down from Heaven. The human person has a given structure, with natural abilities, the reason and will, predisposing to responsible and creative action. These natural talents are not to be buried when a person is moved by grace, but instead are to be set in motion in a responsible, professional, and risky action (Matt. 25:14–30). The spiritual life presupposes the gift of self, a gift given frequently, maturely, and selflessly. In this generosity, in which one engages with one's whole self, the development of inner freedom takes place. If the readiness for total, risky giving is lacking, no spiritual development will come about, and the person will close himself off like the rich young man in the Gospel who lacked detachment from his wealth and lacked inner liberty (Matt. 19:22).

In the theological quest to clarify the mystery of faith about the infusion of human action with God's power, we will therefore be interested only in human acts (*actus humanus*) and not in the acts of man (*actus hominis*). Only those acts in which reason and will are involved are voluntary, so they alone fall within the scope of morality. Stomach movements take place in man, but they are not influenced by reason and so are beyond the interest of the moralist or the theologian. Also, involuntary actions that are the result of pressure, phobias, obsessive compulsions, or strong, uncontrollable feelings are outside the realm of moral choices. When these movements and emotional reactions are antecedent to free choice, one is not morally responsible for them, unless it was in one's power to stop them by making a free choice, and this choice did not take place due to lack of attention. Such neurotic reflexes, prior to free choice, are described in theology as *passiones antecedentes*, and they diminish the freedom of the act.

Reason and will in action

a. Freedom according to St. Thomas Aquinas and William of Ockham

In the fourteenth century, European thought underwent a significant turn in the understanding of the nature of freedom. This theological shift shaped the further development of both theological and philosophical thought. Historians of modern Catholic moral theology view the nominalist theology of William of Ockham as a clear turning point, breaking off from the earlier patristic, classical, and Scholastic moral thinking. This turning point, which Fr. Servais Pinckaers named "the nominalist revolution,"[41] is so radical that ideas about Catholic morality formed in modern times and embraced by both Catholics and people hostile to the Church are very different from earlier formulations. At the root of this nominalist overturn is an altered conception of freedom, which resulted in a complete change in the treatment of moral issues. The concept of freedom, introduced into European thought by Ockham, led to an inevitable tension between freedom and law, freedom and nature, and freedom and God's grace. With this modern theory, it is difficult to imagine the radiation of grace within human freedom.

In Ockham's view, freedom is the pinnacle of man's spiritual faculties. It is treated as an absolute and signifies complete nondetermination, the ability to choose anything at all, independently of the light of reason or the inclinations of human nature. Moreover, truth and goodness, as being

---

[41] See Servais Pinckaers, O.P., *The Sources of Christian Ethics* (Washington, DC: Catholic University of America Press, 1995), chap. 10.

outside the will, although perceived by reason, are regarded as limitations on freedom. Liberty, in this view, is defined by Fr. Pinckaers as a "freedom of indifference," being totally indifferent to values. Since freedom was declared to be an immutable, innate characteristic of the will, completely independent of any values that could direct the will, anything that could somehow shape the will, such as truth, the natural inclinations of the human person, habituation generated by acquired knowledge or gained experience, or, even more so, moral instructions or stirrings of grace coming from God, from that moment started to be viewed as factors limiting the nondetermination of the free will.

Defining *freedom* as the arbitrary indetermination of the will, Ockham by no means was advocating for anarchist license. In his understanding, the human will, completely free and undetermined, meets the unconstrained freedom of God, equally indifferent to values. Reflecting on God's omnipotence, Ockham concluded that God, in order to be omnipotent, must be endowed with just such a will, arbitrarily undetermined and indifferent to values. Ascribing such attributes to God's will made it possible to secure the moral order of this world. Being completely free, God, by the power of His inscrutable decision, imposes externally His will on man, providing him with the moral law. Thus, man may enjoy the unfettered freedom of his will up to the moment he encounters opposition deriving from God's will. Man's moral life was therefore conceived by Ockham as a struggle between human freedom and the obviously more powerful and restricting freedom of God. Since he held that the moral law has its origin in the arbitrary will of God, the only foundation of moral law, and hence of moral obligation, is the will of God. Only the awareness of fulfilling God's will attributes to human deeds their value. If a man performs deeds without this awareness, he is not "in order." God, on the other hand, is not constrained by anything, neither by His nature, His wisdom, nor the nature of beings created by Him. Nothing prevents God from changing the Decalogue injunctions "Thou shall not kill," "Thou shall not commit adultery," "Thou shall not steal!" and then commanding murder, adultery, or theft. And if God were to command those things, they would henceforth constitute moral obligations for us. If God does not perform such moral gymnastics, it somehow makes things easier for us, because we stick to what usually happens, but we have no guarantee that God will not introduce such changes tomorrow.

As we go back to the earlier moral teaching of St. Thomas Aquinas, we find a completely different understanding of *freedom*. Aquinas does not make an absolute out of freedom. Man is not born with a freedom that would be arbitrarily indifferent. Man is born marked by sin. But he develops freedom gradually throughout life as he undertakes increasingly mature and internally free actions. Freedom in its plenitude is the ability to act in accordance with value and perfection. Freedom does not derive exclusively from the will, as it does for Ockham, but it is a common work of the reason and the will. That is why Fr. Pinckaers calls this freedom a "freedom for excellence."[42] Only the person who is self-sacrificing, not out of fear but out of his own free, unconstrained action, because he has been drawn by the value he has recognized, is truly free — and happy. St. Maximilian Kolbe in Auschwitz had greater freedom than a drug addict who cannot free himself from his addiction. The perspective of the Gospel Beatitudes, which are a preface to the teaching of the Sermon on the Mount, resonates only with the one who dares to be internally free. In this view, neither the moral law, which, above all, is a manifestation of God's wisdom and not of His supposedly whimsical will, nor grace, which moves from within a person who is open to it by faith appears as a contradiction of freedom, but precisely as a necessary support for its development.

The nominalist understanding of freedom was followed by René Descartes in the seventeenth century. He thought that God could make two and two be three and not four. Eternal truths, he claimed, depend only on God's will, and so essentially are not intelligible. An error on our part, then, is not an expression of the weakness of reason but a weakness of the will, which makes a decision and is accountable for its actions. Here, cognition has been reduced to a practical order, dependent on the will, which lacks objective criteria of discernment.

And finally, in the twentieth century, Jean-Paul Sartre stated that the intent of freedom is not dependent on reason at all and is not the fruit of any rational

---

[42] Pinckaers, *The Sources of Christian Ethics*, 338–339.

deliberation. Choice in itself is absurd, but to be authentic means precisely to accept this condition — it means to self-generate at every moment the rules of one's conduct. Being absolutely free is a terrible necessity of human destiny. Whenever anyone — another human being or God — looks at us, our freedom may be threatened, because we become an object for someone else. That is why Sartre concluded that "Hell is other people" — because they threaten the arbitrary freedom of a solitary human being, devoid of any light. This means that, through the philosopher's decision, an antagonistic contradiction between freedom and truth has been decreed. Truth has been demoted to the mere status of that which freedom has decided on its own. How very distant this position is from Christ's words: "You will know the truth, and the truth will make you free" (John 8:32).

The trajectory of the development of philosophical thought on freedom has evolved in a way that breaks off any reference of freedom to truth or to any objective values. If today a misunderstanding can be seen between the Church's teaching on freedom and its perception by many in society, the root of this confusion lies in distorted thinking. When the Church speaks about freedom, she grasps freedom in its relation to truth, which has objectivity and splendor. Freedom does not consist in an unconstrained right to think and act according to current preferences. The freedom that God offers a person is a participatory freedom, one that flows from within the person sharing in the life and love of the Blessed Trinity. This freedom enables a person to make a gift out of love, just as Christ, listening to the Father, makes a gift. Demonstrating that such a sharing in the life of God not only does not threaten human freedom but, in fact, it enhances it is a task for theologians — a particularly demanding task because the understanding of freedom is often associated with a denial of God. God is portrayed as a rival of freedom. It is held that recognizing God necessarily involves some loss for man. Freedom is understood as a denial, as a reclaiming of one's rights in the face of God.

The acridity with which this dilemma appears in contemporary culture is, among other things, the tragic result of the dull portrayal of the truth of the Holy Trinity by theologians, as divorced from practical life. The prospect of participation in the life of God requires a theological exposition that outlines the invitation and possibility of union with the Persons of the Blessed Trinity in such a way that man will not feel threatened, will not be apprehensive about the volitional whims and "otherness" of God, and will not wonder whether his freedom will lose anything as a result of this encounter.

b. The will together with reason as the substance of freedom

Before we proceed to analyze freedom and the role of grace within freedom, we must discuss the powers involved in moral acts through which one grows in freedom. What is the relationship of the will to freedom? How do the reason and the will function in the human psyche, in human choices and moral decisions? Having stated in the *Summa theologiae* (Ia-IIae) that moral acts are either voluntary or involuntary (q. 6) and that they are elicited in the context of some circumstances (q. 7), Aquinas proceeds to discuss the will (qq. 8–11).

To grasp Aquinas's teaching on the nature of the will, it is necessary to cleanse one's thinking of the taint of nominalist philosophy. According to Aquinas, the will is a spiritual appetitive power, different from the emotions, which are a sensitive appetitive power. The will expresses the desire for the good that has been apprehended and presented to it by the mind. There is a certain passivity in the will toward the good that attracts it, a certain natural disposition to rest in it. Similarly, the mind is also attracted to the object it apprehends. This passivity of the will toward the object that moves it is metaphysical and not psychological. The intellect shows the good (*bonum apprehensum*) to the will, and, through this, the intellect moves the will — *per modum finis*. The will, on the other hand, can move the intellect *per modum agentis*, stimulating it to cognition whenever it chooses. In order to act, the will requires a rational input that outlines the desired object. Even when we choose an action that is morally evil, we choose that evil *sub ratione boni* because it appears to us as some good, if only partially so. This does not mean that, in a romantic way, the will is incapable of sinning. It only means that in the structure of the will there is an inner inclination toward the apprehended good.

In order to explain the fact that we sometimes choose to do wrong, a further distinction must be introduced between the universal good and the particular good. The passivity of a spiritual power does not necessarily imply a determinism that would undermine moral responsibility. (This is how Aquinas was interpreted by his Franciscan opponents.) Only the universal good, which is happiness in God, necessarily attracts the will.

Aquinas's approach, which recognizes a natural inclination in the will toward an apprehended good, is much more optimistic than the modern approach, which, influenced by Kant's philosophy, sees in the will primarily an energy that urges one toward duty. Of course, there is also a feeling of energy in the human constitution, triggering emotional zeal, courage, and even anger, but this feeling is emotional and therefore sensitive. Its intensity depends on the psychic constitution of the individual. This passion or life energy should not, however, be confused with the will, which is a spiritual power that can be passively drawn by the apprehended good. The will is not a force of pressure that one imposes on others or oneself, or on one's feelings, coercing them to obey an order. Rather, the will expresses a love and desire for the good — that is, a spontaneous impulse toward the good. This passive permission to be attracted by the good is essential for the will. The source of the will's most proper function, which is to love, can be found in the will's attraction to the apprehended good.

The recognition of a drive toward the good in the will amounts to recognizing a natural inclination toward values inscribed by God in the structure of the will. Thus, the will is not, as it was presented in the nominalist view, indifferent to values. In the nature of the will are inclinations toward those goods that fully correspond to human nature. Thus, the will instinctively tends to that which is consonant with human nature. By its nature, the will desires happiness and the universal good. Included in this good is the ultimate human goal of the Beatific Vision of God, the knowledge of truth, the preservation of one's being and life, and the desire for all that which is the proper object of all human powers. Just as the lungs spontaneously need air, so in the will there is a natural inclination toward happiness. This inclination in itself does not determine what a person's supreme happiness is. Particular sensitive goods will trigger an attraction in the emotions. But if reason perceives that some sensitive good participates in a universal good, an inclination toward that good under the aspect of that universal good will then be elicited in the will. If one sees a delicious-looking cake, a desire to eat the cake will arise in his senses, but if one's reason, in connection with this sensory experience, provides the universal rationale determining that it is right to eat a piece of the cake, or that it is right to refrain from eating it because of a diet or because the cake does not belong to the person but is merely displayed in a store window, then there will be a natural inclination in the will to follow the reason's suggestion. This inclination may have to resist the sensual desire, which will prompt the person to ignore the light of reason, but in the will itself, in its structure, there will remain an inclination toward that good that reason has presented in this situation. It follows that particular goods, such as money, power, or pleasure, are not able to draw the will by necessity. A person desires them with the will only when reason has perceived in them some connection with the happiness he desires, but since one may be happy without them, they are not able to attract the will necessarily. There is, therefore, still room for both choice and error with the metaphysical passivity of the will.

Only the ultimate good, that is, happiness itself, and that alone, is able to liberate in the will a drive that precedes all reasoning. There is a certain similarity with the intellect here, which also naturally and necessarily grasps the first principles of thinking.[43] The will's inclination toward the final end is accomplished without any involvement of the cognitive powers, and in this pursuit of happiness, the will is completely free — that is, it finds the fulfillment of the basic inclination of its nature as it moves toward its proper object.[44] In this context, and precisely here, Aquinas uses the term *free will* — *libera voluntas*. In modern thinking, however, marked by nominalism,

---

[43] *ST*, Ia, q. 82, art. 2: "As understanding by its nature and of necessity adheres to first principles, in the same way will adheres to its ultimate fulfillment" (trans. T. Suttor, vol. 11, 1970).

[44] *De veritate*, q. 24, art. 1, ad 20: "When there is question of the objects of appetite, we do not judge about the last end by any judgment involving discussion and examination, but we naturally approve of it. Concerning it there is, accordingly, no choice, but there is will. We have in its regard, therefore, a free will ... but not a free judgment, properly speaking, since it does not fall under choice" (trans. R. W. Schmidt, vol. III [Chicago: Henry Regnery, 1954]).

the expression *free will* denotes the arbitrary nondetermination of the will. It implies that the will can be inclined anywhere at all, that it can choose any course of action according to its whim. Meanwhile, Aquinas perceives freedom within the will precisely when it is in full conformity with its nature — that is, when it experiences the self-determination of its own nature. It is paradoxical that the greatest freedom of the will happens precisely when the will does not undertake any deliberation along with reason, does not make a choice, but, by the power of its natural inclination, it proceeds on its own in a determined way toward its final end. Aquinas perceives such a fully determined, and therefore free, movement of the will only in relation to the beatific final end, which is God. Only when the will is determined from within by its natural inclinations toward its objective object is it truly itself, and in this it is truly free.

Nowadays, it seems incomprehensible, or even self-contradictory, to say that there are natural inclinations within us, and that these inclinations are also found in the will. There is an intellectual impulse today to contrast nature and freedom, implying that whatever comes from nature is in some way a limitation of freedom. In fact, we are free not in spite of our natural inclinations but precisely due to them. An idea of freedom that would seek to bypass nature, or to reform or even deform it, is not an idea of genuine freedom. Rather, it is an ideological manipulation of nature. Denying nature leads not to freedom but to its mutilation.

Speaking of human nature, it is necessary to keep in mind not only its physical dimension but also the spiritual. In human nature, there is an openness to truth, goodness, and beauty. The intellect's natural inclination to truth is the source of contemplation, and the foundation of philosophy and all sciences. This inclination, therefore, cannot be a limitation for man. Just as there is a natural inclination to truth in the intellect, so there is a natural inclination to goodness in the will. It is through these inclinations that we can judge and choose in life. And through an analysis of these inclinations, the natural law is inferred. Since the human will is created by God, that which belongs to its nature cannot contradict God's design, expressed in the natural law. But of course, there is a conflict between the deepest inclinations rooted in the will and the disorder in the inclinations that is a consequence of the wound of sin. This disorder that remains after sin often pushes one to commit further sins. This does not belong to the nature of the will, however, but is a legacy of its malady.

The will thus has a natural inclination within it that determines it to the final good — namely, happiness — and this determined action Aquinas terms the "free will." In the case of all other movements of the will, the will itself is not determined, and it is compelled to profit from the light of reason that determines it. In the will itself, there is an indetermination as to the object of its willing, an indetermination as to the act, and an indetermination as to the alignment of the action to the end. However, in order for the will to will a specific object, in order for this willing to be turned on or off, and in order for this willing to be aligned to the fundamental final goal that is natural to the will (which attributes to the willing a good or bad moral value), the intervention of reason must take place. It is reason that reveals the good to the will and is linked with its movement. In concrete human choices, therefore, reason is always involved, and this presence of reason in choice is the source of personal creativity. The will alone, without the light of reason, would not be inclined consistently toward the good. Thus, the common notion that man has reason and free will, which implies that man is born with reason and free will, and that the will is free regardless of the input of reason, is not entirely correct. Such an understanding mistakenly relegates all moral responsibility for an action solely to the will and restricts the determination of the value of that will to the sole criterion of obedience or disobedience, to the detriment of dash and creativity.

Man is born with basic faculties, but they need to be cultivated in order to develop. Reason is born not as rational but as mindless. It takes many years of education and experience for wisdom to inhabit reason. Similarly, a person is born with a will that is not yet fully developed. It is oriented from within only with respect to happiness, which it necessarily desires. Regarding other goods, the will has yet to learn freedom; it has to accustom itself to make choices deliberately, in conjunction with reason, while becoming independent from the disorder that derives from the stirrings of the senses or from the unwise example or encouragement of other people. It is through these free choices that finally maturity and freedom grow in a person.

If the will has within it a tendency toward the apprehended good, why does it sometimes choose evil? Let us imagine a situation in which the reason flawlessly grasps the true good (*bonum intellectum*) and presents it to the will. Why does the wrong choice sometimes occur? It is because the good shown by reason is not an absolutely perfect good in every respect. Only the ultimate happiness, which consists in the permanent union with God, is absolutely good in every respect, and therefore the will necessarily desires this happiness, whereas every particular good has multiple aspects, some of them good and others bad. And that is why certain aspects may be of greater importance to us; besides, it may be that we are interested in one particular circumstance; and our personal, fluctuating moods may also affect the final choice. Since the will also conditions the reason, it can stimulate it to color the presented object accordingly, bringing out one aspect while concealing another. Over time, people begin to think the way they act. Thus, in the case of a sinful act, Aquinas's analysis sees here not just a "choice" of the act made uniquely by the perverse will, acting in opposition to reason, which has declared that the act is evil. This is how colloquial thought sees it. Aquinas says that reason was also involved in this choice, and it was reason together with the will that made the free choice. In this choice of a sinful act, it was interpreted *sub ratione boni* at that moment — that is, reason saw something good in this act and, prompted by the will, brushed aside other considerations. When choosing an evil act, the will accepts a disregard for the fundamental value shown by reason and fixates on some incidental good, captured *sub ratione boni*. Such abandonment of the fundamental good in favor of the promptings of concupiscence may become frequent. This does not mean, however, that bad habits that are almost automatic are unfree. Free choice is at work in them, downplaying the anti-value of a given choice and stopping at the apparent good, even if there was no long reflection at the time of the decision. Full moral culpability is incurred for repeated sins, including sins of addiction, since they include at least a habitual consent to sin.

In modern thought, also in neo-scholasticism, reason and will were understood to be in sharp opposition. When they are juxtaposed or viewed as acting independently of each other, the decision center of the moral act is then attributed either exclusively to the judgment of reason, to which the obedient will responds, or exclusively to the will, which responds obediently or disobediently to the options presented "indifferently" by reason. Voluntarism, prevalent in modern times, primarily emphasized the will in the analysis of the moral act. It was held that reason was to provide light, and the will was only to accept and implement it. To state it differently, conscience is supposed to indicate the applicability of the norm in a given situation, and the will is supposed to carry out this imperative identified by conscience. In such a view, then, the will gets all the merit or all the blame since it either embraced the imperative or rebelled against it. Such an understanding of the moral act led to the expansion of the reflection on conscience in modern theology. It was said that the moralist has to help the conscience deliver a correct judgment. With respect to this verdict, the will was perceived as either meriting reward or deserving punishment. No explanation, however, was given as to what should be done when the will experiences its limitations, when it feels restrained or even captive. The sole suggestion was that the inept will should try harder. Most often this ended with the exertion of emotional pressure on oneself, with all the neurotic consequences of this error. Aquinas's explication of the moral act is much more nuanced. He did not set such a sharp opposition between the reason and the will; instead, he saw their interdependence in the totality of moral action. He was more interested in the education of the free choice — that is, in the ability of both the will and the reason in their joint creative undertaking of the good, than in the mere question of the will's obedience to the norms handed down by conscience. Aquinas knew that, in this educational process, cooperation with grace is essential. That is why his teaching is not so moralizing as that of modern moralists.

In the case in which a person makes bad choices, it may be that reason is wrong and misjudges the situation. We will say then that the conscience is erroneous. Although erroneous, it is still binding, because a person has no other way of directing the will than through reason. One must, of course, take care to form one's conscience so that the reason will interpret situations correctly, but in the end, it is always reason that directs the choices. It may also happen in the case of evil choices that reason reads the situation correctly, but the drive of the senses turns out to be so great that the will ignores the basic light of reason or prompts the reason to find excuses. The clarity of the light of reason is then buried by a strong sensory impulse, and then an action is chosen that is prompted by the sensory impulse. In such a case, of course, it is a sinful action, which is an expression not of the power of the will but of its weakness. The will agrees to ignore the clear light of reason, which could be its strength, and stimulates reason to find more convenient arguments. The will, along with reason, consents to an action in which it is enslaved by the stronger stirrings of the senses. This is why Aquinas says that the angels, who, living outside of time, are permanently oriented toward God, possess greater freedom than man — precisely because they can no longer sin. Their will is firmly fixed on the supreme good presented accurately by reason, which is God, and for the nature of the angelic will, this means fully "being oneself" and is the source of supreme angelic freedom.[45] It sounds like a paradox, but wherever reason and will are most perfectly aligned with the highest truth and the highest good, that is where there is supreme freedom.

The conclusion to be drawn from these considerations is that the will needs the support of a well-formed reason so that it can free itself from becoming less free. Both reason and will can be culpable for the wrong action. When one undertakes acts of free choice in which both the clear reason and the righteous will are involved, this enhances inner freedom. It is necessary, therefore, that individuals make their own choices, choices that flow from within, in which there is a personal discovery of value by reason and a commitment to that value by the will. Only then does one become truly mature, capable of effective willing, and not just empty willing, or wishful thinking, called *velleitas* in Latin. Mature human action does not consist merely in obedience to an external norm. A mature action is one in which a person has used his reason, which has identified a value worthy of attention, and has used his will, which allowed itself to be drawn by the apprehended value, even if feelings of fear, pleasure, or pressure from other people prompted it

---

[45] *ST*, Ia, q. 62, art. 8, ad 3: "Free choice ... should it make a choice at variance with the order of the end — that is to commit a sin — this would be a defect of freedom. The free choice, then, is greater in angels who cannot sin than in us who can" (my translation).

in the opposite direction. This does not mean that the moral norm is unnecessary. By indicating the direction, it allows the good to be apprehended, and so it educates the reason in the recognition of the good, but the choice itself flows from within, from the personal involvement of reason and will.

c. Free choice as an expression of freedom

When studying the image of God outlined in man by the power of grace, Aquinas focuses specifically on free choice, which is an expression of man's freedom. Witnessing a truly mature goodness that is personally embraced, one wants to "give glory to [the] Father who is in heaven" (Matt. 5:16). Aquinas refers to this free choice by the term *liberum arbitrium*. He uses this expression in his general discussion of the relationship between the reason and the will in free choice. *Liberum arbitrium* should not be confused with the "free will," either in the understanding of Aquinas, where it means, as stated earlier, the self-determination of the will to happiness, or in the modern understanding, in which, following nominalism, *free will* denotes the unconstraint of the will in any direction.

Free choice, which expresses freedom, is the result of the common action of both reason and the will.[46] Since it is reason that passes the judgment grounding the choice, the root of freedom is found in the judgment of reason, which influences choice. We do not always have the external liberty to make a free choice (as it depends on objective circumstances), but the choice is free when it is based on the judgment that is made by the reason.[47] Such personal free choice is at the center of the mystery of the human person, as it describes the person best. In contrast, that which makes the judgment

---

[46] *De veritate*, q. 24, art. 4: "Free choice accordingly does not designate a habit but the power of will or reason—one as subordinated to the other" (trans. R. W. Schmidt, vol. 3, 1954).

[47] *De veritate*, q. 24, art. 2: "Since three elements concur in our activity: knowledge, appetite, and the activity itself, the whole formal character of freedom depends upon the manner of knowing.... Hence the whole root of freedom is located in reason." *De veritate*, q. 24, art. 1, ad 1: "Thus a man is not said to be free in his actions but free in his choice, which is a judgement about what is to be done. This is what the name free choice refers to."

of reason in free choice free is the will. The will urges the reason to make a judgment, and, in turn, the reason stimulates the will by suggesting a suitable object to it. Thus, it can be said that the two powers dialectically influence one another in free choice.[48] It should not, therefore, be claimed that Aquinas's teaching is either intellectualistic or voluntaristic, or that he changed his mind. (Thirteenth-century opposition to St. Thomas Aquinas read him in an intellectualist way; modern Thomism overemphasized voluntarism. Both found passages from Aquinas justifying their interpretations, but, through their one-sided bias, they distorted Aquinas's thought, and, at the same time, failed to capture fully the dynamics of moral action). In reality, Aquinas states that at the decisive moment, which is free choice, the two powers, reason and will, act together.[49] The precise account of the essence of free choice may seem to be an unnecessary speculation. The overemphasizing of either the role of reason or the role of the will, however, consequently results in different visions of morality.

Since free choice is the result of the joint action of reason and will, it is obviously consequential and not prior to the judgment of reason and the stirrings of the will. Nominalist thinking, making an absolute out of the arbitrary will, suggests the opposite direction, as if freedom preceded the reason and the will. The dignity of the human person, who is an image of

---

[48] *ST*, Ia-IIae, q. 9, art. 1, ad 3: "The will moves the mind with respect to the exercise of activity.... But with respect to the form and meaning of activity, which is defined by its object, the mind sets the will in motion" (trans. T. Gilby, vol. 17, 1970). *De veritate*, q. 24, art. 6: "The power by which we freely judge is not taken to be that by which we judge without further qualification, for that is the function of reason; but it is taken as the power which accounts for our freedom in judging, and this belongs to the will. Free choice is therefore the will. The term does not designate the will absolutely, however, but with reference to one of its acts, to choose." Ad 3: "Though judgment is a function of reason, the freedom of judging belongs immediately to the will." Ad 5: "The will in some sense moves reason by commanding its act; and reason moves the will by proposing to it its object, which is the end. Thus it is that either power can in some way be informed by the other" (trans. R. W. Schmidt, vol. 3, 1954).

[49] Daniel Westberg, "Did Aquinas Change His Mind about the Will?" *Thomist* 58 (1994): 41–60.

God, lies not only in the fact that he engages in action but also in the fact that he recognizes the purpose of his action and seeks out appropriate means to achieve that purpose. Mature action is intentional, and all its elements are sewn together for the sake of the desired goal. It is the immature person who acts foolishly and aimlessly. The entire procedure of directing action with respect to the end is performed by reason, which finally passes a judgment and, together with the movement of the will, decides on the action. The act of free choice is thus simultaneously rational and volitional. The use of the light of reason is necessary for the will to be fully itself. Engaging in actions that lack the light of reason and are undertaken without any deliberation, suddenly, as a result of emotional involvement, being intimidated, or purely out of an irrational sense of compulsion, is an expression of a lack of freedom. In such action, there is either a lack of consistency, a lack of persistence, or an uptight, cold voluntarism. The will acting in this way is limited and impaired. It needs to be freed. So, if someone engages in an action that is pointless, poorly thought out, or resulting from external pressure and not his own free choice, he is not a free person. (There have been cases of priests who entered the seminary to fulfill their mothers' wishes. After the death of his mother, such a priest suddenly leaves the priesthood because all his life he felt bound by his mother's will, and finally after her death he feels free — only to discover, after leaving the priesthood, that he is still not free from his own immaturity.)

In order for human maturity to develop, it is necessary that choices are made, choices that flow from within, from a personal discovery of values by reason, and that those choices are not made solely by virtue of obedience to an external norm. A truly Christian upbringing, therefore, is not merely a training based on orders and prohibitions but an initiation allowing one to make his own choices; it necessarily provides room for personal initiatives and room for mistakes. It is only in an atmosphere of freedom and respect for the individual that personal choices are made, choices that include the gift of self. Inner freedom grows with love, with acts in which the gift of self is made, given freely and solely because of the value recognized in it.

A cursory reading of the encyclical *Veritatis splendor* may seem to imply that St. John Paul II is arguing against such an understanding of freedom.

After all, there is a lengthy passage in the encyclical on freedom and law that challenges ethical creativity. In fact, the encyclical speaks out against the claims of some moralists who hold that man is exempt from moral principles and can create his own norms. Such reasoning is patently false. There is no creativity regarding moral norms. They are always necessary, as they direct reason toward the true good. There is creativity in man, however, in respect to action. The ways in which moral values may be responded to are infinite. There is no limit to the creativity of acts of virtue. Inner freedom, in fact, requires full human ingenuity, a full involvement of reason and will in the free choice of good acts. The growth of the capacity for free choice contributes to the growth of freedom and manifests the fecundity of God's goodness. This is why the *Catechism of the Catholic Church*, echoing the intuition of St. Thomas Aquinas, states that "in man, true freedom is an 'outstanding manifestation of the divine image' (*GS* 17)." Further on, it adds:

> Freedom is the power, rooted in reason and will, to act or not to act, to do this or that, and so to perform deliberate actions on one's own responsibility. By free choice[50] one shapes one's own life. Human freedom is a force for growth and maturity in truth and goodness; it attains its perfection when directed toward God, our beatitude. (1712, 1731)

The existence of free choice in man, through which the influence of grace is manifested, is a truth of faith defined by the Second Synod of Orange and the Council of Trent.[51] The prevalence, under the influence of nominalism, of the term *free will* brings a certain ambiguity to modern approaches. Therefore, one must always check what exactly is meant by the term when it is being used. (Some contemporary Church documents employ the term *free will*

---

[50] The Latin text here has *liberum arbitrium*, which is a clear reference to the teaching of Aquinas. Alas, the English translation shows vestiges of nominalism, and the phrase was rendered as "by free will."

[51] DS 378, 383, 396, 1554–1556. Also the English translation given by Neuner and Dupuis erroneously translates *liberum arbitrium* as "free will" and not as "free choice."

most often in the sense of free choice, specifically, the joint intervention of both reason and will.[52])

By choosing a moral action, in which both reason and will are involved, a person in some sense creates a moral order. This is not the creation of an objective moral order, which has its origin in human nature as it came out of the hands of the Creator and in the power of grace given by the Savior. Instead, it is the creation of a subjective moral order — that is, the focusing of all powers and actions toward an end that has been recognized. This focusing of action toward an end generates a certain order — *ordo*, which should be translated not as an injunction (whether of an external or internal imperative) but as the coming together, alignment, or harmonization of a series of actions, in view of the chosen goal. In mature action, there is a certain creativity, triggering joy analogous to the joy experienced by parents when they find out they have conceived a child. From the moment the child has come into existence, something new has come about, something that involves obligations but also brings joy and beauty. Aristotle perceived the manifestation of beauty (*kalon*) in moral action and postulated that the upbringing of children should train them to recognize the beauty of personal acts of kindness, generosity, and fortitude. Aquinas takes up these intuitions of the Philosopher, integrating them into his theology of freedom and virtue. Man is most fully the image of God when he realizes that he is the father of his actions, when he chooses the good consistently, because he has recognized the beauty of the value that is being born.[53] And he can also

---

[52] See Second Vatican Council, Declaration on Religious Freedom *Dignitatis humanae* (December 7, 1965), no. 2: "Beings endowed with reason and free will"; St. Paul VI, encyclical *Humanae vitae* (July 25, 1968), no. 9: "It is not, then, merely a question of natural instinct or emotional drive. It is also, and above all, an act of the free will." *Humanae vitae* 21: "For if with the aid of reason and of free will they are to control their natural drives, there can be no doubt at all of the need for self-denial." St. John Paul II, *Veritatis splendor* 48: "These definitions ... remind us that reason and free will are linked with all the bodily and sense faculties."

[53] Joseph Owens, "Human Reason and the Moral Order in Aquinas," in *Historia Memoria Futuri: Mélanges Louis Vereecke* (Rome: Editiones Academiae Alphonsianae, 1991), 159–177.

courageously undertake actions that are completely beyond his capabilities when he summons the power of the Holy Spirit with his professed faith. Therein lies the magnificence of the Christian spiritual life. It gives the power to abide by the beauty of values, relying only on the imperceptible but real help of divine grace.[54]

Should we not conclude from this argumentation that man is fully free only when he deliberately chooses the good? Undoubtedly, creatively choosing the good makes a person grow, contributes to the development of his maturity, and magnificently images God. But how should we judge situations in which a person has not yet matured enough for such a wonderful freedom? There are, after all, many actions resulting from weakness, actions in which one sees not any beautiful value but merely a pressing compulsion from within or coercion from other people or situations, and there are, after all, also deeds that are simply evil, despicable, stemming from perversion. Is there *liberum arbitrium* — free choice — in them? Or, perhaps, since these acts do not witness to the beauty of God but only express man's confusion, are they outside the realm of freedom and therefore outside the realm of moral responsibility? It is somewhat humiliating for man to be told that he is a just a bundle of contradictory, agitated dynamisms and lacks inner freedom, but, after all, he may recognize himself in this description and may feel absolved from any effort to change, especially if he has no hope for grace, which would unlock the freedom that needs to be liberated.

The Church does not fall into such a despairing judgment even in the case of the most misguided person. The *Catechism* affirms:

> As long as freedom has not bound itself definitively to its ultimate good which is God, there is the possibility of *choosing between good and evil*, and thus of growing in perfection or of failing and sinning. (1732)

---

[54] *De veritate*, q. 24, art. 12, ad sc 6: "Free choice can accordingly have choice and deliberation not only about the matters for which its own power suffices but also about those for which it needs divine help" (trans. R. W. Schmidt, vol. 3, 1954).

Although sin that is committed deprives one of grace and makes it easier to slip into another sin, it does not have the effect of making one permanently incapable of free choice and of choosing the good. In sinful action, there is the joint intervention of reason and will, and so there is free choice in sin, although it is the choice of an apparent good. However, if a person appeals to God through faith, God will grant His grace, which will open the person's eyes to the true good and sustain his ability to choose it. Thus, in any temptation, it is possible to turn to God through faith, asking for help in the given moment. Such communion with God reinforces freedom and helps one to persevere in goodness, despite the difficulty of resisting the oftentimes powerful urges of concupiscence.[55]

The psychological structure of a moral act

Since the sixteenth century, in neo-Thomistic theology generally replicated after Cardinal Cajetan, we find a schematic description of the operation of reason and will in the moral act. This diagram, based on the separation of the functions of reason and will, describes twelve consecutive acts of reason and the will.[56] It implies that reason merely determines the best course of

---

[55] *De veritate*, q. 24, art. 12, ad 12: "Cupidity cannot be understood absolutely to compel free choice, which is always free from force. But it is called compelling because of the vehemence of the inclination, which can still be resisted, though only with difficulty" (trans. R. W. Schmidt, vol. 3, 1954). Ad sc 11: A man in the state of sin can by no means free himself from a sin which he has already committed except by the help of grace; for, since sin consists in aversion, he is not freed from it unless his mind clings to God by charity, which does not come from free choice but is poured into the hearts of the saints by the Holy Spirit."

[56] We find an example of this in Jacek Woroniecki (*Katolicka etyka wychowawcza*, Lublin: KUL, 1986, vol. 1, 104). He presents a diagram in which he lists the consecutive acts: (1) apprehension of an object as good or bad; (2) predilection for it; (3) assessment of the object as an end; (4) intention of achieving it; (5) consideration regarding the means; (6) consent to one of them; (7) discrimination between them; (8) choice of one of them; (9) command of the act; (10) active execution; (11) passive execution by other powers; (12) contentment; (13) judgment of the action performed. Acts 1, 3, 5, 7, 9, and 13 are ascribed to reason; acts 2, 4, 6, 8, 10, and 12 are ascribed to the will.

action, while the actual decision regarding action is made by the will. This diagram is an expression of modern voluntarism. It does not reflect the actual teaching of Aquinas.

Fr. Jacek Woroniecki, as he discusses the consecutive acts of reason and will in this diagram, indicates the questions from the *Summa theologiae* (Ia-IIae) where Aquinas discusses them. It is evident that something is amiss here, as the stated order of questions is chaotic.[57] Moreover, the diagram is overloaded, capturing too many elements to depict properly the process of eliciting moral acts. (Years ago, when I first attended a course in moral theology, my professor said that when one is faced with an important decision, it is good to analyze all the stages of the psychological structure of an act. Many years have passed, and as of now I have not met anyone who would have applied this framework at the time of decision-making!)

More recently, Daniel Westberg[58] has demonstrated that Aquinas's teaching on the structure of the moral act can be presented more effectively using a much simpler diagram:

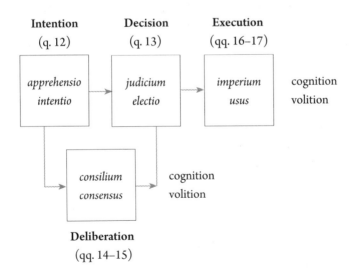

---

[57] Questions 8–10, 12, 14, 15, 14, 13, 17, 16, 16–17, 11.

[58] *Right Practical Reason: Aristotle, Action, and Prudence in Aquinas* (Oxford: Clarendon Press, 1994), 131.

This diagram is based on two basic assumptions, stated by Aquinas: (1) the specification of the act is distinguished from the decision here, with the decision being the essential and basic element of the moral act; (2) the complementarity of reason and will in moral action is here demonstrated.

The most fundamental elements of moral action are intention, decision, and execution. Each of these three stages of action consists of a rational element and a volitional element, which are present together. Influencing one another, the reason and the will act simultaneously and not sequentially. Only when the action is uncertain does a fourth stage come into play — deliberation, which precedes the decision. Deliberation as an additional stage that is not always necessary is discussed by Aquinas after the decision. (The order in which these issues are discussed by Aquinas is thus logical.) When I make a cup of tea, there is an easy transition from intention to decision and to execution. There is no need to deliberate how to make the tea because the matter is obvious. Deliberation is thus optional and not constitutive of the moral act. The terms used here to describe the stages (*intention, decision, deliberation, execution*) are meant to show that in each of them there is both a cognitive and a volitive moment, both of which are present together. The terms are selected so as not to show bias toward either an intellectualist or a volitional interpretation.

Intention is sometimes understood as a certain state of mind, but Aquinas defined it as tending toward something — *in aliud tendere*. Intention is a certain focusing of action toward something. Thus, it also includes the finality of nonrational beings, although, in the proper sense, we apply the term only to human beings. Intention most fully expresses the tending of the will, so it is present in volition — not toward a general goal but toward a specific end that has been apprehended. This end is willed through the intended means. I can wish for health in general, but intention appears only when I consciously plan something, when I go for a bike ride for the sake of the desired health. Since the relationship between the end and the action tending toward it appears in intention, the intellectual moment belongs to the intention.[59] Intention thus

---

[59] *ST*, Ia-IIae, q. 12, art. 1, ad 3: "Consequently 'intention' denotes an act of will, the ordinance of reason directing something to an end being presupposed" (my translation).

involves the intended means and tends toward the object that becomes the end. The difference, however, between intention and choice lies in the fact that intention aims at an end, whereas choice concerns some specific means.

Intention covers the object of the act, i.e., that toward which the action tends in its rationality as grasped by reason, while incidental matters that are beyond intention — *praeter intentionem* — may also emerge in the action. (For example, when commandos seek to free hostages kidnapped by terrorists, their intention, i.e., the object of their action, is the freeing of the hostages; hence, it is a just and valiant act. But an unintended act, which is beyond their intention, may be the unfortunate death of casual bystanders.)

Within *apprehensio*, the cognitive contribution to intention, there is also room for the influence of imagination. Imagination suggests to reason matters that are worth pursuing. The capacity for intention has to be cultivated in a person. It is important to have dreams and to wish good things. Of course, dreamed hopes are one thing, and daydreaming is another. Daydreaming is an escape into an unreal world and a waste of time. Good dreams, however, stimulate the intention; they expand horizons and open the range of possibilities for action. It may happen that subsequent stages of action will not work out, that unforeseen obstacles will stand in the way, and so the dreams will never come into effect. This is not the worst thing that could happen. Much more crippling for a person is a lack of dreams, a lack of horizons.

A well-lived spiritual life will entail inviting God into all stages of moral action, including the stage of intention. It is in this that the virtue of hope consists, as it channels the will toward God's mysterious and great plans. No one will become a saint without having the intention of becoming a saint. So, in the education of the intention, it is worthwhile to examine one's own dreams. What is the thing I care about most in my life? What are the causes to which am I able to give myself selflessly? What do I feed my imagination, my dreams? To define who you are, or to say who someone standing next to you is, your intention, or the other person's, has to be indicated. To say that one's husband is a doctor or an engineer does not yet convey who he really is. To define him as a person, one must point to his personal intention, the inner life's passion that is carrying him. What does he care most about?

It is the inner intentions and personal decisions that lie at the heart of the mystery of a person.

The fundamental moment of any deliberate action is the decision. Every moral action requires a decision, and in this decision, too, there is the joint involvement of both the reason and the will. In the neo-scholastic diagram of the operation of reason and will in the moral act, which is ambiguous due to the inclusion of deliberation, it was assumed that if the matter is simple, requiring no deliberation, there is an immediate transition from intention to execution. (This is how Fr. Odo Lottin, the Benedictine expert in medieval theology, presents simple acts.) This interpretation of a simple act, depriving it of a moral dimension, is obviously false. Every human act requires a decision. Only animals move from their specific intention to execution. Humans always make decisions, even if the matter involves something simple that does not require extensive thinking. Deliberate action always requires a judgment that one is acting for the sake of a specific end and that this act serves that very end. Even if decisions are made spontaneously, habitually, this does not mean that there is no choice and no intervention of reason.

Arriving at a decision involves a certain process of reasoning, which can be called a syllogism. This syllogism, however, has to be distinguished from a logical syllogism. There are two types of syllogisms: a theoretical syllogism and a syllogism tending toward a decision, which can be called a "practical" or "operative" syllogism.[60] Mixing these two syllogisms generates confusion. It is one thing theoretically to consider the various possibilities before us (How could I spend my vacation? What are the arguments in favor of this type of vacation versus another?) and another thing to make a decision (I'm going to the Netherlands!). Deliberation itself does not have the power to move to action. It is merely a deduction derived from knowledge. One can arrive from moral knowledge at a conclusion about the value of a particular act, but this conclusion remains in the realm of general knowledge and not decision. The decision happens only with a practical syllogism, in which the middle premise concerns not theoretical knowledge, but a specific personal

---

[60] *ST*, Ia-IIae, q. 13, art. 3: "Choice follows the decision or verdict which, as it were, is a conclusion to a practical syllogism" (trans. T. Gilby, vol. 17, 1970).

situation. Only a practical syllogism explains the psychological process of reaching a decision. We can demonstrate the difference between the two types of syllogisms with an example:

Theoretical syllogism:
> Evil must be avoided.
> Murder is evil.
> Murder must be avoided.

Practical syllogism:
> Evil must be avoided.
> Murder is evil.
> This action, which I am considering, is murder.
> So I must avoid this murder.

In the practical syllogism, the middle premise proceeds from the level of general knowledge to the recognition of current circumstances. It is the recognition that the general principle applies to the situation here and now. Thus, the practical syllogism combines general knowledge and the particular situation in order to arrive at a decision. The conclusion of a practical syllogism is thus a decision to act. The practical syllogism contains premises that deal not with universal truths but with contingent events. Nevertheless, this syllogism, just like the theoretical syllogism, arrives at a conclusion. In psychological terms, this conclusion can be described as "resoluteness"; and in moral terms, when grounded in right principles, this conclusion can be described as capturing the "correctness" or "worthiness" of the act.

This rendition of the psychology of the moral act differs from the traditional interpretation. The difference is due to the fact that reason and will are shown here as acting together in free choice, rather than as acting sequentially. In the common reading, it is held that the practical syllogism belongs only to reason, which arrives at a moral conclusion and thus makes a judgment of the practical reason regarding the intended action. This conclusion is subsequently either accepted or rejected by the will. In this view, the syllogism does not include the decision, that is, the choice; it is only preparatory, for it provides the input for the decision, which is then made by the will itself. All merit or blame, then, falls solely on the will. This is a false reading not only of Aquinas's teaching but also of the psychology of moral action. It reduces the syllogism merely to the deduction of a conclusion from a principle, a conclusion that remains only a theoretical statement, with no impact on the decision. This approach regards the will as simple volition indifferent to values. The will, in the nominalist view, is "free," indifferent to the contribution of reason. It is free to accept or reject the conclusion provided to it by the judgment of reason.

Aquinas clearly sees the joint involvement of reason and will in the decision. Free choice materially belongs to the will, but formally belongs to reason. The will influences the act of reasoning, and reason acts in the movements of the will. At the root of the reason's making the judgment, the *iudicium*, is the will's desire for the good. And in the will's movement toward the particular good, the *electio*, there is the specifying influence of reason. So both powers are involved in every premise of the practical syllogism, and the conclusion of the practical syllogism, which is the decision, is not just an "intellectual" conclusion but also an expression of the human will. The principle "theft is not to be committed" is not just an intellectual assertion. In order for it to work in a decision, the will must affirm it. The selection of premises in an action also depends on the will. So, when we describe someone as "having" principles, we mean that those principles function as a premise in his syllogism of action, that they play a role in his decisions because the person has adopted them.

While noting the joint action of the reason and the will in a moral decision, this decision has to be distinguished from the judgment of conscience. Aquinas defines *conscience* as an act of the practical reason. The voice of conscience antecedent to the moral act, however, is not the last judgment of reason, for after the judgment of conscience, there is still room for the next act of reason within the framework of free choice, in which reason and will act together. Thus, it may be that a person will not err in conscience but will err in decision. Conscience will truly illuminate the situation for him, but the final decision made by the free choice will be contrary to the voice of conscience.[61]

---

[61] *De veritate*, q. 17, art. 1, ad 4: "The judgment of conscience consists simply in knowledge, whereas the judgment of free choice consists in the application

Since voluntarism has become prevalent in neo-scholastic theology, it was held that the next stage, deliberation or consideration — *deliberatio* — concerns only the choice of means, and so it was said that the function of prudence is to ensure that this deliberation is conducted perfectly. Thus, the virtue of prudence assumed a subsidiary role in the careful selection of means and in warning against action that may involve some doubt. (According to Aquinas, the virtue of prudence is involved in the entire process from intention through decision to execution. It refers more to wise judgment and correct execution than to sole good deliberation.) Deliberation in itself is not a necessary part of human action. Most of the actions we voluntarily perform during the day are simple, and there is no need for a special stage of deliberation. Even when we are faced with many possibilities, if they are all simple, there is no need for deliberation. Deciding which streets I take to walk to the city square requires no deliberation, since there are several valid options. So I simply make a decision and execute my decision. Deliberation takes place only in the case of a complicated situation that requires reflection. (That is why, according to St. Thomas Aquinas, Jesus did not deliberate, because He had no doubts. But He did make acts of free choice — in fact, not only did He do so in the past, but He continues to do so now in His glorified humanity!) Deliberation begins when the end is already determined. In deliberation, as in the previous stages, there is the joint involvement of the reason and the will. Just as choice in the decision involves a rational moment, so deliberation, which is essentially an act of reason open to counsel (*consilium*), includes also a volitional moment, as we consider what we want and give our assent (*consensus*) to the prospective counsel.

---

of knowledge to the inclination of the will. This is the judgment of choice. Thus, it sometimes happens that the judgment of free choice goes astray, but not the judgment of conscience. For example, one debates something which presents itself to be done here and now and judges, still speculating as it were in the realm of principles, that it is evil.... However, when he comes to apply this to the act, many circumstances relevant to the act present themselves from all sides, for instance, the pleasure of the fornication, by the desire of which reason is constrained, so that its dictates may not issue into choice. Thus, one errs in choice and not in conscience" (trans. J. V. McGlynn, 1953).

The basic principle of action is the knowledge of truth and the desire for good. There is no need for an additional motivating force in the form of an externally imposed obligation. Many actions have no need of any special rules of engagement. We greet friends, prepare meals, or hug loved ones affectionately, simply from a perception that this is the right thing to do. How do we know this? Not necessarily because someone instructed us to do so but because we directly perceive the good in it. Of course, this perception of the good also comprises the assimilation of moral instructions that we have received in the past, but there is more to it than that. We have the ability to grasp values directly, even in unforeseen situations. There are also situations in which we do not clearly discern what to do, doubts arise, and then we need to deliberate and have recourse to the moral law, which will instruct us at that moment. As a result of committing sins, reason becomes clouded and often lacks clarity. That is why Aquinas, after discussing sin, gives us a treatise on the moral law. But in the analysis of the psychological structure of a moral act, Aquinas makes no mention of the moral law. The only reference to the moral law in this treatise is made precisely in the context of the doubt that deliberation must address.[62] Daniel Westberg is of the opinion that the function of moral law is limited to the "filtering out" of unsuitable means, and, if necessary, even using sanctions to reinforce this. The law is supposed to assist uncertain reason in its search for the *bonum intellectum*. Westberg also argues that one of the gifts of the Holy Spirit, the gift of counsel, applies not to decision and execution but only to the stage of deliberation.[63] The paucity of Aquinas's references to the moral law in his analysis of the moral act shows how free his thinking is from a moralistic emphasis on obligation. The freedom of free choice is realized in capturing a value directly, because of its own charm, its own splendor of truth, regardless of whether the issue has been mentioned somewhere by some precept!

---

[62] *ST*, Ia-IIae, q. 14, art. 3, ad 2: "Although that which is laid down by law is not produced by the action of the one seeking counsel, nevertheless it guides him in what he does, for the mandate of the law is one reason for doing something" (trans. T. Gilby, vol. 17, 1970).

[63] Westberg, "Did Aquinas Change His Mind?," 173–174.

The final stage in moral agency is the very execution of the decision made. Also at this stage, the rational and volitional contributions are present together. On this issue, there is likewise a great deal of misunderstanding. In the seventeenth century, under the influence of the theology of the Jesuit Francisco Suárez, the *imperium* was transferred from the reason to the will. Suárez held that the rational *imperium* cannot have the necessary impetus for action because this would mean a threat to the freedom of the will. Even in commentaries on the *Summa* of St. Thomas Aquinas, in this matter the theories of Duns Scotus and Ockham, which elevate the role of the will, prevailed.

At the stage of execution, of course, there is no new decision. There is, however, the *usus*, that is, the application of the powers to action, and this is done rationally. Animals use their powers instinctively. They can build nests, but they do not know the relationship of their powers to their members, which is why animals do not use tools. In humans, the application of the faculties is accompanied by a rational input, called *imperium*. A surgeon not only uses his hand but knows exactly why he uses it this way and not in a different way, even if his actions are already habitual. In execution, it is important that what is done is well thought out.

The term *imperium* is somewhat misleading. When one holds, as in the neo-scholastic diagram, that in the process of eliciting an act, the acts of reason and will are sequential, the suggestion emerges that reason issues an "order" that the will must carry out. There is a certain intellectual determinism in this, and it is not surprising that Suárez objected to it. Once one grasps the action of reason and will as occurring concurrently, however, there is no problem of intellectual determinism or unnecessary repetition of the judgment of reason that has been made earlier. Execution means the transfer of the decision that has been made into concrete action, and reason must be creatively engaged in this process. The intellect ensures that what has been decided is carried out and, furthermore, in an interesting and creative way. *Imperium*, then, is best translated as "governing" or "supervising" rather than as "issuing an order." (There is no trace here of the Kantian obedience of the subject to self-imposed moral imperatives.) *Imperium*, therefore, expresses the rational link between the *electio* and the *usus*. The point is to make sure that what the agent has decided is executed — and, even more, executed wisely. This is not obvious, and there are people who struggle precisely with this. They can dream, they can even make up their minds, but when it comes to executing the decision they have made, they do it sluggishly and ineptly, not because they lack the ability to do it but because they suddenly discover that they do not feel like it doing it. "I want to" and "I feel like" are not the same!

The diagram consisting of intention, decision, and execution (and the occasional deliberation) is an accurate presentation of the psychological structure of the moral act. Reflecting on this diagram, we understand better why Aquinas attributes a greater role to prudence than to conscience. Prudence is supposed to accompany a person at each of these stages. It is the virtue that helps one to make decisions and then to carry them out. *Conscience,* on the other hand, is defined by Aquinas only as an act of the practical reason — that is, as the application of knowledge derived from moral instruction and life experience to the moment of decision; hence the Latin term *con-scientia.* In education toward maturity, the cultivation of the virtue of prudence is much more important, since prudence, being present in both the reason and the will, empowers one to act independently, thoughtfully, consistently, and even creatively. In the modern reduction of moral teaching to the presentation of a catalogue of obligations, the importance of conscience, which was supposed to accept the obligation served in the moral law and pass it on to the will, has grown enormously, while prudence has become less prominent. But the model based on obligation does not elucidate as precisely as Aquinas has done the moment of personal creativity and moral maturity. Since Aquinas had in mind the image of God manifested in a mature human being capable of self-giving, it is understandable why he saw the interaction of reason and will in all stages of the free choice.

Having discussed the three or four stages that constitute the psychological structure of the moral act, one can ask which one of these stages is most difficult. Does the greatest difficulty arise at the level of intention, decision, deliberation, or at the final moment of execution? The answer to this question will vary from person to person. Some people have very few ideas and do only what circumstances or other people prompt them to do. Such people need to work on their capacity for intention; they need to expand their horizons, let themselves be fascinated by things and people they have not considered before. It is amazing how many people are unable to dream and simply wish to maintain the status quo in their lives. They respond to any suggestion of a renewal or transformation by saying that it would be better to keep things as they are. Such people contribute nothing to the world. They get through life passively without experiencing anything new. Sometimes they claim that it is better this way because this manifests fidelity to tradition, which must not be changed. (After the fall of communism in Poland, almost everything changed: the currency, the political system, the press, television, parliament, the government, the economy; but not much has changed in the life of the Church — the organists play the same hymns as always. Is not this a sign that the capacity for intention and dreaming was lacking? The point is not to make changes for the sake of change, or to change dogma, but the ways of experiencing life need to be refreshed.) Even if it turns out that one has not moved much further than the sole intention, at least the stimulation of intention has been a mobilizing factor and an invitation to authentic action.

For others, deliberation is the fundamental problem. Basically, they are capable of making decisions, but a disordered emotion of fear interferes with the decision-making process, and so each decision is preceded by paralyzing scruples. The constant search for the opinions of others is supposed to produce certainty, which is inwardly absent. Failure to cultivate the ability to deliberate generates weak individuals who hang on to the opinions of others, or who are psychologically dependent on stronger individuals, whom, as a result, they are unable to view critically.

Other people have no problem with deliberation; they know what can be done and is worth doing, but they cannot decide. A decision entails further decisions and the exclusion of other possibilities. In the upbringing of a young person, the father plays an important role, provoking the adolescent to cross a difficult threshold and assume the risk of a decision. The current phenomenon of adult men who are unable to decide about marriage stems from a lack of education in decision-making. When a young man has been dating a woman for years but delays the decision to marry, he causes her harm. When will she bear children? What will she do with her life when a man has been with her for ten years and then, after all, decides not to marry her? What is the source of this inability to make a decision? Does it lie in the intellectual pessimism of reason, which is unable or unwilling to adhere to the truth and persists in cognitive agnosticism, in which nothing is certain and everything is an arbitrary and mutable opinion? Or does it lie in the failure to cultivate prudence, the failure to cultivate the ability to move from intention through decision to execution? Or is the inner freedom uneducated due to a lack of faith in the empowering presence of God within the decision-making?

Still other people know what they want and are capable of deciding, but when it comes to execution, laziness prevails, some other superficial interest appears, and the execution never takes place, or if it does, the action is performed only carelessly and ineptly. The transition to execution requires the support of a whole range of virtues that channel the psychic forces toward chosen goals. When the practice of generosity is absent, even the greatest ideas come to nothing. The authentic attitudes of solidarity and opposition individuated by Karol Wojtyła[64] along with the inauthentic attitudes of conformity and escape characterize the psychic engagement in action. A person expresses himself in action only when, at every stage of the act — that is, in the intention, decision, deliberation, and the execution — the intervention of reason is creatively manifested. A vision of morality built on obligation, reducing the role of the will to mere obedience to an externally imposed imperative, unnecessarily flattens human action, depriving it of a fully human dimension. It is not surprising that such an inauthentic view has provoked opposition.

In light of this analysis, the following question may be posed: Which attitude is better? Following a genuinely free choice, in which creativity is involved at every stage — intention, decision, and execution — but in which clarity regarding the moral value of the act is deficient? Or the accomplishment of a moral good, but with psychological damage, in which the good is executed in fear of the opinion of others, without personal creativity, in an atmosphere of coercive psychological compulsion that one must be in order in respect to externally imposed precepts? The person who is capable

---

[64] Karol Wojtyła, *Person and Act and Related Essays*, trans. Grzegorz Ignatik (Washington, D.C.: Catholic University of America Press, 2021), 400–407.

of creative generosity, while being somewhat unclear about certain moral principles, will be psychologically healthier than the one who chooses nothing on his own and is a poor carbon copy of what others demand of him, even if it happens that no one demands anything wrong of him, and consequently he does nothing wrong (but nothing good either!).

If we move from this psychological analysis of the moral act to the theological question about the place of the grace of the Holy Spirit in human actions, it is worth reflecting on what kind of natural foundation is needed for grace. Which does the Holy Spirit, influencing human actions and giving them such a quality that bystanders observing them want to glorify the Father Who is in Heaven, invigorate more: individuals who have a rich personality capable of creative intention, decision, and execution, or individuals in whom moral acts are undertaken as a matter of routine, out of obedience to precepts or out of fear of being found noncompliant? What style of action does Christian education promote?

The place of grace in moral action

Going back to the diagram describing the psychological structure of a moral act, one may wonder where God is located in this diagram. The description of the action is philosophical, so it fits the mature action of both a believer and an atheist. How will it be different in the case of a believer? How should one's faith be shaped and applied to life so that one's action is imbued with God's power? Does God appear uniquely as a judge Who punishes or rewards only when one has reached the execution of an action? Do we imagine God as someone with Whom we will argue once the action is completed, demanding our due reward? Or does God, in our religious sensibility, purified by the Word of God, function as a good Father Who rejoices in our resourcefulness and personal mature freedom?

In order to bring a supernatural dimension to our action, which will allow divine fecundity to be manifested within it, it is necessary to invite God into the action. To which stage do we typically invite God? Do we turn to Him only when the execution turns out to be unsuccessful and we need help in putting ourselves back together? Or do we invite Him at the stage of intention, when ideas are born, when the mental horizon seeks greater light, new ideas, and discernment of new challenges? Do we invite Him at the moment of decision, when the decision is made by us, but by faith we call grace to our undertaking? Do we invite Him in moments of doubt, when the light of the Holy Spirit is particularly needed, even when the Holy Spirit does not give clear light and provokes us to make a decision on our own? Do we ask for God's help in the process of execution, so that this work we undertake, great or small, will be supported from within by God's fecundity? Should we not purify our image of God, so that there will be room for Him within the dynamics of our actions? Or perhaps it would be better to visualize God as a good Father who sits quietly on a bench while we race from intention through decision to execution. With patient anticipation, the Father waits for us to pause, to invite Him into our action, to ask what He thinks of our ideas, to listen to His words of encouragement and valor. Like a good father who does not tell his adult children what to do but rejoices when he can accompany them, when he can listen to their worries and give them encouragement, so the Heavenly Father does not give us an app in which the program for running our lives is set. He rejoices in our inventiveness, in our maturing in freedom, and in our self-giving.

We find a wonderful testimony of a trusting relationship with God within a very generous life in St. Thérèse of Lisieux. The theology of grace describes the receiving and applying of God's assistance to one's actions through the category of "merit." St. Thérèse liberates us from an overly mechanical or legalistic understanding of it. She writes:

> Merit does not consist in doing or giving much, but rather in receiving, in loving much.... It is said that it is much sweeter to give than to receive, and it is true, but then, when Jesus wants to take for Himself the sweetness of giving, it would not be gracious to refuse.[65]

That pleasure of giving of God Himself means that He seeks human hands, the human gift of self, in which His divine power may be revealed. But all

---

[65] Letter 142, to Céline, July 6, 1893, Les Archives du Carmel de Lisieux, https://archives.carmeldelisieux.fr/en/correspondance/lt-142-a-celine-6-juillet-1893/, accessed May 27, 2024.

of this is done in great trust and inner peace. We can be the ones who invite God into our actions, or we can exclude Him though our indifference or our perfectionist concentration on self. This is why St. Thérèse was extremely careful not to give herself credit for her actions, in which she perceived a great betrayal of God.

> If I said to myself, for example: I have acquired such a virtue, I am certain of being able to practice it. Because then it would be relying on one's own strength, and when one is there, one risks falling into the abyss. But I will have the right, without offending God, to do little stupid things until my death, if I am humble, if I remain very small.[66]

Therefore, she can say the following about herself:

> I always feel, however, the same bold confidence of becoming a great saint, because I don't count on my merits, since I have *none*, but I trust in him who is Virtue and Holiness. God alone, content with my weak efforts, will raise me to himself and make me a *saint*, clothing me in his infinite merits.[67]

---

[66] Yellow Notebook, CJ August 7, 1897, no. 4, Les Archives du Carmel de Lisieux, https://archives.carmeldelisieux.fr/en/archive/cj-aout-1897/#le-7-aout, accessed May 27, 2024.

[67] Manuscript A, 32r, translated by John Clarke, O.C.D.

4

The Moral Qualification of Human Acts

IN SEEKING TRACES OF GOD'S FECUNDITY within human acts, the main focus was on those human acts in which man is fully engaged. Only acts in which reason and will collaborate in free choice are fully human, and, therefore, it is above all through such actions that God reveals Himself. God's image will be genuine in man only when it flows from man's depths. An action reflecting a mechanical routine or flowing from an uncontrolled passion or a certain compulsion, or a simulated action that is merely a consciously or unconsciously maintained mask — all of these will lack an essential authenticity. The glory of God is an authentic person, rather than someone who is not in control of himself, or who is hiding or acting because he is running away from the truth about himself. Being occasionally tainted by weakness is not an obstacle that prevents something of God's image from being disclosed through one's actions. When recognition of one's own weakness and thus acceptance of the truth about oneself is combined with a trusting reliance on God's mercy, God bestows Himself through this human weakness. "We, with our unveiled faces reflecting like mirrors the brightness of the Lord, all grow brighter and brighter as we are turned into the image that we reflect" (2 Cor. 3:18, Jerusalem Bible). But a lack of trust in the power of grace working within a person results in evasion or in the painstaking hiding behind a façade of an expected but hypocritical "correctness" — or perhaps behind the mask of a shallow wit and escape from true integrity. Running away from the truth about oneself means living a life of falsehood, which generates various repressions and arrested emotional development.

The fact that an action was undertaken sincerely, with the full participation of personal freedom, does not yet mean that it is a morally good action. The proper foundation for a good action is the mature contribution of personality, but to grasp fully the essence of a good action, the reflection must be taken further. How do we judge the moral value of a course of action, particularly when we are faced with difficult life dilemmas? How do we know that one action is good and another is evil? Mere rationality and sincerity of authentic commitment are not by themselves guarantees of goodness. One can, after all, commit crimes sincerely and with a mature commitment of free choice. Thus, the question concerns not only the very entry of a given action into the realm of morality (through the participation of reason and will), but the moral qualification of the act (is it good or evil?). An examination of the way in which the goodness of acts can be apprehended plays a key role in ethical analysis.

A claim can be made, however, that, in the context of Christian moral reflection, this important question will not be the most vital, although it has often been viewed as such in moral teaching. Is the Christian's main dilemma the question of the worthiness or unworthiness of a planned action (or even of its permissibility or impermissibility), or is it the question of how to convey something of the goodness received from God through the action undertaken, how to make the power coming from the death and Resurrection of the Savior bear fruit here and now? In modern moral theology, more concerned with the moral permissibility of an act than with the possibility of its spiritual enrichment, the question of the moral qualification of an act has become too central, and this has affected the manner of deliberation over this issue. The ethical analysis of an act, conducted in a sterile abstraction from the spiritual life, has cast aside questions about the quality of personal involvement and the possibility of its supernatural enrichment. This, in turn, has generated a reaction in the form of teleological ethical theories that are sensitive to the interiority of the moral act but in which the very center of moral discernment is called into question. In an effort to emphasize the wealth of subjective involvement in an act, the understanding of the objective moral character of the act has been diluted. The response to this mental confusion is St. John Paul II's encyclical *Veritatis splendor,* based on the work of many modern theologians, in which the errors of the teleological theories of proportionalism and consequentialism are demonstrated. It is not enough, however, to acknowledge the departure of these new theories from traditional Church teaching. The narrowing of the prevalent perspective in modern Catholic moral theology, which led to opposition and the quest for new paths, must also be noted, along with the perspective of the broader insight found in the older and more evangelical theology of the Middle Ages, toward which the encyclical discreetly points us.

The deficiencies of the approach that has become traditional in modern times lie in the minds. When applying the principles of this thinking to specific moral cases, doubts and misunderstandings emerge. An example of the labor of ethical analysis may be found in the exchange of letters between Fr. Ludwik Wiśniewski, O.P., and Adam Michnik regarding the ethical assessment of the introduction of martial law in Poland in 1981.[68] This dispute, conducted on the pages of the Polish daily *Gazeta Wyborcza*,[69] touches the very heart of the matter.

Fr. Ludwik, intimately familiar with the extent of human suffering during the time of martial law, applies a simple measure that has its source in the teaching of the Decalogue. The self-evident prohibitions of the moral law do not allow him to take any other stand than being against it. Martial law was a moral evil that no amount of equivocation could justify. Contrary to

---

[68] Since the end of World War II, Poland was occupied by Soviet forces and suffered under a dictatorial regime. In August 1980, after much industrial unrest, the communist leadership allowed for the establishment of a trade union, Solidarity, that was independent of communist control. With massive support, Solidarity began demanding changes in the functioning of the state, leading to democracy and capitalism. All the time, there was fear of a Soviet military intervention similar to that which took place in Czechoslovakia in 1968. In December 1981, the Polish communist leadership under General Wojciech Jaruzelski declared martial law and arrested leading figures of the opposition, including Lech Wałęsa, the leader of Solidarity. Later, in 1989, dialogue between Solidarity, Jaruzelski, and the Church in the Round Table Talks led to political and social change.

[69] February 24–25, 2001.

the principle mandating an examination of the three sources of morality, which will be discussed later, Fr. Ludwik's attention is focused above all on the object of the moral act. He writes, "One must answer whether it [martial law] is morally permissible or not. Everything else, including the intentions of the Polish generals, are just circumstances, either aggravating or mitigating." He then proceeds to lay the foundations of his reasoning: "In order for moral judgment to be accepted, there must be, in this case, consensus on two points: first, that objective good and evil exist (although subjective ones also exist), and second, that the principle 'canonized' by General Jaruzelski on that December night, proclaiming that 'it is permissible to do a lesser evil to avoid a greater one,' must be rejected." Referencing the objective good provides a firm foundation to ethical reflection, even though it does happen, as Fr. Ludwik notes, that "someone commits an act that is objectively evil, but [he] is subjectively convinced of its goodness — because he is uninformed, intimidated, enslaved, misguided, convinced of some historical necessity." Further on, he recalls the principle of double effects, in which both good and bad effects follow. "We always choose the good, never evil. But evil is a possibility that we take into account.... One can never do 'pure' evil, even if it were to appear to someone as a remedy for an even greater evil."

Responding to Fr. Ludwik's indignation, Adam Michnik recognizes that the moral assessment of actions is more complex, and he refuses to adopt a moralistic tone. He writes:

> Nor will I ever condone the Manichean, fairy-tale notion that the generals responsible for martial law are the embodiment of pure evil, and that we, their opponents, are and have been the vehicles of good incarnate.... It is difficult to walk "in the generals' shoes."... If I have personally made such an attempt, I was guided ... by civic duty, which mandates the effort to understand another's perspective, and not just the inclination to see the wicked motives of the opponents.

Responding to the principles cited by Fr. Ludwik, he notes the difficulty of their application: "Thus, when you say, 'Objective good and evil exist,' I reply to you: agreed, but none of us should consider himself the bearer of the certainty that he represents 'objective good.' Each of us should keep in mind that in actual politics 'objective good' in its pure form is extremely rare." Examining the complexity of that decision and the fact of the generals' subsequent acceptance of the Polish Round Table Talks, which paved the way for the coming out of communism, Michnik argues for forgiveness, citing the authority of the pope, and he rejects Fr. Ludwik's insistence on promulgating a moral condemnation of the authors of martial law.

Leaving the specific analysis of the political event of martial law in Poland to historians, it is impossible not to notice the difference in the understanding of moral principles in this debate. The dispute between Michnik and Wiśniewski is not just about judging political events, both past and those one would hope to see in the future. The dispute reveals the diversity of approach to moral principles. Using it as an example will allow for a better understanding of the renewal of reflection on the principles of assessing moral acts that is taking place in moral theology. Illustrating the renewal taking place in the Church will require three points: articulating the interpretation of the moral act that has been prevalent in modern theology; discussing the theory of proportionalism; and pointing out the possibility of correcting the traditional scheme of thinking.

The traditional interpretation of the moral act

a. The essence of morality

In every human action, we can identify the physical and the moral being of the act. In the gesture of raising a hand as a signal or greeting, we can see both the physical and the moral moment. When one temporarily abstracts from the physical moment — the raising of the hand — the moral moment alone remains. What does it consist of? After all, there can be two acts whose physical being will be identical and whose moral being will be completely different. To demonstrate the specifics of morality, St. Thomas Aquinas gives the example of sexual intercourse with a wife and with a nonwife. The physical or physiological aspect will be identical in both cases, while the moral dimension of the act will be completely different. So it is also with death. Looking at it from the physical side, death is the end of life. There is an essential moral difference, however, between the death of a patient who dies during surgery, the execution of a convicted criminal, the death of a soldier in war, and the death of someone who has been murdered. Moral qualification, therefore, adds something to the being of the physical act. What does it add? It cannot consist only in the freedom of the act. The fact that an act is done voluntarily merely manifests a prerequisite for the morality of the act. We identify acts that fall within the scope of morality by the fact that they are performed freely. The fact that an act is willed does not yet determine whether it is a good or an evil act.

Morality, then, adds something more to the act. Theology marked by the legacy of nominalism tied morality to a moral norm originating in the will of the One who is the ultimate Author of the moral order. This would mean that good acts are those commanded by God, and evil acts are those that are forbidden. Morality would mean a reference to an externally binding moral norm. And why are some acts forbidden while others are commanded? Because, it was held, such is the will of the Giver of the moral law — namely, God. Such an answer, although it simplifies dilemmas, is obviously unsatisfactory, since it ties morality to a canon of purely subjective decrees arbitrarily imposed from the outside. This theory distorts the image of God and the Church and, in the process, makes it impossible to develop inner freedom.

Another approach to the issue identifies the essence of morality subjectively and internally. The criterion of morality is then found only in the sincerity of desires and in spontaneity, or in the fulfillment of an internal imperative. The encyclical *Veritatis splendor* rejects the recognition of sincerity as the ultimate criterion of conduct:

> To the affirmation that one has a duty to follow one's conscience is unduly added the affirmation that one's moral judgment is true merely by the fact that it has its origin in the conscience. But in this way the inescapable claims of truth disappear, yielding their place to a criterion of sincerity, authenticity and "being at peace with oneself", so much so that some have come to adopt a radically subjectivistic conception of moral judgment. (32)

Still another interpretation, nowadays perhaps more practical than ideological, holds that the criterion for the morality of an act is entirely objective and external. The moral assessment is supposed to derive from society, fashion, public opinion, the policy of the ruling party, the social contract, or merely the procedure to be followed while pursuing solutions. Morality, then, would mean the relationship of an act to this objective and external reference point.

In defining the essence of morality, the encyclical *Veritatis splendor* declares:

> The *morality of acts* is defined by the relationship of man's freedom with the authentic good.... The rational ordering of the human act to the good in its truth and the voluntary pursuit of that good, known by reason, constitute morality.... Activity is morally good when it attests to and expresses the voluntary ordering of the person to his ultimate end and the conformity of a concrete action with the human good as it is acknowledged in its truth by reason. (72)

Morality is defined here as the existing real relationship of free choice to an act characterized by an objective good, knowable by reason. Morality thus adds to the physical act the fact that it was chosen consciously and freely, with the recognition of the truth about it. Since animals do not reason, they do not have moral actions, but only physical actions. Man, on the other hand, not only chooses but also perceives the truth in his action and relates to it, even when he chooses to ignore it at a given moment. Since truth, goodness, and being are interchangeable, being mindful of truth is also being mindful of the nature of things, of their internal coherence. This position on morality assumes that human reason is capable of knowing the objective truth of a planned act and that it can subsequently direct its free choice toward it. Here the encyclical expresses confidence in reason, which is capable of grasping the truth about the good also in the context of various moral dramas. For the moment, the encyclical does not engage the question of the difficulty of getting to know this truth. Nor does it claim that the truth about the good will always be grasped in exactly the same way and without error by every person. Michnik's critique of the hubristic conviction that one is the holder of objective truth does not necessarily contradict the claim that, in a moral act, man is directed toward the truth about the good and that his reason is equipped with the data to recognize this truth. (The question remains whether a person is ready to be inwardly transformed by the truth he has learned or whether he treats it as an object in his possession, by means of which he elevates himself above others and hurls anathemas at them.)

The connection of the essence of morality with truth, knowable by reason, grants to morality a foundation that is lacking in the other ethical theories. By perceiving truth, one perceives the essence of the matter. The foundation of morality is therefore both objective and internal, since nature is an objective fact that is also internal to man. Man participates in nature through his own self. It is possible to perceive in reality an existing order that is internally consistent and subject to rational observation, or an inclination toward that order, that discloses itself even when one acts in a way that distorts that order. Reason perceives in nature a light that reflects the Creator's wisdom. The recognition of this light obviously is not easy. It requires the forming of a certain refinement in the gaze. But assuming, as would seem self-evident, that there is a certain constancy in human nature, which makes it possible to grasp the truth about it, the ultimate criterion of morality, perceptible even without faith, is human nature, whose stability suggests its inner finality. (If one were to reject the reference to nature and to the truth about it, not only would there be no place for objective ethics, but there would be no place for any science at all!) Positing the rational character of reality as the basis grants ethical reflection a foundation, admittedly still remote but nevertheless real, through which more specific deliberations can be undertaken.

Aquinas succinctly captures the whole question of the moral qualification of an act in one sentence. He writes:

> The measure by which we consider the good and evil in human acts is the accordance of the act with reason that is informed by the divine law, whether by nature or by instruction or by infusion.[70]

---

[70] *De Malo*, q. 2, art. 4 (my translation).

So it is not human reason alone that shapes moral principles. They inhere in the nature of things, but reason is capable of recognizing them, and, by virtue of its dignity, human reason is that instance that ultimately passes judgment on the moral value of the performed act.[71] Here Aquinas notes God's great respect for man, since He invests in man's reason so that every individual using his well-formed reason may undertake his moral steps. God does not send down thunderbolts when man grapples with moral dilemmas or when he strays. Furthermore, God assists the perception of human reason through the guidance given in revelation and through His light granted directly. The pointing out of various ways in which the formation of the moral reason takes place, all of which can work together, emphasizes the fact that the apprehension of moral truth involves a series of elements. This truth consists of the nature of the matter, its internal rationality or common sense, additional light coming from revelation, the direct movement of the Holy Spirit, Church teaching, personal experience, the influence of one's culture, social customs, and even some personal conditionings. The recognition of many threads that combine in the process of finding moral truth does not mean that it is arbitrary and that man would fabricate it according to his own needs. Man faces the truth, which obligates him. But it is an indication that man needs various supports in grasping that which will be the best and most righteous solution. It is possible to attempt the working out of moral conclusions through a speculative analysis of human nature and its intrinsic finality. But in the heat of tackling moral dilemmas, philosophical analyses are rarely conducted. That is why, when Aquinas refers to natural law, he often substantiates his conclusions with references to Scripture.

The category of natural law is an expression of the observation of rationality and finality in nature, which bind man. In the practical formulation of the application of the principles of natural law, Aquinas refers to nature,

---

[71] *ST*, Ia-IIae, q. 91, art, 3, ad 2: "The human reason of itself is not the measure for things. Yet principles instilled in it by nature are some general rules and measures for all that men are to do for which the natural reason is the rule and measure, even though it is not a measure of those things that are from nature" (my translation).

rationality, the Decalogue, and the book of Genesis. All these sources of information correct one another and allow for a better reading of the truth about the good. Furthermore, when the seeking reason is open by faith to additional direct movements of the Holy Spirit, it sees better where the beauty and truth of a given moral situation lie. The cultivation of reason so that it will be able to grasp the moral truth and, even more, to be sensitive to the fullness of God's goodness, comes about gradually and slowly. Not every person is willing to let the additional light of God into his moral search, and not at every moment of his life, and sometimes it happens that he smuggles in his own selfish calculations, ascribing them to intuitions that come from God. St. Teresa of Ávila is famous for her harsh observation about people who have prudence but who fail to recognize charity poured in by grace that would transcend the limits of prudence. Divine intervention shaping human reason seeks to enable it to reach out even further than that toward which the observation of nature inclines, so as to go wild with the folly of divine wisdom! "The unspiritual man does not receive the gifts of the Spirit of God, for they are folly to him.... The spiritual man judges all things, but is himself to be judged by no one" (1 Cor. 2:14–15).

A person may reject both the natural light discernible by reason and the intuitions of grace and may not be concerned with forming his conscience. He is then culpable for persisting in error. He may be well aware of where the true value lies, and yet out of laziness or fear he may abandon it. In such a case, he is acting against his conscience. His fault consists in that, although he knows where the good lies, he still decides to do what is wrong. He knows the truth, but he disregards it. It is then an indication of the weakness of the free choice, because the free choice decides on an action, rejecting the previously discerned light. Consequently, then, we distinguish good and evil actions — that is, actions in which the objective good has been recognized and accepted and those in which it has been disregarded. Morally indifferent actions exist only theoretically, independent of circumstances. In practice, all fully human actions are either good or evil. This does not mean, however, that one can easily "enter into the conscience" of others and pass judgments of praise or condemnation. Ethical analysis attempts to capture the relevant elements of reaching a moral decision, but the practice of life is much more complicated and so condemning judgments should be avoided.

The proposal of a double division that is sometimes presented, which distinguishes "good" and "bad" actions and "right" and "wrong" actions suggests that supposedly there are some acts that are simultaneously "good" and "wrong." Such a division is misleading, and therefore the encyclical *Veritatis splendor* rejects it (75). It is certainly true that there may be involuntary acts that are accompanied by a good will. The action then may be bad, although it will not necessarily incur moral culpability. (An example of such an action would be when a surgeon mistakenly amputates the wrong leg.) In such a case, the agent does not actually choose, and therefore does not consciously do what he *thought* he was choosing and doing. Therefore, one cannot formulate a moral principle based on such a mistake. The only relevant distinction is between a technically right or wrong action and a morally good or bad action. A burglar's action can be evaluated as being technically right or wrong, but then it is not a moral evaluation. What is important is to see that some acts are morally evil because their choice is not directed toward a good discernible by reason. Freely choosing an action that reason has discerned as evil will always constitute a choice of moral evil.

To sum up, when we look at the relationship of the act to the will, we are addressing the question of whether the act falls within the scope of morality. An action that is purely bodily or sensual and not subject to the operations of the will does not at all enter the realm of morality. But when we look at the relationship of the act to reason, we find the answer to the question of whether the act is good or evil. Reason is directed toward the truth, and therefore it is capable of evaluating an action and granting it a moral qualification.

b. *The sources of morality*

In capturing the essence of the moral qualification of acts, Catholic moral reflection, certainly from in the Middle Ages, inquires about the sources of morality. This approach appears in all textbooks on moral theology and is echoed in the *Catechism of the Catholic Church* and in the encyclical *Veritatis splendor*. There are three fundamental elements of morality, known as the "sources": the moral object of an act, its end, and the circumstances. For an act to be morally good, it is necessary for all three of these sources to be good. If one of them is bad, ultimately the act will be evil.[72]

The notion of the *object* of the moral act presents the greatest difficulty in grasping this interpretive principle.[73] The manuals of moral theology, in explaining the nature of the object, introduced a distinction that Aquinas knew but did not employ in this context. They distinguished between the *finis operis* and the *finis operantis*, that is, between the end of the act itself and the end of the agent. For example, in giving alms to the poor, the end of the act is the act itself, that is, the alms given, and the end of the agent is the motivation behind the almsgiving. It is possible to help the poor out of pity, out of the love of God, in order to show one's superiority to others, or to set a good example for others. The *finis operis* could be called the proximate end of the act, and the *finis operantis* the remote end of the act. The end of the agent is internal to the will, while the end of the act itself is external to it. Moral action can thus be presented in the following diagram:

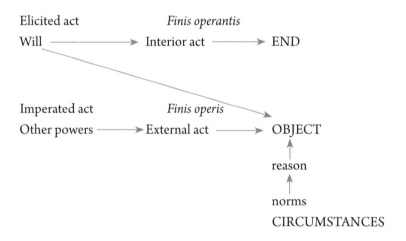

[72] In this regard, the principle of Pseudo-Dionysius is commonly invoked: *Bonum ex integra causa, malum ex quocumque defectu* (An action is good when good in every respect; it is wrong when wrong in any respect).

[73] Martin Rhonheimer, "'Intrinsically Evil Acts' and the Moral Viewpoint: Clarifying a Central Teaching of *Veritatis splendor*," *Thomist* 58 (1994): 1–39.

Ultimately, the act is good only when the end of the agent, the act itself, and the circumstances are all good. If the intention is good, but the object of the act is bad, then the act will ultimately be morally evil. And if the object of the act is good, but it is accompanied by a bad intention, that intention will vitiate the goodness of the act performed.

The *finis operis* in this diagram means that toward which an action tends by its very nature — that is, the end of the action. *The object of the act*, on the other hand, means not only the event itself, the bare act itself that has happened or is about to happen, but also the evaluation of the act undertaken by reason. As the reason judges an act that becomes the object of the will's desire, it reads the internal rationale supporting the act, and, in so doing, it also takes into account the illumination of the situation deriving from the moral law. The moral object of the act does not necessarily mean a physical object. The object may be the car I want to buy or steal, but it can just as well be an emotion I entertain — good or bad.

The diagram becomes clearer when illustrated with an example. Imagine someone taking a knife and inserting it into another person's stomach. The agent's end, and therefore his motive or intention, is to get money. He thinks that by sticking the knife into the other person's stomach, he will be able to get the money he wants. The end of the act itself is to cut open the stomach. There is, however, an important difference between a street thug sticking a knife into a man's stomach to rob him in the process, and a surgeon sticking a knife into a patient's abdomen during surgery. In terms of their physical being, both acts are similar. Morally speaking, there is a significant difference. Where does this difference lie? It lies in reason. If, given the current medical knowledge (which is embodied in the natural law) and the means at his disposal, the surgeon concludes that inserting a knife into the patient's abdomen is a necessary means to heal him, the object of the act will be good. In the case of the thug armed with a knife, the object of the act — that is, the injuring of the victim — is not morally good. Perhaps in the future, with further developments in medical knowledge and different circumstances, making an incision in the abdomen of a patient suffering from the same condition will not be the optimal solution. Perhaps it will be possible to treat the patient through simpler means, and then the incision made by the doctor will be a bad act. Thus, the assessment made by reason is subject to change, taking into account evolving circumstances, but ultimately the power that determines the object of the act is always the reason of the agent.

The will of the agent, when it chooses the object — that is, when it is involved in the free choice together with the reason — always chooses the object of the act and not just the bare physical fact. When it comes to the free choice of a moral act, it is not only the material event itself that is at stake but the object of the act, the object that has been evaluated and determined by reason. The will takes as the object of its willing the action, together with its moral qualification, made by reason.[74] When it is said that it is always inappropriate to choose an act that is objectively evil, even if the intention is good, this means that the act, when it becomes the object of the will's willing, already has its moral qualification, which reason is capable of comprehending. Moral acts do not exist in isolation, estranged from the judgment passed by reason. Reason is involved in every moral choice, and, through this involvement, the end of the action — the *finis operis* — becomes a moral object with a specific moral value. This happens even when the insight of reason into the anticipated act is challenging, when it is surrounded by doubts due to very complicated situations. In the final analysis, however, it is always the reason, even when its perception is vague, that evaluates the action as good or evil, and, as such, it chooses it together with the will.

The agent's intentions, which accompany the act, may be very diverse and may overlap. In our example, a doctor may perform a surgery for a plethora of completely different reasons. He may simply want to make a living and view his work as a means of supporting himself and his family. He may want to test a new medical technique; he may want to use this opportunity to teach a junior doctor; he may want to do research for his academic study; he may want to help the patient, or he may want to serve him out of love, for God's sake. These are all good reasons, although their goodness also varies. But for a surgical procedure to be a morally good act, the most important thing is that the act itself is appropriate. The doctor's basic action must be correct,

---

[74] *ST*, Ia-IIae, q. 18, art. 10: "The species of moral acts are constituted from forms as conceived by reason" (trans. T. Gilby, vol. 18, 1966).

in accordance with the judgment of his reason, which is enlightened by the objective principles of medical knowledge.

It may happen that the object of the act involves pain and suffering. A doctor who decides to amputate chooses a painful and even bloody solution, but if there is no other way to save the patient, the object of the act will be morally good. Similarly, a judge who sentences a criminal to prison chooses an action that is painful for the criminal and his family. But the sentencing does not constitute a choice of moral evil by the judge. It is a choice of moral good and an act of the virtue of justice. The judge issues the sentence with the public good in mind. Thus, it is possible and sometimes even necessary to choose actions that are painful and bring suffering. It is possible to choose actions in which there is what is sometimes called *ontic evil*. But it is never permissible to choose action in which there is moral evil, even if it is accompanied by the so-called higher intention. We can choose actions that are painful, but we cannot choose an evil moral object.

We sometimes hear the argument that, supposedly in some situations, we need to choose a *lesser evil*. Such reasoning is false. One should never choose moral evil directly, neither greater nor lesser, although one may choose an action in which there is physical evil. One should always choose moral good, even if one fears that, as a result, others will choose greater evil. For it is better to suffer martyrdom than to choose moral evil. Of course, in describing actions, precise language is not always used. A person may argue that he chose the lesser evil, and, in fact, he may mean uniquely the physical evil and not the moral evil. There is nothing wrong with this. A surgeon performing an amputation chooses a physical evil that is simultaneously a moral good.

In the discussion on the introduction of martial law in Poland referred to earlier in this chapter, Michnik shared his feeling: "I prefer General Jaruzelski, who called martial law a 'lesser evil,' to General Pinochet, who called the coup d'etat an 'objective good.'" Are both generals speaking the same language? If, at the time of their political decision, they discerned with their reason that, although they were choosing an action that was difficult, painful, executed with the tools and forces at their disposal at that moment (which had their shortcomings and limitations), but nevertheless they were convinced they were choosing a good solution to defend the country and its citizens from impending turmoil and foreign intervention, then, in their interpretation, they were choosing a morally good action. The object of their choice was a moral act judged by their reason to be good. If they were aware that they were choosing a morally despicable solution — that is, an action that their reason judged to be morally wrong in the given situation — and yet they chose it out of selfish motives or out of fear, or for other reasons, then their choice was a choice of a moral evil. One can then shift the discussion to the question of the objective conditions and wonder whether their interpretation of the country's situation was indeed correct and whether there truly was a threat of Soviet invasion in Poland and of Soviet and Cuban invasion in Chile. Perhaps their interpretation of the situation in both cases was wrong, exaggerated, based on incomplete data, and so forth. Then their discernment can be judged as erroneous or correct. Similarly, one can judge the discernment of a surgeon who decides to amputate, wondering whether his assessment of the existing condition was correct. The discussion will then be on the level of the historical analysis of a given political crisis or on the level of medical science. But to make an accusation that somebody has chosen a moral evil would require penetrating the interior of the conscience of the acting person. Michnik's suggestion that Pinochet's judgment was "hypocritically calling 'evil' an 'objective good'" is therefore questionable. On what basis does he think that he may make statements about a person's inner depth?

With respect to capturing the essence of the moral object of the act, the encyclical *Veritatis splendor* sheds a crucial light on ethical analysis:

> The morality of the human act depends primarily and fundamentally on the "object" rationally chosen by the deliberate will.... In order to be able to grasp the object of an act which specifies that act morally, it is therefore necessary to place oneself *in the perspective of the acting person*. (78)

This is a critical point, which closely follows the teaching of Aquinas, even though this moment was not always emphasized in moral theology. The authors of modern manuals of moral theology were concerned about moral subjectivism, which is why they emphasized the object of the act in defense of the objective moral order. They viewed morality from the perspective of ethics built around the central theme of obligations and norms, rather than from the perspective of the virtues, as did Aquinas. They stressed the objective moral order; and the internal moral order, shaped by reason, which judges the anticipated act and assigns it to the will, was forgotten.[75] The manuals presented the moral object of the act primarily through its conformity or incompatibility with the norm, which was mostly understood in a voluntaristic way. This implied that the norms expressed in the Decalogue, in canon law, and in casuistic manuals of moral theology contain a catalogue of evil acts and that the task of reason was merely to determine whether the prohibition of a given act was binding. This led to the premonition that an act must simply conform immediately and without any adjustment to a norm that drops out of the sky without any justification.

The teaching of the encyclical *Veritatis splendor* clearly favors ethics built on virtue. The perspective of the acting person is decisive here. The reason of the agent assimilates the light of the norm, and later, with the help of its instruction and taking into account the circumstances, passes the judgment by virtue of its own dignity. Thus, the final word in determining the moral object belongs to the reason of the acting person. It is not surprising, therefore, that different people interpret the same event differently, because the cognitive sensibility of their reason may detect nuances that others miss.

In analyzing moral dilemmas, therefore, one should not adopt the attitude of a detached spectator. Moral actions are viewed not so much in terms of their physical structure as in their moral species — that is, taking into account their essential reference to values, undertaken by the acting person himself. Moral acts cannot be analyzed purely mechanically, like events that simply happen and produce predictable, measurable outcomes. Ethics differs from physics and chemistry, and therefore it cannot afford to adopt a merely detached approach. The ethics of obligation that was prevalent in the old manuals did not perceive this strictly personalistic character of moral agency; this is one of the reasons so much opposition to the old approaches accumulated over time. It was expected that the moralist would provide an answer to every emerging case, an answer that would be clear and the only

---

[75] Owens, "Human Reason," 159–177.

possible one, applicable to every situation. The reason of the acting person was demoted from a creative role to a merely executive one.

When reason looks at an anticipated act, it must view it in its essence, not just its incidental aspects. The decisive issue is the essence of the act. Other elements may also be anticipated, but that which is done per se constitutes the object. Also, the distinction between a proximate and a remote end, determining what is done directly and what is done incidentally, depends on the personal perspective of the agent. In the chain of factors that make up a complex moral decision, where is the proximate end and where is the remote end? In the case of General Jaruzelski's imposition of martial law, what was the proximate end and what was the remote end of the action? Was it a case of an inappropriate choice of moral evil (imprisoning the innocent out of fear of personal loss of power); or a case of choosing a moral evil, but a "lesser" moral evil than the anticipated greater moral evil to be committed by someone else (imprisoning the innocent by the Poles rather than the Soviets); or finally, a case of choosing a moral good (protecting the Solidarity activists from imminent repression by the advancing Soviet army)? Political dilemmas are complex, so their ethical analysis is particularly difficult because such decisions involve multiple elements.

In moral analysis, the distinction between the object of the act, i.e., that toward which the action tends directly, along with reason's evaluation of that action and the end, or intention, is determined from the perspective of the acting person. It is the one who undertakes the action who perceives what is the proximate end and what is the remote end. It is necessary, of course, to consider not only the intention of the acting person but also the very intentionality of the act, its internal logic and rationality as perceived by the acting person himself. The administering of a pain reliever that may, as a side effect, cause death to a patient is not the same as administering the same medication in order to cause death. The difference between the two cases is not only in the remote end that is in the intention. The difference is in the finality of the act itself. In moral assessment, the object of the act itself and its intrinsic rationality must be examined. When a doctor administers a hazardous palliative drug to a patient, he does so because he understands that it is necessary and because he knows that other, less hazardous means are not available to him. Although the doctor is aware of the risks, he does not choose an act that in itself is evil. He has rational arguments to justify his conduct and is able to articulate them if necessary. He chooses an action that he knows to be good, that is the best way to save the patient, even though this good object is accompanied by some danger. It is completely different from giving a patient a drug so as to kill him. This is not a choice of good; it is murder.

In examining the object of the act, it is crucial to realize that the moral object is not like an immutable lump of rock. The object is susceptible to change; it has multiple layers. The analogous quality of both being and predication prevent us from always seeing everything unequivocally. The fact that there is potentiality in beings means that they can change. We can look at a child acting horribly and see a potential saint in him. When the reason of the acting agent "transforms" the *finis operis* into a moral object, it is susceptible to additional stimuli, such as the emotions, faith in the prospect for growth, or openness to mercy. The mentality of the Enlightenment, with its emphasis on scientific precision, has instilled in our thinking the notion that absolute precision in such deliberations is both possible and necessary. In moral judgments, precision is not mathematical. The moral object is viewed from the perspective of the acting agent, and this person is involved, subject to various conditionings, not all of which may be conscious. In formulating the moral object of the act, it is the reason of the acting agent that has the final word, even if that reason has its limitations or conditionings.

The second source of morality identified in our diagram is the *end*, or the intention of the acting agent. Jesus teaches that the intention in action should be pure: "Beware of practicing your piety before men in order to be seen by them; for then you will have no reward from your Father who is in heaven" (Matt. 6:1). The intention that determines the remote end of the agent expresses the inner stirrings of his will. The difference between the object of the act and its end — that is, the remote intention — depends on the current interest of the acting person. One could say that there is a certain flexibility in distinguishing between the object of the act and the end of the agent. This flexibility is not dictated by carelessness of analysis but springs from the very nature of the moral act that is being analyzed.

The end, or intention, added to the object of the act can make an indifferent act good or evil; it can make a good act better or worse; and it can make an evil act more or less evil. But a good intention cannot make an act that is evil by virtue of its object good. A girl who is sexually active with her boyfriend, telling herself that she is doing it with a good intention because, by binding him to herself, she is also leading him to the Church, is mistaken. One should not "do evil that good may come" (Rom. 3:8). A good end does not justify or sanctify evil means, although undoubtedly a good end sanctifies good means, hence St. Paul's exhortation: "Whether you eat or drink, or whatever you do, do all to the glory of God" (1 Cor. 10:31). This does not mean, of course, that one should necessarily have God's glory in mind in every action. The Church rejected the exaggerated claims of Michael Baius and Cornelius Jansenius, who held that works not performed intentionally for the glory of God are fundamentally sinful. There is no doubt, however, that introducing love for God into all work contributes to spiritual growth.

The third source of morality to be taken into account when considering the morality of acts are the *circumstances*. They can be defined as morally significant accidentals surrounding an act. They are, as it were, added to an act that already has a specified moral value, and they merely encircle the act from the outside. They either decrease or increase or even change the moral value of the act. Fr. Jacek Woroniecki, O.P., captured the primary circumstances as follows: "Who? what? with what? and out of what? how? where? when? and why?"[76] These questions entail more than just the circumstances themselves, as the question "what?" refers to the object of the act, and the question "why?" refers to the end. The other questions capture the circumstances. The moral value of the act will certainly deteriorate if the one drunk in public is the prime minister, or if a brawl takes place in the parliament. The Council of Trent recommended that during Confession, not only sins but also their circumstances be confessed, with the stipulation that this should be done only if these circumstances change the species of the sin.[77]

---

[76] *Katolicka Etyka Wychowawcza*, vol. I (Lublin: KUL, 1986), 265. A similar list can be found in Cicero, *Quis, quid, ubi, quibus auxiliis, cur, quomodo, quando?*

[77] DS, 1681, 1707.

c. The role of the moral law

Reason, when it is making a judgment of the *finis operis* and co-creating the moral object of the act, uses the light provided by the moral law, although it should be noted that reason itself possesses the capacity for moral judgment by virtue of its nature. This is proof of the dignity of human reason.[78] The judgment of reason, directed practically to action, is the conscience. One must have confidence in the judgment of conscience when it passes judgment. It is always wrong to act against the judgment of the practical reason. Even if the conscience is erroneous, it is binding, because man has no other compass involved in a particular act than his own reason.

This does not mean, of course, that reason is inherently infallible, and that man does not need the light of the moral law. Conscience needs to be formed so that it can pass judgments truthfully, according to the truth of the situation. That is why conscience needs the help of the moral law, which steers reason toward true values. Even a vague awareness that a given act is judged by the moral law as wrong is enough for reason to make a judgment that the act is evil.[79] Reason does not need to know all thinkable arguments for the moral evaluation of a given act in order to pass judgment. It is not always possible to know all the arguments. Reason may perceive the intrinsic evil of a particular situation directly, or it may see only that a particular act would cause scandal, or that it is forbidden by God's law, without knowing exactly why.[80]

If human reason lacks clarity to judge the situation, all the more it should have recourse to the moral law, which has its ultimate source in the eternal

---

[78] *ST*, Ia-IIae, q. 19, art. 4: "That the human reason is the rule for acts of human will so that it measures their goodness comes because it derives from the Eternal Law which is the divine reason" (trans. T. Gilby, vol. 18, 1966).

[79] *ST*, Ia-IIae, q. 19, art. 5: "Every act of will against reason, whether in the right or in the wrong, is always bad" (trans. T. Gilby, vol. 18, 1966). Ad 2: "Likewise, if a person is aware that the course his human reason is dictating is against God's precept then he is not obliged to follow it."

[80] *ST*, Ia-IIae, q. 19, art. 5, ad 3: "When the reason grasps something as being evil it always does so as being a special sort of evil, for instance as being against a divine precept or as causing scandal and so forth."

law of God.[81] Sometimes the only argument that can be made regarding the anticipated act is that it is described by the Church as sinful. This may not be very convincing, but it is sufficient for the conscience to pass a judgment. Once reason passes its judgment, the formation of the moral object of the act occurs. And if this object is evil, then it is not right to choose it, even if this object appears as a "lesser evil," relative to another conceivably "greater evil." If spouses know that the Church teaches that the use of contraceptives is wrong, even if they are not really able to explain why it is wrong, then this knowledge of the Church's teaching is sufficient for their reason to pass a judgment. The use of contraceptives in such a scenario would then mean the choosing of an act that is evil by reason of its object. Naturally, if they know the arguments for the Church's teachings, the judgment of their reason will be even clearer.

In discerning the contribution of reason in codetermining the moral object of the act, it is important to be able to distinguish between the judgment of reason that determines the object of the act and the judgment of reason that seeks excuses in order to justify an act that has already been chosen in advance, by the power of a decision of the will that excludes the truth. In such a case, the free choice has already been made, despite the opposition of implicit but nevertheless real conscience. Reason recognizes that the act is evil but seeks a way to free itself from remorse. Such rationalization does not come from the true light of reason and leads to false conduct. Reason, therefore, sometimes needs purification in order to grasp the truth with precision, and it needs liberation from views or even ideologies that could be called an intellectual repression that prevents it from knowing the truth. Moral law plays an important, though not exclusive, role in the purification of reason — that is, in the formation of conscience.

---

[81] *ST*, Ia-IIae, q. 19, art. 4: "Good willing depends much more upon the Eternal Law than upon human reason, and where human reason fails us we should have recourse to the divine reason." Ad 3: "Although as dwelling in the divine mind the Eternal Law is unknown to us, nevertheless in some fashion it becomes known to us either through natural reason, which issues from the divine mind as its proper image, or through some revelation given to us over and above the powers of reason."

The function of the moral law, both the natural law recognized through the effort of individual reason and through the teaching of wiser people, and the revealed law, whether present in the Decalogue or contained in the power of the Holy Spirit moving the Christian from within, is to form reason so that, in the heat of concrete situations, the reason may recognize the proper good, that is, one in which there will be the communication of God's love to one's neighbor. We attain moral maturity when we are able almost instinctively to grasp where the value is and, consequently, which path is optimal. A mature person is in favor of the good through his choices, not because it is prescribed by the law but because it is good. The moral law thus plays a subordinate role in the formation of conscience. The function of the moral norm is to indicate the objective evil that is to be avoided and to show the direction of the good. The negative formulation of the commandments contained in the Decalogue filters out the wrong paths; at the same time, it leaves the whole realm of positive action open. Thus, the norm does not specify how the good is to be realized — for example, how the love of neighbor is to be expressed. This is left to the creativity of the individual human being. God does not want people to function as puppets in His hands; He desires free, creative human responses that express the wealth of individual love. Although no one has the right to invent his own moral norms, man's reason must be creative with regard to the act he chooses. This is what living a virtuous life consists in: that man embraces the talents received from God and engages them in action for the sake of the good, according to his own inventiveness. In the final analysis, then, when it comes to determining the object of the moral act, it is reason that decides — the reason of the acting person.

In comparison with modern manuals, Aquinas's teaching in this regard is characterized by a much greater confidence in reason. Aquinas does not think that every human act, good or bad, depends strictly on the moral law. In contrast, casuistic manuals of moral theology suggest that every act is characterized by a dependence on the moral law, which can be deductively inferred from it. In Aquinas's synthesis, we find no attempt to develop such deductive patterns. The moral law has an educational function, and that is why educated reason has its dignity. If one had to wonder about every act's relationship to a particular commandment, there would be no room in human life for a sense of humor!

d. Intrinsically evil acts

The setting together of reason, which evaluates the act and contributes to the articulation of its moral object, with the moral law, which educates it, calls for a careful balance so as to avoid falling into two false extremes. One extreme denies the intrinsic role of reason and reduces it merely to the role of a rubber stamp that prints out the instructions of the moral norm for the given moral issue. In this view, conscience has merely to render the stance of moral science, which is credited to have the ability to foresee all possible situations and circumstances. This was the temptation of the old casuistry. Moral theologians of the eighteenth and nineneenth centuries aspired to offer a definitive answer to all possible moral situations. Although their concrete solutions, marked by the social context of the era, were mostly correct, such a view of morality entailed a mutilation of the most significant gifts of the gospel. The other extreme into which several Catholic moralists of recent years have fallen is the denial of any meaningful role for the moral law. If the moral law is reduced merely to the role of an external incentive, toward which reason or conscience assumes a position of utter indifference, then every individual will consider himself infallible and all moral norms will be replaced with nihilistic relativism. The encyclical *Veritatis splendor* voices the Church's protest against the denial of the possibility of knowing moral truth.

Although the treatment of the role of the moral law and its reception in previous approaches requires some adjustment, one should not fall into the trap of anomy. The Church's continuous emphasis on the need to refer to norms reminds us that there are some acts that in every situation are evil. The Decalogue, in its core message, insists that murder, theft, lying, and adultery are always evil acts. The contribution of reason in determining the moral object of the act does not occur within an indifference to objective values. Reason needs the signpost of norms that show which acts are always evil, regardless of intentions and circumstances. The individual's inventiveness in undertaking various virtuous acts does not justify the ignoring of norms.

As demonstrated earlier, defense against an aggressor, whether in the form of engaging in defensive warfare or the sentencing of a criminal by a judge, is not a denial of the light of the moral norm but an eliciting of an act of the virtue of justice. The fact that justice occasionally requires drastic measures does not authorize the mistaking of physical evil with moral evil and the conclusion that intrinsically evil acts are unrecognizable. The arguments promoted by proportionalists, linking moral goodness exclusively with the intention of the agent rather than with the object of the act, amount to a denial of the possibility of determining the moral value of an act — that is, to a denial of the role of moral norms, leading thereby to moral agnosticism.

e. A universally human or exclusively Christian diagram?

When we look at the sources of morality and at the diagram that has been worked out to describe the fact of morality, we can raise the question: Is this a universally human presentation, or is it a Christian one? Or we can extend the question further and ask how this diagram is changed when we are dealing with the free choice of an act, made not only by a righteous atheist but by a Christian and, even more, a Christian who wishes to live to the full according to the grace he has received. What new elements, if any, does Christianity add to the process of resolving moral questions?

The virtue of faith, which is the humility of reason, is infused in the spiritual powers of a Christian. Faith does not negate reason, but it opens it up to God's revealed mystery. This means that in the believer's evaluation of the *finis operis*, which co-creates the moral object of the act, there is also room for a supernatural intuition given by the Holy Spirit, especially through the gift of wisdom. Among the norms that a Christian considers, there is room not only for the natural law or the Decalogue but also for the new law of grace — that is, for the direct intervention of the Holy Spirit, Who, using the teaching given in the Church, guides human reason to that judgment that will be most Godlike and will express most fully the charity received from God. Moreover, the influence of grace is not limited to reason alone. It also extends to the will, pouring supernatural love into it and inciting it to the good. The good, recognized and accepted for the love of God, assumes then the characteristics of an act that is simultaneously human and supernatural. In human works, the fecundity of God Himself is made manifest!

f. Acts with double effects

So far, in reflecting on the moral qualification of acts, we have been focused on the anticipated moral act itself. It is clear, however, that life is much more complicated than an ethical analysis suggests. How should the consequences of elicited acts be assessed? They cannot always be predicted. Sometimes unplanned evil follows from a basically indifferent act. There are also times when the opposite is true. It happens that good consequences result from evil acts. For many people, a serious sin may be an opportunity for humiliation, repentance, and later conversion.

If the consequences of an act are foreseen, and, as such, willed, they belong to the object of the act and the agent is fully responsible for them. If the consequences are not foreseen, one is responsible only for those consequences that usually occur. An accident caused by a tipsy driver falls within his responsibility, since such an outcome is foreseeable. These cases are quite straightforward and do not present difficulties. Problems arise, however, with such acts in which many collateral outcomes can be foreseen, some of which will include evil acts. Assuming that General Jaruzelski wanted to protect Solidarity activists from an imminent deportation to Siberia, does he bear moral responsibility for the collateral casualties that occurred as a result of the imposition of martial law?

If it were always necessary to eliminate all anticipated evil consequences, making moral decisions would be torture. Every good action always may be accompanied by some evil side effects. Modern manuals of moral theology have therefore developed rules that are to be followed in such cases. First, the action undertaken cannot, in itself, be evil; the object of the act must be good. Second, the evil and good effects must derive from the act equally. The direct effect must be good, although it may be accompanied by an indirect, further, undesirable evil effect. Third, the intention of the agent must be good. He must not desire a bad effect. And fourth, there must be a proportionately serious reason for accepting the indirect evil effect.

The rules for the evaluation of acts with double effects have been criticized by some today as not being very practical. We do not find them presented in this form in the works of St. Thomas Aquinas. They were developed in the sixteenth century by Spanish Thomists. This list of four rules was presented as universally binding only in 1647 in a manual of the Salamanca Carmelites. From then on, these rules were commonly repeated in manuals of moral theology up to the Second Vatican Council. Undoubtedly, we find in these rules an echo of the casuistic mentality of the modern era.

The starting point for this reasoning was Aquinas's teaching on killing in self-defense.[82] Aquinas seems to have applied this principle without actually spelling it out. He had to reconcile two traditions. The legal tradition allowed for killing in self-defense, while St. Augustine thought that killing an attacker constituted a sinful attachment to one's transient life. St. Thomas Aquinas allowed the defense of one's own life during which, as an unintended consequence, the killing of the assailant occurred. The object of the act is self-defense, and the unintended side effect is the killing of the assailant. Today, of course, we can see that all this reasoning was developed at a time when there were no firearms. It is much more difficult to apply this solution with a machine gun in hand!

It is instructive to examine the examples offered by the Spanish Thomists as they explained these rules. Medina presents several examples: a student who reads Latin love poetry and has impure thoughts in the process; a butcher selling meat to the Jews who use it for their non-Christian religious practices; a maiden who, walking down the street, arouses impure desires in boys because of her looks. It is clear that the rules about acts with double effects were developed so as to free penitents from unhealthy scrupulosity. What was the beautiful *señorita* supposed to do? Was she supposed to sit at home and not go to the well to fetch the water? John of St. Thomas repeats the same examples, but he also adds the example of killing in self-defense.

There is a certain clash in these moral calculations. The early Christians who lacked systematic ethical speculation refrained from offering a pinch of incense before the statue of Caesar, and, in the twentieth century, Christian

---

[82] *ST*, IIa-IIae, q. 64, art. 7.

moralists reflected on the moral justification of bombing cities.[83] How are such calculations to be made? How does one judge that there are reasons to justify performing acts that will have collateral evil consequences among the good consequences? Aquinas refrained from providing detailed, speculative deductions derived from the basic intuitions of the moral law, and this is a sign of his prudence and understanding of life. In a moral decision, there is always a creative moment, some attestation of value. It cannot be merely the product of pure calculation. Moral choice always entails espousing a value, and in every marriage there is more than calculation. There is also risk. This is why Aquinas did not deliberate on moral case studies and concentrated exclusively on describing virtue — namely, that inner transformation that enables one to respond creatively, in the manner of God, to moral dilemmas.[84]

The theory of proportionalism

In recent decades, especially after the promulgation of the encyclical *Humanae vitae* by St. Paul VI in 1968, theologians in some countries have started to question the very foundations of the moral qualification of acts.[85] It seems that the theories propounded by them were developed in order to justify the abandonment of Church teaching, especially in the area of sexual ethics. St. John Paul II's encyclical *Veritatis splendor* rejects a current of thought that has emerged recently, which links the moral qualifications of acts to

---

[83] John C. Ford, "The Morality of Obliteration Bombing," *Theological Studies* 4 (1944): 261–309.

[84] Stanley Windass, "Double Think and Double Effect," *Blackfriars* 44 (1963): 257–266.

[85] The encyclical *Humanae vitae*, 14 invokes the principle of arriving at the moral qualification of acts and applies it to the issue of contraception: "Though it is true that sometimes it is lawful to tolerate a lesser moral evil in order to avoid a greater evil or in order to promote a greater good, it is never lawful, even for the gravest reasons, to do evil that good may come of it —in other words, to intend directly something which of its very nature contradicts the moral order, and which must therefore be judged unworthy of man, even though the intention is to protect or promote the welfare of an individual, of a family or of society in general."

the intention of the agent, rejecting any reference to the object of the act.[86] Such an approach leads to the denial of the existence of intrinsically evil acts, and consequently it amounts to a revolution in the very foundations of Christian morality.

The encyclical does not mention the names of Catholic theologians whose views have been rejected, but identifying them is not difficult. Among the most vocal proponents of proportionalism we find mainly American and German theologians, such as Charles E. Curran, Richard A. McCormick, S.J., Louis Janssens, Peter Knauer, S.J., Joseph Fuchs, S.J., and Bruno Schüller, S.J. There are some minor differences among them, but their positions can easily be considered together. Many of these authors, such as Louis Janssens, have tried to prove that a proportionalist argument can be found in the works of St. Thomas Aquinas and in Catholic tradition. However, it seems that these are merely attempts to defend a previously adopted position without any foundation in Catholic tradition. It is interesting to note that among the Anglo-Saxon theologians most involved in polemics with the proportionalists we find four lay theologians: Germain Grisez, William May, Joseph Boyle, and John Finnis. For many years, they have been engaged in a sharp scholarly dispute on the pages of theological journals in defense of the traditional tying of the morality of acts with the moral object. Among French-language authors who demonstrate the errors of proportionalism, Fr. Servais Pinckaers, O.P., should be mentioned.[87]

The proportionalists took the final, fourth rule of the principle of acts with double effects, as it was stated in traditional manuals, as the starting point of their reasoning. This rule, as previously stated, stipulated that there must be a proportionally serious reason in favor of executing an act when it is anticipated that an indirect evil consequence will occur. This fourth rule was always provided at the end. The rule applied exclusively to ambiguous situations,

---

[86] Of course, this is not a new way of reasoning. Over the centuries there have been people who wanted to free themselves from moral requirements in this way. What is new, however, is the widespread propagation of these theories by theologians employed at Catholic universities.

[87] Servais Pinckaers, O.P., *Ce qu'on ne peut jamais faire: La question des actes intrinsèquement mauvais: Histoire et discussion* (Paris: Cerf, 1986).

in which a number of consequences were anticipated, among which an evil consequence could come about. This rule was invariably preceded by the earlier assertions that, first, the elicited act cannot be intrinsically evil (for the object of the act must be good); second, that evil and good consequences must equally derive from the act, while the direct consequence must be good, although it may be accompanied by an indirect, remote, undesirable evil consequence; and third, that the intention of the agent must be right.

Thus, the principles of double effect did not elevate the search for a proportionally serious reason justifying an evil consequence to the status of a basic principle of morality. The search for a proportionally serious reason was undertaken only in cases in which the direct consequence of an act was good, and it was only incidentally accompanied by an unintended, indirect evil consequence. These rules were rooted in the conviction that there are intrinsically evil acts that should never be committed.

The proportionalists, however, shifted the center of gravity of the moral qualification of acts: moving away from the analysis of the object of the act, they transferred the attribution of the moral quality to the intention, and therefore to the will of the agent. Proportionalism boils down to the moral acceptance of acts that, by virtue of their relationship to the object of the act, will be evil, whereas, due to a good intention, they will be considered good, especially if the intention aims at a proportionally higher good. Although the adherents of proportionalism differed in the solutions they suggested, their reasoning, when applied to sexual ethics, led to the acceptance of the moral permissibility of contraception, abortion, premarital sex, and even marital infidelity and homosexual acts, if the persons committing these acts had "good will."

The proportionalists did not interpret their solutions as permitting morally evil acts but as permitting acts that they viewed only in their materiality, as events devoid of any moral connotation. They sometimes referred to these acts as *ontic evil* and subsequently accepted them just as one accepts physical evil, provided that some greater justifying reason is found. Summarizing their position, *Veritatis splendor* concludes:

> The criteria for evaluating the moral rightness of an action are drawn from the *weighing of the non-moral or pre-moral goods* to be gained and

the corresponding non-moral or pre-moral values to be respected. For some, concrete behaviour would be right or wrong according as whether or not it is capable of producing a better state of affairs for all concerned. Right conduct would be the one capable of "maximizing" goods and "minimizing" evils....

[Proportionalism claims that] *it is impossible to qualify as morally evil according to its species — its "object" — the deliberate choice of certain kinds of behaviour or specific acts, apart from a consideration of the intention for which the choice is made or the totality of the foreseeable consequences of that act for all persons concerned.* (74, 79)

Using such reasoning, the claim was made that abortion could be justified when a proportionally higher reason emerged (such as saving the life of the mother). The proportionalist current has not worked out any guidelines for the assessment of the value of goods. How do we know which goods constitute a proportionally higher good? How do we know that saving the life of the mother at the cost of murdering the child is supposed to constitute a proportionally higher good than accepting a life at risk, together with the increase in faith and trust in God and the Christian witness to the hope and sanctity of human life embodied in the birth of a child?[88]

There is no way to measure the moral value of acts and to determine which one is proportionally better when the moral qualification of an act based on its relationship to the moral object is rejected. So, on the grounds of proportionalism, the final judgment was made in an intuitive way. This means that proportionalism was unable to provide a coherent theory applicable to specific moral quandaries.

Another theory, stemming from the same teleological trend, based on the intention rather than the object, has been called *consequentialism* because it considers, above all, the consequences, that is, the outcomes of the act. Moral

---

[88] In 2004, St. John Paul II canonized an Italian doctor, St. Gianna Beretta Molla. During her pregnancy she was diagnosed with cancer, but she refused an abortion and a treatment that would have killed the child. She died shortly after giving birth to her daughter. Years later, the daughter attended her mother's canonization along with her father and her siblings.

judgment according to this theory consists in comparing the good and evil consequences of an action and compiling them together so as to examine which ones prevail in light of the agent's intention. Judging the consequences of an action is, of course, far from straightforward. Some consequences are immediately apparent, while others may not emerge until the distant future. According to this view, the moral decision considers the social, political, and historical consequences of an act. Is this practically feasible? How far into the future should predictable and unpredictable consequences be factored in? Proportionalism differs from consequentialism in that proportionalism is not concerned about the consequences. Both approaches, however, are related because they rely on the same internal logic.

The proportionalist position, with its emphasis on the agent's end itself rather than the object, is close to the relativist position of utilitarianism. That which proves useful for the sake of the chosen end is considered morally permissible, while the existence of man's objective finality, his nature, and his ordering to the ultimate end are questioned. In proportionalism, reality is divided into two categories: (1) premoral physical or ontic good and evil and (2) good and evil with strictly moral meaning. The ontic goods are health, life, property, knowledge, and so on. Ontic evil is the privation of these goods. Moral order occurs only when these goods are willed. Moral judgment, according to proportionalists, consists only in comparing various ontic goods or their absence in the light of the anticipated willed action. This comparison basically is just a technical process, similar to that of comparing the efficiency of machines. The transition from the ontic order to the moral order is accomplished solely through a decision of the will. Moral "goodness" is judged only by a reference to the will of the agent, while "rightness" is judged on the basis of anticipated consequences and their interdependence. The introduced division between moral "goodness" and "rightness" thus touches the very core of morality. Confusing the technical rightness of an action with moral judgment is a fundamental error. Officials in concentration camps may have displayed technical efficiency in their work and may have thought their intentions were good, but that still did not warrant a positive moral judgment of their conduct!

To free themselves from the demands of moral norms, proportionalists introduced distinctions between different sets of norms. They referred to some as transcendental or categorical norms, and others as concrete or material norms. The former purport to describe intrinsically evil acts, but they remain only at the abstract or general level. On the other hand, in concrete conduct, the concrete norm emerges. It cannot become a universal norm, prohibiting some behavior always and everywhere, since it would have to provide for all concrete cases, all the circumstances of all times and cultures. Since this is not feasible, proportionalists declared that it is impossible to formulate concrete norms that would always and everywhere prohibit certain acts that are intrinsically evil. Thus, they stripped moral norms of their universal and binding character.

Proportionalism as a moral doctrine was rightly rejected by the Magisterium of the Church. The tearing apart of the unity of the moral act by discarding the reference to a rationally apprehended moral object, and the exclusive consideration of the intention, even if formulated most nobly, deprives ethical reflection of its basic foundation. From there, the path to moral relativism and an endorsement of all forms of depravity is clear.

A suggested revision of the ethical analysis

The emergence of the proportionalist theory among Catholic theologians should provoke a deeper reflection. It is not enough simply to state that "it is good that the pope condemned foreign innovators" and consider the matter settled. The proportionalist theory was born partly out of dissatisfaction with the approaches that prevailed in traditional manuals. Theological inquiry, then, should prompt further questions: Why has proportionalism become a contemporary problem, and what direction should the renewal of moral theology take? Our search for answers to these questions will be aided by suggestions contained in the encyclical *Veritatis splendor*.

a. The shortcomings of the traditional model

The interpretation of moral agency through the three sources of morality (object, end, and circumstances), in which the object, understood through the distinction between the *finis operis* and the *finis operantis*, gains primacy, is an achievement of moral theology of the modern era. The outline presented above was worked out as a safeguard against interpretations that undermined the objectivity of morality. Since the main emphasis in ethics was on obligation, having its root in an external law, that law supplied the reason with a basis for the passing of a judgment about the anticipated act. The emphasis placed upon the object, formulated by reason, which invokes the law, was a defense against the subjective blurring of clarity in moral problems. The diagram provided earlier was developed with the help of texts taken from St. Thomas Aquinas. It serves as a safeguard against attempts to link moral value with the intention — attempts that always appear as a temptation to justify wrongdoing. Furthermore, the diagram reminds us that there are acts (such as murder, theft, and marital infidelity) that are always intrinsically evil, and a good intention alone can never confer moral goodness on them. But this diagram, however legitimate, is not an accurate rendering of Aquinas's view and his contributions to the study of Christian morality.

The diagram of the moral qualification of acts presented earlier has several shortcomings. Like all of modern Catholic moral theology, it is still tainted by a nominalist vision of morality, built on obligation rather than on virtue and the desire for happiness, as is the case in Aquinas. In this manualistic approach, the intention or end of the agent has been moved outside the essential moral qualification of the act, which is grasped primarily through the rationally apprehended object. The moral act is conceived in this diagram in its unitary existence, abstracted from the basic life aspirations of the acting person. These may be of different kinds, including those that are spiritual, done for God's sake, or completely down-to-earth. The act is studied here as an atomistic entity, which can be rationally analyzed as such. Is it righteous for a waiter employed by a restaurant to eat there? Is it theft or not? Such was the perspective of casuistry, which studied individual cases without reference to the person's calling or his inner spiritual dynamics. The outsider's perspective allows for a dispassionate analysis of the morality of each act. But is this a true picture of the way moral dilemmas are resolved?

Additionally, the introduction of the distinction between the *finis operis* and the *finis operantis* often resulted in wrongly identifying the moral object as the *finis operis* while ignoring the contribution of reason in shaping the moral object. While the manuals occasionally treated the moral object somewhat factually, directly attributing to it a moral quality by virtue of a mere verdict supplied by the moral norm, leaving no room for the contribution of a personal perspective of the agent's reason, the proportionalists went even further in identifying the object with a bare *finis operis* perceived uniquely in its moral physical being. They then held that this object as such is devoid of any moral value and should only be treated as a "premoral event."

b. Return to St. Thomas Aquinas

A careful reading of the work of St. Thomas Aquinas demonstrates that, for him, the end — that is, the intention residing in the will — is of vital importance in the moral qualification of an act. St. John Paul II's encyclical *Veritatis splendor* reminds us, albeit in a subtle way, of the neglected teaching of Aquinas. In the previously quoted passage from the encyclical, there is a clear reference to the teaching of Aquinas:

> The morality of the human act depends primarily and fundamentally on the "object" rationally chosen by the deliberate will, as is borne out by the insightful analysis, still valid today, made by Saint Thomas (cf. *Summa Theologiae*, I-II, q. 18, a. 6). In order to be able to grasp the object of an act which specifies that act morally, it is therefore necessary to place oneself *in the perspective of the acting person*. (78)

A reading of the indicated article from the *Summa* of St. Thomas Aquinas is at first surprising. It seems that here Aquinas presents us with a teaching that is a complete opposite of the fundamental message of the encyclical *Veritatis splendor*. In this article, Aquinas poses the following question: "Does an act get a specific kind of good or evil from the end intended?"[89] It is well known that Aquinas's didactic method entails posing a question and then identifying arguments against the position he wishes to defend. In the *Summa theologiae*, we usually have at the beginning of each article three or four objections that we know Aquinas disagrees with. Then, an opposing opinion

---

[89] Trans. T. Gilby, vol. 18, 1966.

is given, usually drawn from tradition, and finally, in the body of the article, we find Aquinas's fundamental position. The responses to the objections, provided at the end, offer additional explanations.

Article 6 of question 18 (I-II), then, starts off with a tricky affirmation, and we know in advance that it does not represent Aquinas's position: "It seems that good and evil from the end intended do not vary acts in their species." Does this sentence not state precisely that which we proved at length in our earlier argument against the proportionalists? Therefore, it looks as if the proportionalists' position will find the support of Aquinas. The first objection of the article affirms:

> For this they have from their objectives. An end, however, lies beyond what constitutes an immediate objective. Therefore the good or bad arising from their ends does not vary the species of acts.

This objection sounds exactly like the teaching that has been presented for centuries in Catholic manuals on moral theology. And yet we know that Aquinas does not accept this statement. Could it be that St. Thomas Aquinas is not concerned that the analysis of an act through its end will lead to subjectivism — that is, to the moral qualification of acts solely by referring to the intention, where a good end would justify bad means?

The second objection supplements the reasoning provided earlier:

> Moreover, an incidental factor does not constitute a specific type, as already noted. That an act can be motivated to an ulterior end is purely incidental (*accidit*), as when somebody gives to charity to earn applause. Hence acts are not differentiated into different specific types on account of the good or evil of their ends.

This is because the intention is added on from outside the act, which has its moral quality from its object. The objection thus confirms the well-known and established doctrine.

The third objection states:

> Furthermore, specifically different acts can be ordered to the same one end; thus the acts of diverse virtues and vices [can be ordered]

to a show of vanity. The specific character of acts, then, is not varied by the good or bad of motives.

Thus, it seems that the author of the encyclical *Veritatis splendor*, in writing that "the morality of the human act depends primarily and fundamentally on the 'object' rationally chosen by the deliberate will, as is borne out by the insightful analysis, still valid today, made by Saint Thomas (cf. *ST*, I-II, q.18, art. 6)," made a fundamental mistake that could happen only to novice readers of Aquinas, taking the objections provided by him as an exposition of his thought!

As we read on, the issue seems to become even more complex, and later it becomes clearer. In the *sed contra*, St. Thomas states:

> Human acts get a specific character from their ends. Hence the good and bad taken from ends will make for acts of different kinds.

Thus, a doubt arises. When Aquinas speaks of the "object" of the act and the "end" of the act, is he talking about the same thing that is said in modern Catholic theology when it identifies the sources of morality: the object, the end, and the circumstances?

The solution to this puzzle is to be found in the body of the article. Aquinas first provides an obvious fundamental principle. Acts are referred to as "human" only if they are voluntary. That which happens outside the voluntariness of man does not fall within the scope of interest of moral reflection.

In a voluntary act, there is a twofold movement, one that is the interior act of the will, and the other that is external to it. Both of these movements of the will have their objects. That which is the object of the interior act of the will is named the *end*; while that which is the object of the external act is named the *object*. Therefore, just as the external act receives its species from the object on which it bears, so the interior act of the will receives its species from the end, which is the proper object of the will.

Thus, we see that both acts have their proper objects, one of which, corresponding to the internal movement of the will, is given the name *end*, and the other, corresponding to the external movement toward the act, is given the name *object*. In drawing this distinction, Aquinas does not bring in the expressions *finis operis* and *finis operantis*, which have appeared in the modern diagram.

St. Thomas goes on to explain:

> Now the part played by the will shapes the performance of the external deed, for the will applies members like instruments to the execution of an action; indeed our outward acts possess no moral significance save in so far as they are voluntary. Hence the specific character of human acts is assessed as to its form by the end intended and as to its matter by the objective of the external deed.

Aquinas's argument becomes clearer when it is parsed out through a diagram, and illustrated with an example:

Is the end compatible with the final end?

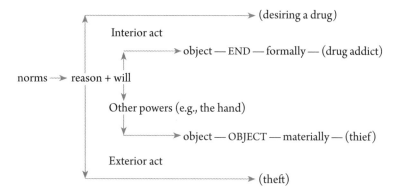

Is the object compatible with the truth of the situation as is taught by the moral norm?

This diagram shows that Aquinas views the moral act in its totality, without overemphasizing the role of the object. Both the inner stirrings of the will and the external action together constitute moral conduct. The influence of reason extends both to the inner workings of the will, when reason poses the question of the compatibility of the recognized end with the will's innermost orientation to its final end, and to the external act performed at the urging of the free choice by the other powers, when reason instructed by the moral law poses the question about the essence of the anticipated act.

Thus, we see that the inner stirring of the will is not burdened here with the suspicion of making the moral act subjective, nor is it excluded from the analysis of the morality of the act. Both that toward which the act relates directly and the inner motivation for the action have vital moral significance, and, as matter and form together, they constitute the wholeness of the act. Moreover, that which is formal is somehow more important than that which is material. The intention — that is, the inner movement of the will — plays a decisive role in the moral act. That is why Aquinas then devotes two whole questions to a more detailed analysis of both the external act and the internal act. In this way, the study of morality is not limited to the study of merely atomistic external acts, as is the case in casuistry. It considers the internal dynamics of the acting person.

In our example of the drug addict who steals, the fact that he steals is not the most important fact about him. Of course, it is true that theft constitutes an evil act. It is clear that when theft is considered in the light of reason appealing to the moral norm, its moral qualification is negative. If I am the one who was robbed, I certainly view the act as a moral evil that I have suffered. However, when one looks at the agent, that is, the drug addict who committed theft, that which is formal about him is far more important than that which is material. Theft is an individual evil act, but a much more important truth is that this poor drug addict is trapped by his addiction, which makes him steal, and most likely not just steal, but also commit many other evil acts (lie, fail to work, disrespect his family, fall into despair, contract HIV, etc.). Why does he commit so many evil acts? Because he is a drug addict, because, in the inner stirrings of his will, the direction toward that which may give him the supreme happiness is missing, since it has been substituted by its semblance, the drug. An examination of this case in its plenitude will, therefore, not stop uniquely at the fact of theft. It will point to the need for spiritual and psychological inner healing of the drug addict and the need to free his inner life dynamics from the bondage of addiction.

Therefore, in order to describe the essence of moral action properly, it is necessary to consider both the external and internal movements of the will. When viewing the morality of the external involvement of the will, the question of the truth of the anticipated action can be raised. Experience, the light of the moral norm, and the unique circumstances of the action are relevant factors in determining the moral object of the act. And in viewing the morality of the inner act of the will, one can ask to what extent that which is willed is wanted for the sake of the final end. Are the acting person's deepest desires distinguished by courage and momentum? Does he dare to have the "impudence" to recognize that nothing, no drug, no power, no money, no human ambitions will limit the horizon of his volition because he has deposited his deepest desire for happiness in the hands of God Himself, Whose promises he has trusted? Has he, through his faith, allowed his will to be transformed in its volition from within by the prospect of evangelical beatitudes? Or has he perhaps limited the horizon of his desire to the minimal dimension of immediate gratification or even forgetfulness of everything through the taking of this or some other drug?

For the formation of man's ethos and the development of permanent dispositions to goodness, it is important to pay attention to the inner moral dynamics, and not just to the external acts. Hence the pertinent question is: What is man's deepest desire? It is true, of course, that sometimes human desires are illogical and immature and that they are implemented mindlessly and abruptly, but what is most important in Christian morality and spirituality is precisely the introduction of charity deriving from God into the deepest desires. In the examination of conscience, therefore, it is helpful to look not only at individual acts but also at the inner motivations for the actions. A mere examination of acts, good or bad, does not yet define a person. The deepest question has to be asked: Where is he heading? What is the fundamental direction of his life?

The recognition that both the internal act of the will and the external chosen act have their proper objects means that the evaluation of moral action will not be accurate as long as it focuses uniquely on the external act as it is judged in the light of the moral norm. Sensitivity toward the internal dimension of an act necessitates a regard coming from the perspective of ethics built on virtue, and not just obligation. The dominance of obligation ethics in modern moral theology has shifted the focus above all toward the external act, interpreted through a reference to the externally applied norm. From such a detached outsider perspective, casuistic questions could be posed.

Is a given act permitted or forbidden? Acts were viewed in their atomistic singularity, abstracting from the particular person who performs them, and judged by means of an external rule. Such moral theology had no need of virtues! If moralists mentioned virtues, it was only as a catalogue of moral obligations, and not as the qualities of a mature, independent, loving person. Meanwhile, in the perspective of Aquinas, without denying the importance of the moral evaluation of the external act, accomplished through the interpretation of the object in the light of the norm, the external act is treated as uncovering that which is formal, that which is happening within the person. Stealing exposes the drug addict in a person. Generosity manifests a loving person, one who is transformed by the charity of God Himself!

In response to the deficiencies of the limited and obligation-centered moral theology of modern times, finally an additional theological discipline was developed, variously called *spiritual theology, ascetical-mystical theology,* and *the theology of the interior life.* Is this not in itself a symptom proving that moral theology had been reduced to the status of a mere theology of the exterior life? The old manuals fell into this pitfall. The emphasis on the exterior life combined with a disregard for the interior life led to a vision of morality that was concerned only with the correctness of external acts. Thus, moral teaching was built uniquely on the Decalogue, with injunctions and proscriptions inferred from it by way of deduction regarding increasingly wider dimensions of life. A reflection on sexuality, marriage, and all sexual dysfunctions was derived from the commandment "Thou shall not commit adultery." A reflection on social ethics, economic life, the morality of banking, the stock market, and so on was derived from the commandment "Thou shall not steal." The enumeration of forbidden acts and the justification of the prohibitions through a reference to a specific commandment were not always convincing and had little to do with initiation into Christ's salvific work. It was a depressing, fundamentally Pelagian vision, devoid of reference to grace. Within the framework of moral formation, nothing was said about the life of grace and about allowing divine grace into one's inner life. Only the select few among the faithful who were exposed to the elite perspective of the inner life could hear about this. The experience not only of hardship but indeed the impossibility of leading a righteous life without a practical initiation into the supernatural inner life led many to the abandonment of the moral norms that, humanly speaking, are impossible to fulfill without grace.

We cannot accuse St. Thomas Aquinas of endorsing a subjectivist vision of morality due to his strong emphasis on the inner act, nor of ignoring that which is most interior and personal in man because of his objectivism. His vision of morality captures both the objective and the subjective aspects of moral action. Aquinas's view, despite its rather technical language, is profoundly personalistic. This dual perspective is then continued throughout the second part of the *Summa theologiae*. Aquinas is mainly focused on the power of grace manifested in the acting human person. Therefore, the special moral theology of Aquinas is grounded in the study of the virtues, the gifts of the Holy Spirit, and the new law of grace — that is, those supernatural realities that transform man inwardly, making him receptive to divine intervention. When he discusses each of the virtues, Aquinas refers to the corresponding gift of the Holy Spirit so as to suggest how God's personal guidance of man is accomplished. He then introduces also a brief reference to the relevant commandment merely to show the convenience of the teaching contained in the precept for the development of the virtue in question. The commandments mostly capture that which is measurable in the prohibited external act, but by no means do they exhaust the description of moral dynamics. Aquinas does not allow for an attitude that would invent one's own norms for personal use, but he also does not burden the ethos with a too strong connection with norms and obligations. The emphasis placed on the internal nature of moral choices in the context of the whole person's journey toward the final end allows for an integral presentation of the fully human action transformed by grace.

In response to the objections presented earlier, Aquinas provides additional clarification. The first reply reiterates that the end also has the character of an object, except that it is the object of the movement of the will. This means that the terms *end* and *object* should not be understood in a mechanical way. Both terms refer equally to the internal movement of the will and the external act.

The second reply clarifies that the subordination of an external action to an internal intention may be an accidental matter for that action (*accidit* — "it happens"), but it is not accidental to the internal act of will. A beggar who receives alms may not care that they were given for motives that are not completely pure, but tainting the motivation with vanity is not an accidental matter when the act is examined from the perspective of the giver. The adding of an improper intention to a good act vitiates the ultimate value of that act.

The third response explains that when many different actions are linked by a common motive, that motive connects them all, although, naturally, each external act has its own specific essence. The drug addict from our example may commit many evil acts, but it is his drug addiction that is the root of all these acts.

In conclusion, we can see that, in assessing moral acts, it is necessary to look at the act itself, its nature and its motivation. Aquinas, recognizing both the internal and external dimensions of human actions appreciates the richness and dynamism of the human person who elicits good action out of a spiritually transformed and rich inner life. This insight has its deepest source in Aquinas's fundamental theological intention. In his moral theology, he is seeking God — the God Who, through grace, is present in the mature human being. Not surprisingly, with this perspective he must look at the entire person in his good moral action, and not merely at whether the person's external acts conform to the moral norm.

The theological tradition that preceded St. Thomas Aquinas looked at morality through the eyes of a metaphysician. Theologians posed the intriguing question of the metaphysical goodness of all beings, including also sinful acts. How is it possible that there are acts that, metaphysically speaking, are good — because everything that God sustains in being is good — and at the same time are morally evil? Aquinas changed the approach. Starting from a theological fascination with God, Who, by His grace, is present in the charity of a good person, he viewed moral action from the perspective of the spiritual life. He looked for traces of the fecundity of God's grace within human moral choices, in their inner richness, which comes about in an engaging generosity that enhances freedom. The good chosen consciously by a mature person, who knows where he is heading and knows the relationship between what he is choosing and his final end, manifests the goodness of God. The good embraced out of love for God, with faith in His accompanying presence, becomes supernatural, enriched from within by the dynamic of God Himself! The post-nominalist tradition of the modern centuries was so focused on defending the objective moral order from the dangers of subjectivism[90] that the dynamic approach of Aquinas was forgotten and replaced by a static analysis of individual acts considered in the context of normative ethics. If God appeared in this moral reflection, it was only as a voluntaristic source of obligation — and not as a Savior or Sanctifier!

c. The recommendations of Veritatis splendor

The encyclical *Veritatis splendor*, responding to teleological theories that link the moral qualification of acts exclusively with the intention, emphasizes the importance of the object of the act. On this point, the encyclical is fully in line with the modern manualist tradition. While it is not the intention of the encyclical's author, however, to give a complete description of morality (for the encyclical only responds to pressing issues), he places also an emphasis on the inner character of acts. This is a certain novelty and a suggestion to correct the conventional teaching that has been quite prevalent up to now. Both the reference to Ia-IIae, question 18, article 6 and the statement that "it is therefore necessary to place oneself *in the perspective of the acting person*" (78) point to this internal perspective. Moreover, the encyclical asserts that:

> Activity is morally good when it attests to and expresses [a] the voluntary ordering of the person to his ultimate end and [b] the

---

[90] This approach could be found as recently as 1961 in the text *De ordine morali*, prepared for the Second Vatican Council. The authors of this document, Frs. L. Gillon, O.P., F. Huerth, S.J., and E. Lio, O.F.M., wanted the Council to affirm the objective and absolute character of the moral order. They wanted a repressive document, rejecting any moral teaching that did not flow strictly from nineteenth-century casuistry and the natural law as conceived by neo-scholasticism. They rejected the centrality of charity, fearing subjectivism, and their main emphasis was on the commandments. Happily, the Council Fathers rejected this document in its entirety. See Pierre d'Ornellas, *Liberté, que dis-tu de toi-même? Une lecture des travaux du Concile Vatican II 15 janvier 1959–8 décembre 1965* (Sainte-Maur: École Cathédrale, Parole et Silence, 1999).

conformity of a concrete action with the human good as it is acknowledged in its truth by reason. (72)[91]

This is sufficient evidence that in the encyclical we find an affirmation of the need for a virtue-based ethics that is open to the spiritual depths of the acting person.

A claim could be made that the followers of proportionalism, by pointing out the importance of the end in the moral act, demonstrated the lack of faithfulness of the post-Tridentine textbook tradition to the teachings of St. Thomas Aquinas, although they overreacted in their response. But did proportionalists understand the finality of acts in the same way as Aquinas? St. Thomas saw the need to coordinate the interior act of will with the ultimate end and the exterior act, forming an integral whole composed of matter and form. That is why Aquinas began his moral theology by examining the final end and intrinsic finality of all things. Proportionalists attributed the entire moral qualification to the intention of the agent, simultaneously denying the existence of an inner finality of things, the existence of intrinsically evil acts, and the existence of the moral quality of the object of the act. This reduced the understanding of finality merely to the rank of a personal attitude, possibly a noble one, accompanied by a purely technical choice. In this view, moral choices were not treated as acts through which a person matures spiritually and discovers the true value of things, becoming increasingly open to the inner transformation wrought by God. For the proportionalists, moral choices were reduced to the level of technical procedures, undertaken by spiritually flat individuals who justify their moral evasions through allegedly higher intentions, formulated in a purely verbal way.

The proportionalist theory remained limited to a casuistic perspective that analyzes specific individual acts, even though it got rid of the moral norms that would be still universally valid. The theory also rejected the theological and moral virtues, which are redundant in its framework.

---

[91] The matter becomes clearer when [a] and [b] are added, which is not what we find in the encyclical.

Proportionalism remained locked in the system of obligation-based ethics against which it rebelled. It still failed to combine its ethics with spiritual theology, and the system lacked any links with the great tradition of the Church Fathers, Scholasticism and, above all, the New Testament.

St. John Paul II's encyclical *Veritatis splendor*, while drawing abundantly from St. Thomas Aquinas, does not treat his teachings as its only resource. It points first and foremost to the Word of God, and, referring to Aquinas, it shows how he should be read: in full continuity with the Word of God and the teachings of the Church Fathers. It is not by accident that the entire straightening out of erroneous ethical theories in the encyclical is rooted in St. John Paul II's biblical meditation. In response to the young man's question in the Gospel: "Teacher, what good must I do?," the pope says, "Do not be conformed to this world," and he immediately explains why, "lest the Cross of Christ be emptied of its power." The pastor shows solicitude not just for the lost sheep, nor is he focused on the moral order that should be preserved at all costs, but he is concerned about the mystery of grace flowing from the Cross, which, unrecognized and not received, seems to be poured out in vain. The reception of this grace calls for an opening of man's inner self by faith, and not just the correct execution of external acts. "For by grace you have been saved through faith" (Eph. 2:8), and grace, in order to bring fruit, requires a trusting faith, rooted in the spiritual depths of man, that is then reflected in generous acts of charity. It is not just an external reward given for the correct fulfillment of a moral duty!

Increasing in favor with "God and man" (Luke 2:52)

Going back to Fr. Ludwik Wiśniewski's discussion with Adam Michnik about the declaration of martial law in Poland, in light of the presented theological perspective, two moral layers of this political event should be identified. The first moment will be an analysis of the exterior act, which was General Jaruzelski's decision to impose martial law. This opens the field for historical research, which will show whether the threat of a Soviet invasion was real, or whether it was just a bluff, and to what extent the brutality of the imposition of martial law was foreseeable or avoidable. In light of this evidence and the information that the general had in 1981, one may try to gain insight into his dilemma and the solution he chose. It should be remembered, however, that this decision, like any other moral decision, can be truly analyzed only from the perspective of the acting person. Only he himself could reveal which reasons and considerations were at play when he made his decision. With these reasons and data, one can wonder about the reasoning applied at the time and the moral qualification of the decision made. The objectivity of this consideration, however, will not embrace the totality of the drama, nor will it allow us to pass a judgment on the internal dispositions of the main actor of the event. How was the general's interior act formed? What was his deepest intention? What was he striving for? In the heat of the difficult decision, did he ask God for light, for the purification of his will from selfishness? And did he hope that Divine Providence would steer events in such a way that, among the numerous consequences of his act, goodness would triumph above all? It is not for us to pass judgment on this matter, but we must not forget this deeper dimension of moral actions.

Christian formation cannot limit itself merely to defending the moral order and emphasizing a minimalist understanding of obligation. To be faithful to the perspectives that have been revealed to us, this formation must open up to the dynamics of grace, which shapes actions from within. Only when the moment of referring everything to God, the Giver of grace, is made present in the context of executing even the most trivial external actions, only then will the mysterious operation of divine power happen. An awareness of our own infirmities and sins is no obstacle to this radiation of divine life. The fact than the Savior assumed the consequences of our sinfulness and overcame them with a power stronger than death lays the foundation for human trust that, in the context of all great and small dramas, may expect the spiritual enrichment of even the least grand action. Christian tradition has many images symbolizing this mysterious percolation of grace in the hands of men. The Gospel tells us of a boy who offered his five rolls and two sardines to feed thousands (see John 6:9). The Lord Jesus blessed this boy's gift. The good given freely and blessed by Jesus bore fruit, inviting each individual to open his heart and also share whatever he had. St. Thérèse of Lisieux gave us the image of rose petals, symbolizing minute gestures of kindness, smiles, good words — such small things in which there is love for God's sake. God blesses these petals, which are quietly and discreetly dispensed, and sends them down to earth as a new leaven of love.

A moral life accompanied by a generous love for God's sake contributes to spiritual growth. "God's love … poured into our hearts through the Holy Spirit" (Rom. 5:5) solicits a human gift so that it may grow. There is no limit to the unfolding of the dynamics of grace in a person, except for the one and only barrier that each individual himself may erect against God by giving up generosity. Aversion to the gift of self precludes the heightening of divine love; the giving of oneself to God allows for the mysterious fecundity of divine charity. Aquinas's theology describes the intriguing increase in the fruitfulness of grace within man through the concept of "merit," transferred analogously from human relationships to the supernatural order. By virtue of our tie with other people, our actions assume the character of merit. If the reference group is a political community, we merit reward or punishment. But the political community does not permeate the entire human person with its influence; it has a limited scope of operation, and therefore not all human acts deserve either punishment or reward in the political order — but everything that man does can be referred to God's love.[92] A person may be sick, paralyzed, or completely disabled physically — but if he loves with divine charity, he is able to contribute admirably to the growth of the Church. The smallest acts of charity prove to be immensely fruitful in the mystery of the Church. Therefore, the involvement of the interior act is of vital importance in the spiritual life.

The fact that human works have supernatural power does not originate from man. Good acts executed beyond grace have natural value, but they do not contribute to spiritual growth. A doctor who cures his patients but is not

---

[92] Aquinas, with his usual brevity, formulates a principle that has critical implications for social life when the moral order and the political order are balanced properly: "A human being is not subordinate to the political community entirely in his whole self and with all he possesses, and therefore it is not required that each of his acts should be well or ill deserving within the political order. But all that a man is, all that he can do, and all that he has is within God's order." *ST*, Ia-IIae, q. 21, art. 4, ad 3, trans. T. Gilby, vol. 18, 1966.

in a state of grace, does not cultivate a relationship with God, and does not make present in his interior act the orientation toward God, is nevertheless doing good, and he deserves credit in the temporal order for his treatment. He may even, apart from payment, deserve an order of merit. If, however, he is vigilant about doing his work in communion with God, there will be a mysterious Christian dimension in his work that spiritual people will recognize. There is no natural possibility in us to transit into the order of grace. That is why, the first grace, which makes it possible to merit in grace, is always given completely freely. *Principium meriti non cadit sub merito.* But the human response in which the love received from God is instantiated depends on the human gift, and God grants further grace commensurate with this gift. Merit within grace contributes to the growth of love. We can somehow illustrate this mystery with the example of a child asking his mother for money. With this money he buys a flower, which he then gives to his mother for her name day. The mother may be more pleased with this flower, which, after all, she herself paid for, than with an expensive gift bought by her older son with his own earned money, but given without love. God issues the first grace, but He expects our response, given out of love.

Growth in love depends on the quality of the given gift. There are people who, for years on end, live honest lives, who do their best to avoid sins, yet they do not grow spiritually. They fulfill good deeds, but nevertheless spiritually they do not move forward. Why is there no development of holiness in them? It is absent because there is a lack of full dedication. Theology describes such a good deed that lacks the dynamic of love as an *actus remissus*. The imperfection of these acts is not a sin, but the power of the virtue that one possesses is not used to the full. It is as if someone possessed a virtue with a power of sixty degrees (if it were possible to measure it!) but executed the acts with a commitment of only thirty degrees. The failure to surrender everything to God, like that of the rich young man in the Gospel, inhibits spiritual growth.

Spiritual life, therefore, requires that we look into the interior act of the will to see if the will is transformed from within by the theological virtues and a total gift of self. The giving of oneself to God allows Him to enter the soul and transform all human actions, granting them a spiritual fecundity.

St. Thérèse of Lisieux tells us that the novelty of Christianity consists not so much in loving one's neighbor as oneself (which was already prescribed in Leviticus 19:18) but in loving *as Christ loves* — that is, loving with His freely given love. About this mysterious divine love, granted to her heart and known only by faith, she told Christ: "Your love has preceded me and from my childhood, it grew with me, and now it is an abyss the depth of which I cannot fathom."[93] Becoming open to the gift of divine charity — that is, allowing it into the nitty-gritty of practical actions — is the most important task of Christian life. And the discernment of this mystery — that is, the articulation of the laws of the unfolding of divine love in man — is the most important task of moral theology. Moral theology is true to itself only if it somehow, to the best of its ability, names and elucidates this mystery of God's presence within human actions.

---

[93] Manuscript C, 35.

5

Liberating Freedom[94]

NEITHER FREEDOM NOR OBEDIENCE is the goal of Christian life. Nor are they the ultimate goal of educational endeavors. The ultimate end of the Christian life is union with God, and this takes place through the encounter of human weakness with the power of divine grace. The fruit of this encounter is charity, which, St. Paul wrote, is "poured into our hearts through the Holy Spirit" (Rom. 5:5). This love demands a response, a generosity that brings the dynamism of divine power to the world. A human response to the stirrings of the Holy Spirit, concrete, sensitive, involving the whole personality, and at the same time prudent and responsible, is a sign indicating that God is a living, true God, Who makes human hearts, attitudes, and actions flourish. God does not seek merely dispassionate executors of His divine will; rather, living people who, like the Son of God, enrich supernatural love with the distinctive contribution of the wealth of their personalities and talents. Thus, we can say that inner freedom, although it is not the end of Christian life in itself, is undoubtedly a necessary condition for its authenticity.

Neither licentiousness nor obedience

The problem of liberating freedom and enabling it to develop in a genuine way in a person is therefore an important component of education. It should not be assumed that freedom is automatically given to a person. One grows in interior freedom, which is acquired through the courage of independent steps,

---

[94] This chapter was published in the Polish quarterly *Pastores* 2 (2001): 9–19.

through the quality of the personal gift of self. It requires daily nurturing, transcending oneself in risky, occasionally innovative, and always generous actions. For freedom can sometimes be inhibited, blocked by emotional repression, by fear and pusillanimity, by lack of confidence in oneself or in one's abilities, or in the possibility of knowing the truth, and by lack of faith in the reality of God's grace.

It is not only emotional repression, which neurotically closes man in on himself, that blocks freedom. Intellectual repression of the enslaved mind, which, by a decision of the will, accepts only half-truths, also prevents the intellect from reaching out further, beyond thought patterns, beyond comfortable mental shortcuts and the limitations of one's own pessimism toward the truth itself, and this, in consequence, cripples personal freedom. It is also restrained by the repression of the supernatural life caused by the underdevelopment of faith, by its failure to lead the soul out toward God's unfolding mystery.

How can the desire to give oneself completely to God grow in a person if grace is treated only as a cliché, and not as a reality that affects daily life and has the power to change that life in surprising ways? The liberation of freedom is necessary for the development of Christian love. Without inner freedom, shaped by recognized values, charity will remain merely a theory, a façade, with an insert of falsehood within. The leaven of divine love will then be like a seed that fell on rocky soil. It will grow quickly, but since it has no roots, it will soon succumb to external forces that will warp it (see Matt. 13:21).

When we speak of charity, we refer to the kind of love that empowers one to become friends with God, and to treat one's neighbors as God's friends. This love is essentially different from a love of a lower kind, grounded in human friendship, sentiments, or even physical attraction. Growth in divine love also requires schooling because, before it can bear fruit, it has to pass through the threshold of faith, which acts like a sieve, filtering out that which is unworthy of it. Only breaking through the darkness of faith purifies love from the impurities of selfishness and consciously or unconsciously maintained illusions, dreams, or ambitions.

Sometimes a suggestion is made that superiors in religious orders should reshuffle the members of individual communities in such a way that each one would include only people who get along well together and are capable of forming a friendly community. Such reasoning is fundamentally flawed, because it is based on uniquely human friendship, and such cannot guarantee the stability of a religious community.

Only charity, in which the other is accepted in faith as God's friend, even if he or she is a difficult, humanly limited, or even unpleasant person, confers a real supernatural dimension to the community. Only challenges that are embraced in faith purify love and bring out of it its supernatural foundation. Thus, supernatural obedience, accepted by virtue of a vow made to God, plays a vital role in relation to love, as it habituates a person to decisions grounded in faith. The vow of obedience, like freedom, is not an end in itself but is a great aid in the development of supernatural love. While inner freedom is a necessary background for a mature gift of self to be born, professed obedience is not absolutely necessary for the development of charity. Those who have not professed obedience also grow in supernatural love. But those who have freely taken up the consecrated life have in the vows of obedience, chastity, and poverty a useful aid that steers them directly toward God and makes it easier to become friends with Him.

Mature freedom

The Belgian theologian Fr. Servais Pinckaers, O.P., distinguished two understandings of the nature of freedom that have prevailed in European culture.[95] He called the first, classical kind "liberty of quality." This freedom is the fruit of the joint action of the reason and will, and it manifests itself in the independent undertaking of acts in which there is a personal recognition of value. Man is not born with this freedom, but he gradually learns it throughout life. A necessary aid for growing in this freedom is the formation of virtues, which — as constant habits — channel the volitional and emotional dynamics toward the chosen ends. The acts of virtue always contain novelty and inventiveness. The virtuous individual amazes with his creativity in taking up values that he has personally recognized. Growth in the liberty of quality allows one to respond fully to God through numerous expressions of love.

---

[95] Pinckaers, *Sources of Christian Ethics*, 327–378.

The life of grace requires the development of this freedom and it also develops it further because grace takes root in the spiritual powers that become more and more themselves and increasingly capable of creative, loving action.

Since the end of the Middle Ages, in philosophical thinking and consequently also in theological and moral reflection, a completely different understanding of freedom has prevailed. Fr. Pinckaers traces its origin to the nominalist philosophy of William of Ockham. Freedom, in this theory, is said to be a property of the will itself, which — in order to be free — supposedly does not need the light of reason, or education, or the dynamics of the virtues. In this theory, the will is always free, from the moment of birth; and any directing of it, whether by education, by truth, by the instruction of divine law, or by the inner workings of grace, is said to be its restriction or even enslavement. Such an understanding of the nature of the will and of freedom necessarily results in the will's positioning itself to resist and revindicate its solitary freedom, in indifference toward all external factors. The "liberty of indifference" requires no education; it is supposedly a fundamental quality of the spiritual being that protects its isolation and its rights. Classical theology attributes such an understanding of freedom neither to man nor to angels nor to God. But in modern theology, such an understanding of freedom was attributed, above all, to God, Whose omnipotence was said to consist in not being bound by anything at all, not even by truth or law that He Himself established. In this theory, God, being completely and arbitrarily free, imposes on lower beings His will, which appears as a cold, binding obligation. The fallacy of this theory distorted people's relationship with God, Whose image became nonpaternal, absolute, imposing obligation by virtue of the higher authority of God's indifferent will, and also their relationships with other people.

When the concept of the liberty of indifference took over people's minds, the revindication of the space of freedom became a fundamental program, embraced by some to the point of absurdity (Sartre's "Hell is other people") or, among the less courageous, to the limits of an externally imposed obligation. From then on, God and all authority became an enemy of freedom, imposing a restrictive obligation simply by virtue of their higher power. As a result of this distortion of the understanding of the nature of will and of freedom, the teaching of morality was reduced to a precise quantification of the limits of the binding power of norms, and morality itself, in the practice of life, was reduced to the fulfillment of mandatory rules, which, in turn, generated attempts to defend oneself from excessive obligations. Not surprisingly, the joy of personal generosity disappeared from moral reflection, in which obedience — rather than love — became the fundamental attitude.

Freedom versus obligation

Understanding the will in a nominalist way seems to exalt freedom, elevating it to the rank of a fundamental quality of the will. In practice, however, making out of freedom an absolute indifferent to the light of reason brings to the forefront obligation, one that has its origin in the arbitrary, not necessarily rational, will of someone who happens to be more powerful. The will is considered free to the point that it encounters another will, which is also free and simultaneously more powerful. Hence, the following questions arise: To what extent can I defend my independence while simultaneously fulfilling the minimum of the prescribed obligation? What must I absolutely do so as to be in order? Which matters are within the bounds of prescribed obligation, and which are left to individual freedom? The way in which these questions are formulated manifests the false approach to the problem, where all power — and ultimately also that of God — is viewed as restricting freedom. In posing these questions, are we mindful of St. Thomas's view that it is blasphemy to claim that the essence of justice consists in a dispassionate obedience to the divine will that has no regard for reasons?

When the will of the lawgiver is considered to be the source of all law, especially God's law, then this perception generates either a feeling of fear or, in the case of a more resolute individual, a feeling of coercion, of being compelled by an obligation that is binding uniquely because it has been commanded. Will there still be room for love? True love is born when one recognizes the harmony and expediency of the good toward which one is striving, and when this fascination with the recognized good triggers a movement of the will, prompting it to make a free choice, which is a joint effort of the reason and the will, and as such, a creative endeavor. The discussion on the nature of the will and freedom on the surface may seem to be a play of Scholastic distinctions. In fact, the various positions taken on this issue result in entirely different understandings of Christian morality.

Obligation is not the principle and center of the moral order. Nevertheless, there is a place for it in the ethos.[96] It should not be treated only as a basic fact, as a self-evident principle. Obligation exists, but it finds its justification and basis in the spiritual structure of the human being, who naturally desires happiness and friendship, and in the objectivity of goodness, which triggers an attraction to itself in the will. Of course, this presupposes the ability of the mind to recognize the good and then, together with the will, to make a free choice. At the root of the attraction to the good that shapes obligation is man's natural pursuit of happiness as his final end and the reality of the good. Thus, one can posit moral obligation expressed in the moral law as a sapiential support and guidance in the right direction of the basic desire for happiness and ultimate finality, which inherently are located in the will. The subordination of moral obligation to the desire for happiness by no means removes its absolute qualities. This is because obligation does not depend on a dubious hypothesis, such as "If you desire happiness, you must . . ." The desire for happiness is not a hypothesis. It is categorically inscribed within the nature of the will. It manifests itself also in sin, when the individual seeks happiness in some good that turns out to be apparent. The principle that underlies all moral action — *bonum est desiderandum* — is indisputable, since it expresses the natural inclination of the will toward the good. So deriving obligation from the desire for happiness is not some reduction or contestation of obligation.

If one were to capture the relationship between the will and the good solely through the category of obligation, this would be an incomplete and merely fragmentary picture. In the good that attracts man, there is more than just obligation. Obligation captures only an aspect of the influence of the good and the instruction that the moral law provides to the will — that is, it draws attention to factors that are external to the will. It does not show the relationship from the other side — that of the will tending toward the good.

---

[96] Cf. S. Pinckaers, "L'obligation morale," in St. Thomas d'Aquin, *Somme théologique: Les actes humaines*, vol. 2 (Paris, 1966), 265–268.

Obligation highlights the opposition of the good and the will, rather than their mutual unity and complementarity. If we focus primarily on obligation, then in this perspective the response of the will is framed incompletely, as if it were truncated. What is then missing is that which is the greatest richness of the will. The point is that the will may respond to obligation not by virtue of an external compulsion, but by its own spontaneous initiative, which is most proper for the will, because it expresses its spiritual nature best. Education for freedom, therefore, requires the development of the ability to judge, to recognize where the value is, and to respond creatively to the recognized good. One should not think that this is a difficult matter, reserved exclusively for extraordinary people. Even a child, if he is raised to do so, will know how to choose the good because it is good, recognizing joy and experiencing the excitement that comes from self-directed generosity. Similarly, the child will know how to discern that certain acts are evil simply because they are evil, and not just because they are forbidden. An eight-year-old child confessing that he has watched forbidden movies on TV, when prompted with a question, will admit on his own that a particular movie is not just forbidden but simply bad.

If we were to consider all the actions we perform on any given day, they could be divided into three categories. First, some actions are mandatory. Our religious and moral life is governed by laws and commandments that prescribe certain things (such as the Sunday Mass obligation). Secondly, forbidden actions may also happen. Sin is part of our existence. Most of the day, however, is filled with actions that are neither commanded nor forbidden. These are neither sinful nor expressly mandatory. Which of these actions are the most interesting, and which express our identity the most: actions that are commanded, forbidden, or free? Which of them does God find to be most interesting? Undoubtedly, of most interest are the fully free actions, which manifest personal invention and generosity. Perhaps there is some recurring weakness in us, some recurring sin. Perhaps — by virtue of our position or vocation in life — we are forced to undertake certain tasks that we perceive only as mandatory, as a burden that is tiresome because it is obligatory. But life consists of more than that. Of most importance is that which we do because we want to do it, because we have recognized a compelling good, because an inner impulse of the soul has driven us to creativity and invention. Does Christian education, and, even more so, the formation of seminarians and religious, prompt free, personally chosen actions in its students? Or maybe this education is especially fearful of independent inventiveness?

We find a profound description of personal freedom, which may serve as a practical example of the teachings of St. Thomas, in an author who would probably be surprised to find himself quoted in a theological work. In his memoirs, Jacek Kuroń, a prominent Polish social and political figure wrote:

> When growing up, a young man must rebel against authority figures — in order to stand on one's own feet, and not to be crippled for life. I have seen many who did not rebel, and there is a serious psychic defect in them: the inability to make decisions of their own. If I didn't like my father, I probably would have chosen to go to the political right, but he fascinated me so much that I went to the left and opposed him only in the sense that I wanted to straighten out his life with mine, to make it consistent. I had no idea that in this way I was choosing such a complicated biography for myself. A person who is growing up should rebel against the established order of the world. For this order always betrays the ideals in which children are raised. The alternative to any youthful rebellion is conformity, that is, obedience and imitation, and yet every person, especially during his youth, wants to be the subject of his life.[97]

The education of a young person should engage his enthusiasm, his impatience, and his readiness to fight for a better, more authentic life. If this enthusiasm is extinguished in the name of obedience, however devoutly defined, this will produce not a mature person but an individual with the psychic defect mentioned by Kuroń, in whom conformism and escape will destroy personal subjectivity.

---

[97] Jacek Kuroń, *Wiara i wina : Do i od komunizmu* [Faith and fault: To and from Communism], (London-Warsaw: Wydawnictwo ANEKS — Niezależna Oficyna Wydawnicza NOWA, 1989), 29–30.

Developing personal maturity is not easy. It requires courage and a willingness to defy established customs and patterns. Kuroń writes about his own political struggles:

> It takes an awful lot of strength and courage to negate your entire life. Not only that, you need to have some other idea for your life. And what did I have to choose from? After all, not the attitude of my dad, who was a party activist, and would talk back at me at home. I was not fortunate enough to know the other leftist alternatives. To conclude that I was right rather than the entire movement, the quiet whisper of my dad at home was not enough.[98]

Should not similar questions and struggles emerge in young candidates for the priesthood when they are worried that pastoral approaches are no longer captivating, and when they read the Word of God and try to relate it to the realities of their world?

Three types of obedience

Inner freedom and the life of grace flourish when they are supported by properly understood obedience. But what does obedience consist in? There are three types of obedience that need to be carefully distinguished.

The first type is neurotic obedience or, to put it more bluntly, communist obedience. It was in this obedience that Polish society was kept until St. John Paul II called out, "Take courage, be not afraid!" Psychic reflexes do not disappear immediately, and one should not be surprised that such an understanding of obedience can still exist. Communist obedience may be defined as the repression of the will undertaken by fear or an emotional sense of duty that has been imposed by force.[99] Instead of the will tending toward the good, so as to provide the enthusiasm for a courageous and creative free choice, an irrational inhibition of the will occurs, accomplished by the pressure of fear

---

[98] Kuroń, *Wiara i wina*, 48.
[99] Marshal Zhukov declared that "in the Red Army, it takes a very brave man to become a coward," which means that there the fear of their own superiors was much higher than the fear of the enemy. See Norman Davies, *No Simple Victory: World War II in Europe, 1939–1945* (New York: Penguin, 2007), 266.

or a sense of compulsion. The psychic reflex emerging from the feeling that personal initiative is frowned upon by the authorities constitutes a psychological mutilation. The defect that such obedience generates is all the more dangerous in its consequences the higher the authority that causes it. If the pressure applied by educators is sanctioned by religious motives, it will result in the repression of the will, which will produce a dull, rigid, uninteresting personality. A person who implements a prescribed obligation in a neurotic way has an immature will, with a weakened capacity for personal free choice. In such a person, a material internalization of the imposed obligation takes place, and gradually, it infuses his will with its content, as it were, supplanting the will with the obligation. When this occurs, the obligation penetrates the subconscious level and takes over the personality so much that the person may think that he is acting on his own initiative, whereas, in fact, he is enslaved by an external will. The fulfillment of the good is then at best mechanical, undertaken out of compulsion, and with no spontaneous impulse. It does not contribute to the flourishing of personality.

The second type of obedience can be called military obedience or one that takes place in an office or business. It may be defined as the restraint of the will under the direction of reason. Reason is rational and therefore it knows its limits. It understands that there are matters in which others are more competent, and therefore it is reasonable to obey a superior. A soldier at the battlefront experiences fears and may not like his commander, but he knows that if he disobeys an order, he will be in an even greater danger. Similarly, an employee who follows his manager's orders understands that his work will contribute to the success of the company. Such obedience does not entail a repression of the will. It is free of the perverse deformity that characterizes neurotic obedience, but it is not yet supernatural obedience. A similar role is played by obedience in the early stages of moral education. The child knows the kindness and solicitude of his parents. With his still underdeveloped but already functioning reason, he comprehends that the wisdom of his parents has to be trusted. So when, at the beginning of the moral life, there is a lack of clarity of cognition in free choice and a lack of effective desire of the good for its own sake, the will needs a nudge imposed by an external power that is demanding. The child needs the nurturing influence of his elders and imposed requirements (as long as they are intrinsically rational and not the result of an arbitrary emotional outburst). Obligation imposed by the power of rational obedience characterizes the first stage of moral development, which could be called the period of moral infancy. As the will progresses toward the good, the coercive nature of obligation diminishes until there is a conversion of sorts, in which there is a transition from compulsory obedience to personal love that is a feature of moral maturity. Love will not override obligation, but it will reach out much further. Under the influence of growing love, the external compulsion to obey will disappear and a personal contribution to one's own life, given with conviction, will develop.

The third type of obedience is one that is a vow made to God. The whole point of this obedience is supernatural. It grows out of supernatural love, in which, by the power of the gift of grace, one communes with God. This obedience may be defined as the humility of the will undertaken in view of faith, whose light allows one to hear the voice of God. In pursuing such obedience, one responds with love to God's love. Divine guidance is often surprising, bringing out hidden talents in unexpected ways and opening completely new horizons. The humility of the will is by no means its repression. This type of obedience recognizes the dignity of the will and its role within personal free choice. It also recognizes the function of the reason, which creatively shapes every act of free choice. Just as faith does not negate reason but leads it out toward the mystery that surpasses it, so obedience by faith does not negate creative willing but leads it out toward the mystery in which God is recognized.

The embarking on the adventure of surrendering one's creativity to God is not always automatic. The *fiat* spoken to God every day sometimes has to contend with the darkness of faith, but then other motivations give way and only the sheer willingness to give oneself to God remains. In following the path of this obedience, difficult moments happen, forcing a more mature faith and a greater availability for God, but they never bring psychological mutilation. When God guides a person, He never deforms. One should not think that God holds in His hand the computer data for our lives. Being guided by God does not mean that He sends us detailed instructions from Heaven for every moment of our lives. God wills our initiative and the richness of our gift.

The obedience of consecrated persons does not deny personal inventiveness, the creative use of talents received, and the recognition of new challenges. God is a Father, and like any good father, He delights in our personal steps.

A comparison of these three types of obedience may be made in a theoretical manner. In the practice of life, they are often mixed, and it is not always immediately possible to distinguish between them. An important factor in education, however, is the recognition of how obedience is received. A young person's experience, whether at home or at school, may sometimes cause a reflex of neurotic obedience. When such an individual finds himself in a seminary or a house of religious formation, which, by their nature, impose a more stringent framework of life than do the exigencies of life of other young people who are in college or have professional careers, he or she may experience obedience in a fearful way or perceive it as an imposed imperative. The requirements will then be met externally, there will be care not to get into trouble, but will personal subjectivity develop in such a person? The style of formation has to be structured in such a way so as to leave room for personal inventiveness, for an independent organization of one's time, for the development of one's inner freedom. The living out of the vow of obedience should stem from a personal relationship with God. If this relationship is not nurtured through individual prayer and through the generosity of giving oneself to God, then the vowed obedience will turn out to be a façade and, at the slightest difficulty, will be renounced. Educators and formators, therefore, have to be attentive to what is going on inside a young person and not be satisfied with external appearances alone.

6

Let Us Drink, to Conscience First, and to the Pope Afterward![100]

THERE ARE FUNDAMENTALLY TWO MAIN ISSUES that can be identified in the questions posed by the editorial team of *Znak* regarding conscience. The first one concerns the very nature of conscience. What is it? Is it different from consciousness, memory, an emotional feeling of guilt or complacency? To what extent is conscience "the voice of God," as it is commonly described, and to what extent is it merely a product of social pressure and nurture? If it is the voice of God, why is it that some people appear to have no conscience? Does God not speak to them? Thus, in order to determine properly the role of conscience in moral behavior, it is necessary to grasp precisely its nature and its position in the human psyche and ethos.

The second series of questions posed by the editors points to a certain dissatisfaction with the popular interpretation of the role of conscience, which appears to limit and even threaten human freedom. In religious experience, should we rely on external law or on the freedom of conscience? What should we do if they are in conflict? Does the existence of social and historical circumstances not work in favor of relativizing the power of the categorical imperatives of conscience? The association of the inevitable conflict of conscience with the moral law (and also with the changeable canon law) demonstrates that conscience and law are sometimes interpreted

---

[100] This chapter was published in the Polish monthly *Znak* 494 (July 1996): 37–51.

as being in opposition to each other. The same is true when conscience is assigned the role of a passive and obedient spokesperson for the moral law, which also stands in sharp contrast to freedom, defending its distinctiveness. The answers to the difficulties that emerge here are to be pursued through a correction of the understanding of the nature of freedom, so that its development and susceptibility to signals coming from within a person or to instructions coming from outside can be grasped. It is only when the nature of conscience and its place in the moral act are captured correctly that it is possible to escape the daunting perception that conscience is no more than a cliché, meant merely to punch out mechanically acts that are all identical. Having liberated the concept of conscience from its extreme connotations, one can adequately depict its dignity and the path of Christian transformation of conscience by the accompanying presence of the Holy Spirit.

The nature of conscience

St. Paul, in describing the moral orientation of the pagans who are ignorant of revelation, appeals to the common experience of conscience. He concludes that the pagans "show that what the law requires is written on their hearts, while their conscience also bears witness and their conflicting thoughts accuse or perhaps excuse them" (Rom. 2:15). The Second Vatican Council refers to this verse when it states that "conscience is the most secret core and sanctuary of a man. There he is alone with God, whose voice echoes in his depths."[101] The encyclical *Veritatis splendor* recalls the comparison of St. Bonaventure, for whom the conscience is "like God's herald and messenger; it does not command things on its own authority, but commands them as coming from God's authority, like a herald when he proclaims the edict of the king" (58). All these designations are descriptive and do not settle the Scholastic dispute over the placement of conscience in the human psyche. This leaves room in theology for a certain plurality in the interpretation of the interaction of powers at the moment of the emergence of good actions. It may seem that the differences in the understanding of the essence

---

[101] Second Vatican Council, Pastoral Constitution on the Church in the Modern World *Gaudium et spes* (December 7, 1965), no. 16.

of conscience among Scholastic doctors pertain only to the nuances, but, applied consistently to the ethical system, they generate a diverse spiritual climate. In the quest for paths of liberation from contemporary resistance to moral teaching, it may be useful to examine older formulations that have a place in Catholic theology. A variety of approaches does not necessarily contradict the fundamental teaching of both *Veritatis splendor* and the *Catechism of the Catholic Church*, which attribute a crucial role to conscience in making the judgment of practical reason both before and after action. Both sources emphasize the binding nature of the judgment of conscience.

The first preliminary remark regarding conscience is that fundamentally it belongs to the order of cognition rather than the order of appetition. A judgment of conscience, which is a judgment of reason, is different from an emotional feeling of guilt or satisfaction. The judgment of conscience should not be confused with the experience of remorse, although, in a mentally healthy person, this judgment is supported by an emotional reaction. It may also be the case, however, that the emotional feeling of guilt does not coincide with the judgment of conscience. It happens that the reason does not perceive falsehood in behavior, while the emotions feel guilty; or conversely, reason perceives falsehood, while the emotional reproach is completely lacking. These are, of course, partially pathological situations, but they are by no means rare. The formation of conscience should therefore facilitate the development of a mature autonomy, in which the judgment of practical reason will be able to clearly read the truth of the situation, liberating itself, if necessary, from incidental emotional inhibitions originating from psychological habits or from some external pressure.

The second fundamental preliminary remark regards the necessity of distinguishing two levels of the judgment of practical reason in moral agency. The judgment of conscience is not the sole and final act of reason in the process of eliciting moral acts. (The popular interpretation of the moral act, deriving from the perspective of neo-scholasticism marked by nominalism, suggests that the conscience issues the final judgment of reason, which is then only passively executed by the sole obedient will.) The reality of the act requires a much more nuanced description, although basically the issue is quite simple. Reason makes a judgment regarding moral action twice. The first judgment of reason is that of the conscience, in which a simple reading of the truth of the anticipated act is made. This is followed by a second judgment of reason, which occurs together with the will in the joint act of the free choice, which St. Thomas calls the *liberum arbitrium*. It is at this point that the actual decision regarding the act takes place. The moment of free choice, which is a manifestation of the person's inner freedom, can be divided into several stages, all of which are characterized by the joint operation of reason and will. A person is not to be reduced to the role of an animal, which executively submits to the instincts of its nature. In the free choice following the verdict of conscience, there is room for the reflection of reason. In the case of a simple act that presents no difficulties, there is a standard transfer from the stage of intention through the stage of decision to the execution. In the case of a complex action, involving some difficulty, there is an additional, random stage of deliberation. In all of these three or four stages of the free choice, the cooperation of the practical reason with the inclination of the will is necessary. Even in the case of a simple act, the involvement of reason is needed at the stage of intention, in which there is the perception of the truth about the good suggested by the conscience. It is also needed at the moment of decision about the action, in which the reason and the will condition one another, and finally, it is needed at the stage of the execution of the act, when reason provides a certain oversight of the course of action. Free choice is thus always simultaneously rational and volitional.

Just as, in appealing to fundamental values and their designation by the moral law, we can speak of an "objective moral order," so, in eliciting moral action for the sake of a recognized end, an analogous "subjective moral order" is worked out, that is, a certain stitching together of a sequence of actions, carried out by the subject himself in the moment of free choice. This simultaneously rational and volitional aligning of actions to a consistent and coherent *ordo* is done not on the level of pure theory but in the particulars of a unique and consciously intentional moral agency.

The distinguishing between the two moments of intervention of the practical reason — only the first of which is strictly the judgment of conscience, while the second contributes to the act of free choice — is essential because it allows for a wealth of inventiveness in the moral act. Moreover, it may happen that the judgment of conscience is correct, while the free choice is wrong.[102] This error is not necessarily uniquely the fault of the will, for in free choice, throughout all its stages (intention, decision, possible *deliberatio*, and execution) the contribution of reason is essential, and this reason may also be blinded. St. Thomas, who reserves the term *conscience* for the act of reason at the initial moment, attributes to the virtue of prudence the function of rectifying reason and the will at all the stages of the free choice. In his theological and moral synthesis, he devotes much more space to the virtue of prudence than to conscience. Modern moral theology adopted a radically different perspective. The main emphasis was laid on the conscience, while prudence was shelved and reduced to the status of an uninvolved, external observer, offering admonitions concerning only the means of the action. As a result, the need to nurture the ability to make decisions and to persist in them until their final execution was forgotten. But the inability to make decisions and to execute decisions that have been made manifests a moral weakness, and this, in turn, gives rise to the temptation to question the judgment of conscience. Indeed, the immaturity of the free choice undermines the willingness to accept the judgment of conscience.

Paying close attention to these different moments of the reason's involvement in a moral action is significant because a cursory reading of *Veritatis splendor* might make it seem as if St. John Paul II is questioning the right to make decisions. After all, rejecting the position of theologians who advocate a "creative" interpretation of conscience, the pope writes:

> But those norms, they continue, cannot be expected to foresee and to respect all the individual concrete acts of the person in all their uniqueness and particularity. While such norms might somehow be useful for a correct assessment of the situation, they cannot replace the individual personal decision on how to act in particular cases....
> In their desire to emphasize the "creative" character of conscience, certain authors no longer call its actions "judgments" but "decisions":

[102] St. Thomas Aquinas, *De veritate*, q. 17, art. 1, ad 4.

only by making these decisions "autonomously" would man be able to attain moral maturity. (55)

Could it be that the pope questioned an individual's right to make decisions? Was he unaware that a person matures precisely through personal moral decision-making? It is important to note carefully what the pope is *not* saying here. He is not questioning the ability or the need to make decisions. The blade of the encyclical is directed against claims that deny the objectivity of the moral order, not against moral maturity. The encyclical does not provide us with a comprehensive textbook analysis of moral acts. It only responds to those false claims that need to be corrected. Thus, St. John Paul II rejects the position claiming that man has the right to be "creative" in respect to the moral norms.

Man does not create moral norms for himself because they are objective, rooted in the very nature of things. Moral law is a manifestation of wisdom, which discloses objective truth and protects against dangerous paths, whereas conscience has to read the objective truth of the anticipated situation on the basis of the light shed by the norms, and it is to apply this truth to the specific moral dilemma. This does not mean, however, that an individual should not be "creative" in respect to the act. The agent needs to think, to make decisions and be creative in the way he reacts to values. The questioning of the "creativity" of the conscience in respect to the objective norms does not undermine the "creativity" of reason within free choice. A person who is internally creative in his good choices becomes capable of eliciting virtuous acts. He then grows in maturity, and, as St. Thomas puts it, through his *liberum arbitrium* he becomes a living image of the living God!

Reason does not create truth for its own purposes in the process of eliciting the act of free choice. In the joint action of the reason and the will in free choice, it is the act that is elicited, and the more creative the act — the more it manifests inventiveness, richness of talent, and persistent responsibility in responding to moral dilemmas — the better. The ultimate value of the act, however, extends deeper than the mere creative daring of the agent and depends on the will's inward tending toward the most fundamental ends and on the conformity of the chosen action to the truth of the situation as interpreted by the conscience. The reason and the will can therefore, according to their respective natures, be characterized by "creativity" in jointly undertaking acts of free choice, as long as, in doing so, there is no denial of the truth of objective reality as it is illuminated by the moral norm and perceived by the conscience. This is possible because, within the spiritual powers of the reason and the will, there is an inner spiritual attraction toward that which is true and good.

It is also important to note that the creative moment in free choice does not disappear in the case of supernatural action. When a believer gives himself to God, allowing himself to be led by Him, even through mysterious tribulations that resemble Christ's Passover, and he recognizes the inner movements of the Holy Spirit urging him to be giving and to be generous, he is not to react to God's will with mindless and blind obedience. Openness to divine guidance requires the full and free intervention of the reason and the will in free choice. That is why St. Paul, exhorting us to offer "your living bodies as a holy sacrifice, truly pleasing to God" he stresses that it should be done "in a way that is worthy of thinking beings" (Rom. 12:1, Jerusalem Bible). And we should add even more here. Supernatural life develops the human mind, broadens the horizons, and allows one to view things from God's perspective, which extends beyond time and is distinguished by its depth: "that Christ may dwell in your hearts through faith; that you, being rooted and grounded in love, may have power to comprehend with all the saints what is the breadth and length and height and depth, and to know the love of Christ which surpasses knowledge, that you may be filled with all the fulness of God" (Eph. 3:17–19). (If someone who declares himself a Christian displays an embarrassing narrow-mindedness, with aggressiveness and insularity rising to the forefront, this is sure proof that his spiritual life is yet to be developed, and he still has a long way to go in opening his mind and heart to "all the fulness of God"!)

Having introduced the essential distinction between conscience and the rational input in free choice, we can now further outline the nature of conscience. Following St. Thomas, we define *conscience* as uniquely an act of practical reason. Aquinas differs in this regard from his contemporaries. St. Albert the Great defined *conscience* not as a judgment of reason, but as knowledge — *scientia*. In this knowledge, he held, are contained the inherent principles of the natural law along with acquired life experience. St. Bonaventure, on the other hand, defined *conscience* as a disposition, a *habitus* that perfects the practical reason and also contains within it a volitional dimension. He held that conscience cannot be a mere expression of moral knowledge, because the final judgment of conscience is an echo of the mindsets and attitudes in life, and not merely the conclusion of a rational deduction. St. Thomas Aquinas, familiar with these opinions, deliberately restricted conscience to an act of the practical reason. According to him, the function of the conscience is only to apply the possessed moral knowledge to a specific act. This application of moral knowledge to an act presupposes, of course, the possession and development of that knowledge, along with the possession of moral virtues that dispose the reason to fulfill its function of illuminating a particular act. In the case of the Christian who, through faith and hope directed to Christ, develops an openness to the intuitions of the Holy Spirit and takes up these intuitions in active charity, the gift of wisdom will expand his reason to the deeper perspective of faith and will generate in him a certain connaturality (*connaturalitas*) with the truest good, shown by the Holy Spirit.[103] In the eyes of an individual guided exclusively by natural reason, this supernatural perspective may seem to be absurd, but the Christian whose conscience is formed by the dynamics of the Holy Spirit is ready to adopt positions and take actions that embrace the folly of the Cross. This is possible because his reason is permeated by faith and his will is submissive to the inner stirrings of charity infused by God.[104]

All the Scholastics linked conscience with an antecedent disposition called *synderesis*, derived from erroneous Greek (Fr. Jacek Woroniecki suggested that it should be rendered in Polish as *prasumienie*, "proto-conscience"). St. Thomas, just like St. Albert, defined *synderesis* as an innate disposition that captures the first principle of moral conduct. Just as the first

---

[103] *Veritatis splendor* 64 highlights this moment of St. Thomas's teaching.

[104] *ST*, Ia, q. 1, art. 8, ad 2: "Since grace does not scrap nature but brings it to perfection, so also natural reason should assist faith as the natural loving bent of the will yields to charity" (trans. T. Gilby, vol. 1, 1964).

principles of theoretical reason are at the basis of all thinking, so the first principle of moral conduct is at the basis of all moral agency. St. Thomas narrowed down this principle to one simple statement that "good is to be pursued and evil is to be avoided." This principle does not lend itself very readily to the derivation of a complete system of moral pronouncements, but, for St. Thomas, that is not necessary because, for him, conscience is not a body of knowledge but only an act of reason. So, for St. Thomas, synderesis merely provides the proper direction within which the judgment of the anticipated action is made by the practical reason. St. Thomas's position on this is close to that of St. Bonaventure, who linked synderesis to the will. St. Thomas, in stating that synderesis incites to the good and protests against evil, recognized that there is also some affective element in it, i.e., a certain contact between the reason and the will. Thus, synderesis expresses the metaphysical interchangeability of the true and the good. As St. Jerome put it, it is a spark that comes from the divine fire and is alight in the human mind. This makes it the most fundamental basis of moral intuitions. Beginning with the statement that "good is to be pursued and evil is to be avoided," St. Thomas looks into the deepest inclinations of the human being in order to discern where precisely the good inherent in human nature lies and what constitutes its absence.

The examination of these inclinations in light of the synderesis impulse enables one to grasp the basic rulings of the natural law. St. Thomas, however, never developed a coherent and detailed deontological system based on synderesis and the fundamental inclinations of human nature (nor also based upon the revealed law). This means that the reception of the fundamental instructions of the natural law, and of the precepts contained in the Decalogue and in the teaching of the new law of grace, serves merely as a leading guidance to the conscience, which is just an act of reason. Examining and reflecting on the fundamental inclinations of human nature, as well as the external instructions of the revealed law, assists the reason in its capacity to "grasp" where the splendor of truth lies. When this truth of the situation is "grasped" and directed to action by the judgment of the practical reason, it becomes the judgment of conscience that subsequently has a bearing on the final free choice of action.

Such an understanding of the nature of conscience, confined solely to an act of the practical reason, explains the internal logic of Thomas's moral synthesis. For he primarily considers the virtues, starting with the most basic theological virtues, which unite a person with the living God, because it is through the virtues that, in free choice, the response to objective values is manifested, and it is in this that St. Thomas recognizes the fecundity of divine grace present in the divine image that is man. The commandments of the Decalogue feature in this synthesis only very briefly as "affixed" to each virtue and explained through their convenience. The engine of moral conduct, therefore, is the good itself, which, in more modern language, can be called the value. It is the value that attracts man in its truth. The moral law has an educational function, opening the eyes to the splendor of the truth inherent in the value, but in the final perception of the beauty of the compelling value, the reason itself makes its judgment, and this act of reason, called conscience, provides the necessary background for the subsequent act of reason in conjunction with the will within the free choice. No wonder, then, that St. Thomas sees mature freedom of an individual in his responding to values, and not merely in responding to external obligations.[105]

Does such an interpretation of conscience, reduced to an act of practical reason, an act admittedly marked by the intuition of synderesis, the educational influence of the moral law, and the knowledge and virtues possessed, justify elevating it to the rank of the voice of God? Is it not perhaps somewhat impudent to link the judgment of one's own reason with the voice of God? This concern is legitimate, albeit one that stems from the experience of confusing conscience with inhibitions, suggestions, or whims foreign to the pure light of reason. By calling conscience an act of the practical reason, St. Thomas recognizes in it an orientation toward the truth, and all truth, regardless of who proclaims it, ultimately comes from the Holy Spirit. That is

---

[105] *Super II ad Cor.*, c. 3, l. 3 (112): "Therefore, one who avoids evils, not because they are evil, but because of God's commandment, is not free. But one who avoids evils because they are evils is free. But this is done by the Holy Spirit." *Commentary on the Letters of St. Paul to the Corinthians*, trans. F. R. Larcher, B. Mortensen, and D. Keating (Lander, WY: Aquinas Institute for the Study of Sacred Doctrine, 2012).

why recognizing a reflection of God in the judgment of conscience, whether in the case of a conscience interpreting the light from nature or from the perspective of faith and the wisdom of the Holy Spirit, is fully justified.

The tying of an act of reason that is the conscience with synderesis involves referring it to the fundamental intuition of the good, which, since it is created, cannot come from anyone else but God. Cardinal Ratzinger therefore proposes the replacement of the term *synderesis*, commonly used in theology since the Middle Ages, with the term *anamnesis*, for he sees in the proto-conscience a reminder of the deepest orientations inscribed in human nature by God:

> This means that ... something like an original memory of the good and true (both are identical) has been implanted in us, that there is an inner ontological tendency within man, who is created in the likeness of God, toward the divine. From its origin, man's being resonates with some things and clashes with others. This anamnesis of the origin, which results from the godlike constitution of our being is not a conceptually articulated knowing, a store of retrievable contents. It is so to speak an inner sense, a capacity to recall, so that the one whom it addresses, if he is not turned in on himself, hears its echo from within. He sees: "That's it! That is what my nature points to and seeks."[106]

A particularly powerful testimony to the modern Catholic tradition attributing divine prerogatives to the conscience may be found in Newman's *Letter Addressed to the Duke of Norfolk*. Both the *Catechism of the Catholic Church* and *Veritatis splendor* include references to this magnificent text. In 1874, shortly after the First Vatican Council proclaimed the dogma of papal infallibility, the British prime minister William Gladstone accused Catholics of alleged political disloyalty. Newman responded to this with an elaborate open letter in which he took the liberty of comparing the authority of conscience with that of the papacy. With a single stroke of his pen,

---

[106] Cardinal Joseph Ratzinger, *Faith and Politics* (San Francisco: Ignatius Press, 2018), 123–124.

Newman distanced himself from the ultramontanists, whose understanding of papal power was too political; he reassured concerned non-Catholics; and, employing the beautifully clear language of a seasoned polemicist, he outlined the nature, dignity, and primacy of conscience. It was obvious to Newman that the whole point of morality, religion, and even the papacy rests precisely on the dignity of conscience. There would be no point in listening to the voice of the pope if a person did not first confront the inner voice of his own conscience, where God speaks. After all, the final

> rule and measure of duty is not utility, nor expedience, nor the happiness of the greatest number, nor State convenience, nor fitness, order, and the *pulchrum*. Conscience is not a long-sighted selfishness, nor a desire to be consistent with oneself; but it is a messenger from Him, who, both in nature and in grace, speaks to us behind a veil, and teaches and rules us by His representatives.[107]

Newman compares conscience to the threefold function of the papacy, modeled on Christ. In doing so, he grants conscience the same attributes of power that the pope enjoys, except for the charism of infallibility:

> Conscience is the aboriginal Vicar of Christ, a prophet in its informations, a monarch in its peremptoriness, a priest in its blessings and anathemas, and, even though the eternal priesthood throughout the Church could cease to be, in it the sacerdotal principle would remain and would have a sway.[108]

These are powerful words. Is not the experience of Siberian Christians, deprived of priests for years, proof of the survival of the Church wherever the voice of conscience is heard?

Citing the opinion of multiple Catholic theologians, Newman states the following principle:

---

[107] *A Letter Addressed to the Duke of Norfolk on Occasion of Mr. Gladstone's Recent Expostulation*, in Alvan Ryan, *Newman and Gladstone: The Vatican Decrees* (Notre Dame: University of Notre Dame Press, 1963), 129.

[108] *Duke of Norfolk*, 129.

> Conscience is ever to be obeyed, whether it tells truly or erroneously, and that, whether the error is the fault of the person thus erring or not.... Of course, if he is culpable in being in error, which he would have escaped, had he been more in earnest, for that error he is answerable to God, but still he must act according to that error, while he is in it, because he in full sincerity thinks the error to be truth.[109]

This principle expresses respect for the dignity of the individual conscience. Man has no ultimate authority other than his own reason, which captures the truth. The main issue is that the reference of reason to truth will not be poisoned. Newman recognized this danger, which is why he states:

> Conscience has rights because it has duties; but in this age, with a large portion of the public, it is the very right and freedom of conscience to dispense with conscience, to ignore a Lawgiver and Judge, to be independent of unseen obligations.... Conscience is a stern monitor, but in this century it has been superseded by a counterfeit, which the eighteen centuries prior to it never heard of, and could not have mistaken for it, if they had. It is the right of self-will.[110]

In the discovery of the truth by conscience, Newman saw an openness to signals coming directly from God. Therefore, he remonstrated:

> When men advocate the rights of conscience, they in no sense mean the rights of the Creator, nor the duty to Him, in thought and deed, of the creature; but the right of thinking, speaking, writing, and acting, according to their judgment or their humor, without any thought of God at all.[111]

Since the voice of God speaks in the conscience, great care, experience, and also courage are necessary so as to develop a sensitivity to this voice. This is possible at the level of purely natural reason, as illustrated by the attitude of the Greek Antigone. At the level of grace, in openness to the mystery

---

[109] *Duke of Norfolk*, 137.
[110] *Duke of Norfolk*, 130.
[111] *Duke of Norfolk*, 130.

of faith, the intuition of God's voice in the conscience is sharpened. The guidance of the Holy Spirit, accomplished in the darkness of faith, is subtle and conditioned by the human readiness to respond. God does not impose Himself; instead, He invites.

Forming the conscience

While it is true that a person should act in accordance with his conscience, since human dignity is expressed in being guided by reason, it is also true that a person is responsible for his conscience. Conscience needs to be formed — that is, reason needs to be trained so that it can recognize the truth of moral situations and, referring to the truth, can illuminate even uncomfortable and yet binding dilemmas. Certain people seem not to have moral dilemmas because they are indifferent to values. When confronted with injustice and dishonesty, or presented with an opportunity to get involved in the cause of good, they just walk on because they simply do not see the problem. Their conscience has not been formed to respond to values. This is a defect, indicating immaturity and spiritual mediocrity. Along with educating the practical reason to read the truth, what is needed is the simultaneous cultivation of the ability to move from the judgments of conscience to decisions that are truly made and executed with perseverance. Without this further ability, true intuitions of conscience will prove to be no more than a straw enthusiasm.

Seeking and finding the truth in order to be guided by that truth in life helps develop a moral backbone. When St. Thérèse of Lisieux told a novice, "You may hate me, but I will tell you the truth until I die,"[112] this may have at first triggered her opposition, but with time, it evolved into understanding and respect. We are not indifferent to the truth. When it is perceived, it grants a certain satisfaction, a sense that finally we are standing on firm ground, because truth is not a deforming alienation for the reason. As a

---

[112] Quoted in St. Thérèse de Lisieux, *Oeuvres complètes* (Paris: Cerf, DDB, 1992), 1289 (my translation). "Je vous dois la vérité, *me disait-elle*, détestez-moi, si vous voulez, mais je vous la dirai jusqu'à ma mort," Marie de la Trinité, *Procès Apostolique*, 1915–1917 (Rome: Teresianum, 1976), 475.

result of intellectual and spiritual mutilation, it may happen that the draw toward truth is weakened, but when, due to proper education, the reason's orientation toward the truth is restored, it rediscovers itself in the truth. This does not, however, come about easily. The recognition of that toward which truth compels requires effort and clarity of thought.

The temptation of liberal thinking retreats from this challenge and suggests that truth may be sought as long as one does not claim that it can be found. Such agnosticism prefers to stop at the threshold of truth in order to free itself from the demands of conscience. For once discovered, truth is binding, whereas the agnostic prefers to avoid obligations and therefore exalts sincerity rather than truth. Sincerity alone, however, is no guarantee of the integrity of conscience. Furthermore, the bringing to the fore of only sincerity makes one incapable of making binding decisions in life. In order for a person to be able to make decisions about his life or vocation, he must be convinced that the truth can be known by reason, even though this requires humble training and the learning of truth, for conscience, by its very nature, is not infallible. The false theory of the supposed infallibility of conscience, which implies that an individual may ignore the truth, by no means elevates the conscience but rather degrades it. If each conscience is considered infallible "in its own way," this means that a dual status of moral truth has been introduced: there is objective truth, which is general, unknowable, and separated from reality; and there is personal truth, which everyone works out for himself. In other words, there is no truth at all. Conscience reduced to personal sincerity is then lost in a nihilistic vacuum. When conscience absolves itself of the truth, it ascribes to itself the power to justify. Since it is not seeking the truth, it does not indict for falsehood, nor does it open itself to the justifying grace of Christ. Instead of being a window open to God, it becomes a device for self-justification. In practical terms, this means that truth is replaced by social pressure. Whatever fits social expectations and does not require taking a stand seems good and fitting. Such an approach does not develop character and fosters mediocrity.

True formation of conscience, therefore, implies a constant striving for the truth — not just truth in the realm of ideas but truth in life. Do everyday decisions, reactions to existing situations, or asually uttered words or gestures express the truth? Does one resist in them moods, fads, anxieties, and cravings — in the name of truth? And in the name of the gospel? Does the light of Christ illuminate daily decisions? Can we repeat after Our Lord, "For this I was born, and for this I have come into the world, to bear witness to the truth" (John 18:37)? Through practice in learning the truth and adhering to it, maturity and independence are developed.

Only by referring to the highest reasons does one find wisdom. Traditionally, three levels of wisdom are distinguished: philosophical wisdom, attained through the efforts of a seeking reason; theological wisdom, grounded in God's revealed mystery; and wisdom given in grace, the fruit of the direct intervention of the Holy Spirit in the human mind. At each of these levels, experienced in the realm of practice and not just theory, the root of the issue must be addressed, and the most fundamental questions must be posed: What is the issue? What values are at stake? Where does the truth lie? What am I really striving for? Posing such questions is not easy, because going against the flow to the source requires effort, and those who stand by the truth experience loneliness. People are more willing to opt for an easy solution than for the truth. But only going deeper to the highest reasons of truth develops the character because this liberates a person from social simplifications, from seeking refuge in legalistic formulas, or from escaping responsibility. Remaining merely at the level of habit or heeding other people's opinions does not develop reason and independence and will not protect one from subjugation, gossip, or fads. Only in discovering the truth does a person become free. This then entails a dependence on reality itself, together with a freedom from other people's opinions, from seductive schemes and catchy slogans. More so, being anchored in the truth contributes to the development of true friendship. That which binds friends most is the truth. The motto that is constantly repeated in the Dominican Order and is taken from the writings of St. Thomas, *Contemplata aliis tradere*, may be translated as "sharing with others the values that have been discovered." Showing truth to one's neighbor, the truth about concrete practical life matters, attributes a firm foundation to friendship precisely because it concerns truth. The more one loves a friend, the more one wants to give him or her the best that one has, and the best thing we can give is precisely the discovery of truth.

Recognizing the truth by the conscience and transferring it into action requires fortitude and courage and perhaps even playing some sort of game with oneself so as to protect oneself from laziness, fear, or cowardliness. When St. Thomas More recognized in his conscience that taking the oath required by Henry VIII meant severing the Church in England from the universal Church, he knew well that by refusing to take the oath he faced the death penalty. So he made up jokes in order to assuage his fears and force himself to be faithful to the judgment of his conscience. His sense of humor defended him from pusillanimity. As he was mounting the scaffold, he asked the executioner to give him a hand, and he immediately added that he would not need assistance on his way back. Martyrdom does not exclude fears, but it means transcending them by being faithful to the truth recognized by conscience.

Failure to develop the ability to make decisions and implement them — that is, the underdevelopment of the free choice — lies at the root of moral subjectivism. Some people are capable of making the right judgment of practical reason. This means that their conscience is functioning well, but they lack the ability to act creatively and responsibly. If this weakness is not overcome, in time they will begin to question the first judgment — that is, the very recognition of truth. We are complex beings, and if we lack perseverance in implementing the judgments of conscience, over time we will begin to retreat from the truth. One may wonder to what extent moral subjectivism has its roots in embracing philosophical positions that question the objectivity of truth, and to what extent it stems from a lack of moral vigor, which may have quite different causes. The ubiquitous absence of fathers in parenting, the low representation of men among teachers, and the climate of intimidation (in families, society, and religious communities) all contribute to the underdevelopment of the assertive emotions. When the emotions of courage, enthusiasm, and anger, that is the capacity to be indignant at evil are underdeveloped, it is difficult to be relentlessly consistent in pursuing the good. But what cripples an individual most is the lack of spiritual life. This is because a personal communion with God enables one to accept the truth about one's own weaknesses without blowing it out of proportion. It allows one to receive forgiveness and gives the power to face emerging challenges. When there is no living relationship with God, the person then closes in the weakness and is unable to face the disturbing challenges of truth.

It is in the context of developing a mature conscience that the Church's teaching should be received. Newman was right. The Church's preaching serves the interior development of man. In a maieutic way, it brings out a resonance in a soul hungry for truth and God. Speaking to men who already have experienced the grace of faith that opens to the living God, the Church brings out the sense of the deepest truth purified by faith. And when a nonbeliever hears the Church, he may not grasp the most magnificent and profound prospects of being a child in the arms of the Father, but if he is diligent in his search, he will find in the Church's fundamental moral teaching a confirmation of his intuition of the natural law.

> It follows that the authority of the Church, when she pronounces on moral questions, in no way undermines the freedom of conscience of Christians. This is so not only because freedom of conscience is never freedom "from" the truth but always and only freedom "in" the truth, but also because the Magisterium does not bring to the Christian conscience truths which are extraneous to it; rather it brings to light the truths which it ought already to possess, developing them from the starting point of the primordial act of faith. The Church puts herself always and only at the *service of conscience*. [113]

The teaching voice of the Church is an ally of the conscience. It guides the conscience toward that truth that reason seeks in its deepest layers. The Church, after all, preaches nothing else but Christ, Who is "the way, and the truth, and the life" (John 14:6).

Since Christ has the ability to penetrate the interiority of a person's conscience, Newman concludes his essay with a somewhat playful but profound remark:

---

[113] *Veritatis splendor* 64.

If I am obliged to bring religion into after-dinner toasts (which indeed does not seem quite the thing) I shall drink — to the Pope, if you please — still, to Conscience first, and to the Pope afterwards.[114]

---

[114] *Duke of Norfolk*, 138.

7

Conscience or Superego?[115]

FATHER, I DID NOT GO TO MASS on Sunday.
Why?
Because, Father, I am a waitress, and once a month I work on Sundays. Then I can't go to Mass. But I did go to Mass on Saturday night. The priest said that it was a Sunday Mass, that it was valid.
The priest was right. Nowadays the Church allows the faithful to participate in Sunday Mass on Saturday evening. It is an accommodation that the Church introduced for people in situations like yours. You have not committed a sin, so you don't have to confess it.
But I prefer to confess that I did not attend Sunday Mass.
You did attend Sunday Mass, except it was celebrated on Saturday night.
But I don't feel good, if I don't mention it during Confession.

Occasionally, we run into such reasoning. To be precise, it is not actually reasoning, because the penitent mentioned here is not guided by reason. She knows, of course, that the Church has changed the law and has the power to do so, and she understands that she has not transgressed any divine or canon laws, but she still feels uncomfortable. She may be guided by reason in her everyday life, but in her moral life she is guided by feeling rather than reason. And the feeling cannot keep up with the reason. When reason considers a

---

[115] This chapter was first published in the Polish monthly *W drodze* 162, no. 2 (1987): 3–10.

new situation, feeling continues to be guided by the habit insisting that one needs to go to Mass every Sunday. The penitent in question will probably want to confess that she missed Mass if she happens to be lying on an operating table in a hospital on Sunday! Going to Confession does not necessarily manifest a mature conscience. Sometimes it is simply the result of feeling bad.

A mature conscience is an act of reason, not of a feeling. The Latin *conscientia* means knowledge that is applied to a specific situation. That is why St. Thomas Aquinas defined *conscience* as an act of practical reason that precedes conscious action and later evaluates it in light of this knowledge. The truth perceived by conscience is not purely theoretical, since it is the truth of a given situation, which demands a response. Thus, when a voluntarily chosen reaction to a recognized truth takes place, it comes about through a free choice that can be broken down into the stages of intention, decision, sometimes deliberation, and finally execution. In this free choice, at each of its stages, reason once again recognizes the truth, and, together with the will, it responds to it creatively, either by undertaking that which affirms the truth or by deciding on an action that ignores or denies the recognized truth. Free choice, being simultaneously rational and volitional, is an expression of the ingenuity and resourcefulness of a person who has been affected by a moral dilemma and has responded to it. In traditional moral theology, the sustained ability to respond genuinely, creatively, and at the same time responsibly to the truths indicated by conscience is known as the cardinal virtue of prudence. It is the virtue that drives moral action. Its task is to ensure that the truth of the situation recognized by antecedent conscience has indeed been honored and that it has elicited an adequate, creatively developed response.

And so, conscience belongs to the order of cognition. It considers moral principles and values, which it respects and discerns in concrete situations. Through conscience, the objective moral norm, which is intrinsically general, becomes subjective and concrete. Each operation of the judgment of conscience is an independent act of reason, provoking a further voluntary and creative act of free choice. Reason, both at the antecedent level and within free choice, requires initiative, perceptiveness, courage, proper self-confidence, fidelity to the truth, and trust in one's own verdict. Conscience has no legislative power; it does not make the rules: these rules are given by nature and are expressed in the objective moral norm. It does, however, have administrative power, since it determines the application of the norm, and when, despite everything, that norm has not been applied, the consequent conscience has judicial power. It evaluates the conformity or nonconformity of an act with a previously rendered verdict.

A sound, well-formed conscience is guided by objective principles and is able to distinguish between apparent and proper values. It is not guided by prejudice, preferences, or other people's opinions but by objective reality. This is not always easy — sometimes, even for an adult, it is difficult to distinguish the judgment of one's own conscience from the opinions of parents, grandparents, or a teacher that linger somewhere in the memory, shape the emotional response, and enter the realm of reason, blurring the picture.

Properly speaking, in the conscience three overlapping layers that together form its final verdict should be distinguished. The first layer is the fundamental conviction that good should be pursued and evil should be avoided. This is the simplest verdict of practical reason, unquestionable and inherent in the very nature of reason. St. Jerome called this *proto-conscience*, the spark that flew from God's fire and took up residence in the human soul. Proto-conscience, also known as *synderesis*, is a natural impulse that directs us toward the good, but, due to its generic nature, it calls for further specification. Everyone agrees that good should be done, but not everyone knows what should be regarded as good.

Therefore, this fundamental layer of the proto-conscience is augmented by a second layer — one that is specific to conscience. Practical reason makes judgments, creatively analyzes principles, considers particular circumstances, and ultimately determines how one is to act. It is receptive to the illumination that comes from outside. Reason accepts sound instruction and explanations — that is why conscience needs to be formed; ethical formation, which provides reason with principles so that it can render an adequate verdict, is necessary.

Practical reason is also receptive to further illumination that belongs to another order, the order of grace. The Christian conscience shows sensitivity to direct inspirations coming from the Holy Spirit. It surrenders not only to the objective principles of the written moral law, but also to the rulings of the unwritten law of the Spirit that is equivalent to grace. And these rulings of the new law, which are always concrete — showing how to mediate God's love *hic et nunc* (here and now) also constitute an objective order for practical reason. Reason accepts them when it persists in humble recognition of its limitations. Receptivity to grace depends on faith, which is the humility of reason. And this is why the Christian conscience opts for the folly of the Cross, for acts that are a scandal to some and folly to others but to the conscience are "the power of God and the wisdom of God" (1 Cor. 1:24). But for this, a sensitive ear, sophisticated spiritual antennae, and skill in relying on grace are necessary so that the stirrings of grace are discerned and followed. The discernment of divine inspirations takes place within the conscience, in the atmosphere of faith, and therefore within reason. We are still at the level of cognition.

It is only as a result of the cognitive act of reason that there is a reflection of it on the level of appetition. When the act has followed the verdict of conscience, an internal joy arises in the sphere of emotions. It is natural for the emotions to be led by the directions of reason. Every act, if it is in accord with the verdict of conscience, produces interior satisfaction. Even in the case of righteous indignation at evil or wholesome lamentation over one's own or someone else's misery, internal joy follows; for emotions, when they follow the directives of reason, bring joy. Their satisfaction is a bodily echo that supports the conscience.

However, in the case of an act that did not follow the judgment of conscience, the emotions also react. The sinner not only knows that he has done wrong but he also feels uneasy. The negative judgment of the subsequent conscience supports the psychological feeling of guilt. A person feels remorse, and this feeling is corporal. It is reflected on the face and causes blushing. This psychic feeling of guilt does not belong to the judgment of conscience per se but to the emotional, bodily realm, which is shared with animals, but it is a huge additional incentive, stimulating us to follow the judgment of conscience. When this emotional support for the conscience is lacking — as is the case of psychopaths — a person knows that he has done wrong but does not feel guilty. A psychopath will avoid an evil act because of the threat of punishment, but not due to an inner feeling of guilt, because in him a separation of the rational and emotional spheres has taken place. His judgment of conscience does not find support in feelings — but this is a morbid, pathological phenomenon. In a normal person, the judgment of conscience is enhanced by a physical feeling, but it is not reduced to it.

The Swiss researcher of conscience Hans Zulliger describes the following situation: One of the boys at camp stole some money. Since the issue of the theft was troubling everyone, the camp director told them about the Abyssinian method of finding the culprit. Each of the suspects was to drink cold water in front of everyone else. The culprit would surely choke and not be able to swallow. So a cup of water was circulated. All the boys drank from it, and one of them choked. Indeed, he confessed his guilt and returned the stolen money. The feeling of guilt, which is inherently physical and emotional, impacted him so much that it even affected the functioning of his esophagus.[116]

It is erroneous to think that conscience is limited to this feeling of guilt. This feeling is only an external, emotional expression of the judgment of conscience, which is inherently rational. If the feeling of guilt is compatible with the mature judgment of conscience, it enhances that judgment and facilitates a righteous life. If, on the other hand, it supersedes the judgment of conscience and is contrary to it — as in the case of the penitent mentioned at the beginning — or if it substitutes the operations of conscience, it becomes destructive. Instead of supporting conscience and leading to personal maturity, it causes neurotic self-centeredness. Due to the intensity of its involvement, a misplaced feeling of guilt encroaches upon the sphere of operation of the conscience, precludes development, prevents the creative operation of reason, and is a source of neurotic repression. By contrast, a feeling of guilt that is in its proper place, subordinated to the judgment of conscience is a useful tool that encourages integrity and supports the pursuit of responsibility and freedom of the children of God. But a feeling of guilt that replaces conscience leads to interior slavery.

Thus, for a complete picture of the conscience (with the three layers being proto-conscience; the judgment of practical reason — which for the

---

[116] Hans Zulliger, *La formation de la conscience morale chez l'enfant* (Mulhouse: Éditions Salvator, 1971), 80–83.

Christian is enlightened by faith; and a supporting feeling of satisfaction or guilt), it is necessary to add a fourth element that does not belong to the conscience but is often confused with it: the *superego*. This term does not have a Christian origin. It was introduced into modern thought by Sigmund Freud, who saw the superego as the main culprit behind the formation of neuroses. In its classical Freudian interpretation, the term is of little help to us because it is not very precise. Freud understood the superego as a cluster of conscience, feelings of guilt, and ideas imposed by educators and society. This cluster, in his understanding, can repress the sexual drive. Hence, in order to be liberated from neurosis, Freud advocated rejecting the pressure of the superego so that the repressed drive could develop freely. The rejection of conscience and moral norms in the name of liberation from repression, however, proved to be a disaster.

Nonetheless, if we narrow down the meaning of the term *superego* to a misplaced feeling of guilt, which becomes the determining factor of moral behavior in lieu of the practical reason — that is, conscience — then the term will prove useful. It will allow us to distinguish between conscience and neurotic guilt. A feeling of guilt may concern both a past and a future action. A fear or a sense of energy ordering one to fight some other emotion generates repression. The essence of neurotic repression lies in the fact that some other emotion enters into the sphere of influence of reason and will and assumes the responsibility of repressing the emotion that is deemed undesirable, thus cutting off the way for the reason and the will. To use the language of rational psychology, the factor that perpetrates the repression is an emotion of the *appetitus irascibilis*, the utility appetite, which, in turn, is stimulated by the sensory usefulness judgment — the *vis cogitativa*. For example, someone may feel the desire for sexual pleasure, and subsequently a flawed sensory usefulness judgment tells him that the sensation is inappropriate. Before reason can pass any verdict, the neurotic person feels that the sensation of pleasure is inappropriate and immediately turns on fear or the emotion of energy so as to suppress the desire for pleasure. This, of course, gives rise to neurosis. The entire process takes place on an emotional and not a rational level.

In the forming of the conscience, therefore, it is crucial to pay attention to the way moral principles are received. Freud was right when he said that moral norms generate neuroses, but this only happens when they are interpreted in an emotional, sensual way. Moral norms do not give rise to neuroses when they are apprehended by reason — that is, by the conscience — and when they affect the free choice, which is simultaneously rational and volitional. Freud failed to make this distinction.

Thus, the superego, in a restricted sense, is a movement of an emotion that replaces the proper conscience. It mimics both the antecedent and consequent conscience, assuming the position of a director of moral life. Sometimes it dons a devout suit, feigning a stirring of grace. A feeling of guilt, instead of playing a subservient role to the conscience, then takes on a leading role. The abandonment of the use of reason in directing moral life in favor of an all-determining feeling of guilt is invariably a certain diminishment, restricting a person. Sometimes it may seem to be a convenient shortcut, but, in fact, it is a stop in the journey. Sometimes, deep down, we prefer to be guided by a weepy feeling of guilt rather than a mature call to personal responsibility. A feeling of guilt may become a convenient veil behind which one may hide, an excuse that justifies inaction and spiritual stagnation.

Let us attempt to compare the workings of the superego and the conscience. The superego commands an act so as to obtain approval. At the basis of its functioning is fear that the sympathy of an authority figure will be withdrawn. Conscience, on the other hand, invites to creative love, to the gift of self. The superego has an introverted attitude; the center of its attention is one's own sense of value. The conscience has an extroverted attitude; the center of its attention is the value itself; feelings about one's own value are secondary. The superego is static; it does not develop. In a new, unforeseen situation, it cannot act creatively; it can only repeat the order. Conscience is dynamic and sensitive to value. It knows how to encourage the taking of risks, and it is capable of judging in a new situation. The superego follows the authority. Frequently, this authority is subconscious. It does not want to discern the situation and respond creatively to it but, instead, is guided by blind obedience toward a heteronomous principle. The conscience is searching for the value irrespective of whether the authority has suggested it or not. The superego directs all of its attention to individual acts. The conscience pays more attention to the overall attitude and reflects on how the individual acts fit into the general pattern of behavior. The superego is focused upon the past; it strives for a clean slate at any cost and wants to be punished so that past actions will be absolved. The conscience is focused on the future; it recognizes the need to heal certain attitudes, but for the sake of the future — although it also sees that wrongs committed in the past need to be rectified. The superego is distinguished by a quick transfer from a deep feeling of guilt to a sense of self-value, as a result of confessing the guilt to some figure that is an authority. Conscience generates a feeling of gradual spiritual growth that encompasses all dimensions of personal maturity. The feeling of guilt in the superego is more dependent on the rank of the authority figure and the way he expresses disapproval than on the merit of the issue, whereas conscience experiences a feeling of guilt that is proportionate to the weight of the value that had been violated, even if the authority figure may have never mentioned it.[117]

The superego, which is an unhealthy feeling of guilt, takes away freedom, keeps one in the grip of immaturity, and prevents the development of responsibility. We are supposed to be free, self-determining people who base their decisions on confidence in oneself and sound judgment, taking into account principles that have been consciously and internally adopted. It is not always possible to evaluate the evil or goodness of an act on the basis of the presence or intensity of a feeling of guilt. Sometimes this feeling is completely absent. Take, for example, the realm of "bad, dirty thoughts." Many people immediately associate them with the sexual sphere, as if this sphere were the worst. This is because, due to their defective upbringing, they experience the greatest guilt in this area. Meanwhile, a sexual thought does not always have to be sinful. God has given us sexuality, which appears in the consciousness and this willed by the Creator. How much more a "dirty thought" is the vision of God as a terrible Judge, Who is just waiting to punish us. Such a perspective is certainly false and quite inconsistent with the image of the merciful Father that Christ gives us in the parable

---

[117] John W. Glaser, "Conscience and Superego: A Key Distinction", *Theological Studies* 32 (1971): 30–47.

of the prodigal son. Should we not feel guilty when we attribute to God qualities that are not His; perhaps taken straight from the image of our own strict father or a bitter, stubborn catechist from our childhood? Those who were once authority figures for us may linger in our emotional reactions for years, stifling the development of the personality, preventing the forming of a healthy conscience, or even distorting it.

When the superego takes over the function of conscience, it usually causes theological distortions. The emotional reaction then does not match the content expressed in the dogmatic formula. It is necessary to study revelation, to get to know Jesus Christ, to recognize His actions in one's own life, to look for traces of His grace. Intimacy with the Savior is the best means of healing flawed emotional reactions because Christ liberates the conscience from the clutches of the superego.

It is good, therefore, to check the image vision of God that we have and compare it with revelation. Is God really a merciful Father in our perception? Do we think of Him primarily as a kind, loving Father to Whom we can call out, "Abba" — "Father," or rather "Daddy"? Or is He instead perceived as a guardian of perfection, all the more threatening because He is all-seeing and all-punishing? If that is the case, then such a God has become an idol that deserves to perish.

Let us note how Christ treats sinners: the woman caught in adultery, the good thief, and the Samaritan woman at the well. Christ loves us whole, together with our bodies, male or female, together with our sexuality and everything that constitutes our "self." He wants us to be transformed by grace — but as free, authentically loving men or women — and not as well-programmed robots, stripped of their own wealth. This is why Christ first affirms the basic goodness of the sinner; He shows him that He is convinced of his goodness. He does not allow the feeling of guilt to be paralyzing. We know that we are sinners, but that is why He has loved us. Christ's conviction of our fundamental goodness is not just a theoretical assumption, but it is reflected in His emotions. The pattern is always the same with Christ: He first recognizes the goodness of the sinner and makes it felt; He shows the sinner his worth. Then He heals the body and the soul, and only at the end does He say, "Go, and sin no more!" This order is important.

Christ does not start by enforcing the moral law; He starts by affirming the goodness of the sinner, and this affirmation is reflected in His personality. This is what His mercy is all about. Christ does not manipulate our feeling of guilt. He does not threaten to deprive us of His kindness. He finds greater joy in granting us His forgiveness than in receiving homage from us. After all, He said, "It is more blessed to give than to receive" (Acts 20:35), and He was talking about Himself. The image of God that we have in Christ should not paralyze us the second we fall into sin. On the contrary, a healthy feeling of guilt brings us back into God's embrace with a renewed trust. Peter's feeling of guilt cleansed him of pride and refined his love for Jesus. Judas's feeling of guilt drove him to the tree because it was self-centered. Deep down, Judas remained a Pharisee impervious to charity.

The encounter of our misery with the merciful Jesus transpires most fully within the Sacrament of Reconciliation. And this is exactly how this sacrament should be described. The traditional term *Confession* is misleading because it emphasizes the confessing of sins, as if that were most important. Meanwhile, the essence of the sacrament is the celebration of divine mercy. The priest is a minister of divine mercy, which is transmitted "from generation to generation" (Luke 1:50). The penitent comes to rejoice with the priest in the goodness of Christ, Who humbles Himself, Who sits lower than we do and washes our feet. Delight in God's humility should captivate us emotionally more than the feeling of guilt caused by our transgressions.

I have the impression that many of our penitents who come to Confession regularly are not aware of this. They do not come to rejoice in God's goodness; they come because they are tormented by bad feelings, and they want to confess them to an authority figure, and they leave feeling reassured for a certain time. In this, they make a firm purpose of amendment — but this resolution is grounded exclusively in their own strength. They do not walk away with the realization that it is God's grace that makes the purpose of amendment possible, that Christ is the One to Whom the moral successes are to be credited. Confession is then only a mirror in which the penitent looks at himself and decides to change, and Christ is completely absent in this perspective. Such a confession is practically pagan. It is intended only to make a person feel better.

And what is it that makes a person feel bad? Most often it is the things that were severely stigmatized in childhood, which are completely trivial for an adult. And so, adults confess trivial matters: that they did not listen to Mom, that they smoked cigarettes, forgot to say their prayers, and so on. They do not, however, go deeper into their lives, their relationship with God and their neighbors. They fail to confess their focus on evil, their suspicion devoid of hope, their sense of entitlement, their irresponsibility, and their pride — that is, their self-sufficiency before God.

Every infantile confession of an adult aggravates the neurotic feeling of guilt, because it stems not from an honest examination of conscience and from giving God an opportunity to grant His grace gladly but from a feeling of the superego. An adult who thinks that Confession is primarily about confessing disobedience to his parents or other childhood infidelities or that it is about the periodic placating of a punishing God in the hope that it will finally make him feel better does not attain maturity and learn responsibility, and so he becomes a psychic wreck, incapable of independent management of his own life and that of his family. And when life forces a person to become independent — when, for example, the husband or the wife expects a break of the psychological dependence on in-laws — the infantile feeling of guilt will keeps the individual chained and enslaved. The reduction of the Sacrament of Reconciliation to a relic from childhood effectively often leads to its complete abandonment. This does not necessarily bring Christian maturity. Sometimes it reinforces a profound lack of responsibility for oneself and for others, selfishness, resentment toward the world, an entitled expectation that others will carry the consequences of one's own mistakes in life, and generally a shallow life. Meanwhile, "for freedom Christ has set us free" (Gal. 5:1). "You will know the truth" — that is, you will use reason to discern who you are, what you are really striving for, what you really care about, and Who your Savior is, and you will not be guided by mere feeling — "and the truth will make you free" (John 8:32).

The French Jesuit who wrote religious songs, Fr. Aimé Duval, shortly before his death confessed how an external manipulation of his feeling of guilt drove him to addiction:

I came from a poor and humble background. But instead of telling me, "You are the son of a peasant, be proud of it; you have received the calling of Jesus Christ, so go and preach the Gospel!," the superior tried to humiliate me even more, forcing me, for example, to kneel before the entire community for walking too fast in the hallway or for looking around suspiciously. For such foolishness, for such trifles he spoke from the height of God's authority! Well, first there is fear, followed by distrust. After distrust comes escape. After escape comes an even greater distrust, until it leads to escape into alcohol.[118]

---

[118] Aimé Duval, S.J., "Biedne zwierzę, które jest w nas [The poor animal that is in us]," interview with Claude Coure, *Powściągliwość i Praca* (February-March 1985): 5.

8

Integrating the Emotions into Moral Life

The cult of emotions

WE LIVE IN A WORLD that values the expression of emotions. People want to experience their feelings both individually and as a crowd, where no effort is needed to build human connections. Whether it is a crowd watching a soccer game, a love parade in Berlin, a crowd attending a rock concert, or young people at a world meeting with the pope, people enjoy being in large gatherings. They enjoy the experience of being absorbed into the crowd's mood. The issue that draws the people is less important. What matters is the experience of rapture, as in dancing, in which now there is no human contact, no dialogue, no flirting, no making friends. There is only the motion of the body and emotions following the rhythm of the deafening noise. Is this something good or bad?

On the one hand, maybe it is a good thing; maybe there is some enrichment in this because, in a society built on technology, rationalism, and the laws of economics, people are feeling lonely and lost, so they respond by demanding passion and emotions. We are finding out today that man is not just a *Homo sapiens*. A certain rehabilitation of the emotions is taking place. They are no longer seen as just a biological obstacle that interferes with the functioning of the reason and the will. Today, the importance of emotional intelligence is emphasized. The functioning of emotions affects the functioning of the mind. Intelligence demands a balanced emotional life. We are also a *Homo sentiens*. The recognition of the value of the emotional sphere is a positive fact.

But on the other hand, there is something deeply unsettling about the cult of emotions that we see today.[119] It seems that what is now cherished is the mere power of sensation, rather than a lasting emotion or a committed attachment to values. When we look back to nineteenth-century Romantic literature, which emerged after the rationalism of the Enlightenment, the characters in the novels experienced emotions that were vehicles for values. Sentiments were described, with all the colorful and, at times, painful aspects of love, sorrow, passion, concern, hope, overwhelming joy, or tragic tears, but this always served the purpose of expressing values such as service, patriotism, loyalty, solicitude for others, and authenticity in interpersonal relationships. Romanticism demonstrated that these virtues are not just cold decisions of the reason or the will; they need the bodily and sentimental contribution provided by the person's emotional sphere.

Today we observe the exaltation of emotional sensation, but without a moral or virtuous component. The sensation itself is being sought, the excitement or gratification that the emotion provides. It is just about the cry, the stir, the sensation, without any reference to values. The cry-inducing shock of a sensation is valued more than the contemplative feeling that elicits a sigh. Contemporary cinema and, even more so, the ubiquitous commercials focus on experience itself. "Buy this cell phone, and you will be moved to tears!" "Buy this new kind of yogurt, and your kids will squeal with joy!" "Buy this cream, and your soft skin will feel voluptuous!" "See this thriller, and it will really scare you!" It seems that people today need their emotions to be aroused, excited, stimulated so as to experience more and more sensations, new surprises and experiences, which may sometimes border on hysteria and may be completely artificial. Violence, shouting, blaring music, and extreme risks seem to be all the rage. It matters little whether sexual experiences are linked to real human bonds or whether they are stimulated by pornography or by Viagra, if pornography no longer works. The important thing is to feel their power. The emotion, as it is experienced, is severed from the deeper foundation of values, true relationships, authentic choices, or concern for others. The emotional sensation itself is treasured. But this

---

[119] Michel Lacroix, *Le culte de l'émotion* (Paris: Flammarion, 2001).

emotion has no depth; it is shallow. It is a lie, because it pretends to express something, whereas, in reality, it does not deliver any content, and as such, it does not offer satisfaction. And that is why it has to be stimulated, if only artificially — because it leaves an insatiable hunger. And so the pursuit of emotional sensations continues to lead to increasingly strong experiences, to extreme sports, new thrills, and drugs. Emotional life seems to be centered on movement rather than on focus, on action rather than on contemplation. It is concentrated on the physiological sensation of feeling, rather than on cordiality, which adds a warm, human dimension to ties built upon values.

After such extreme stimulation of the emotions in the name of shallow sensations that are dull in their banality, will we be able to be touched by simple yet genuine experiences? Can a child's smile, a mountain landscape, the beauty of a poem, the smell of a flower, or the joy of having dinner with friends still move us? Are such simple experiences that involve real, authentic values capable of touching us, or do they leave us with a feeling of indifference, because the emotions have been used so much and have been exhausted to the point that they are unable to react when they come into contact with something that is real and valuable? People are moved by strong sensations, but are they capable of feeling? Can they be moved by real sentiments that mean something? Are sensation seekers really human? We are witnessing a real cult of sensation and strong emotions, and these feelings are idolized. And every idol, because it is an idol, destroys the one who worships it.

In the light of the global social, political, and economic changes, people feel powerless. It seems to them that they can do nothing. We can see that people have lost their zeal "for a cause," for service in the name of an idea. Ideologies, trade unions, political parties, local associations, scouting — all these types of movements are dying out. People are no longer attracted to nationalism or class struggle. They are less and less ready to devote their time, service, minds, and choices to public affairs. Since it appears in advance that their efforts are doomed to failure, people turn to themselves. This is a turn not toward the inner life — that is, spiritual life, which is an encounter with Another, with God. It is a turn toward the experience of being moved, the experience of emotions. Just as a drug addict escapes into his drug fantasy, so many people escape into sensations. Taking enjoyable vacations and spending money seem to be the goal. Since wars today are remote and require specialized armies, the average person who, in the past, would have to defend his homeland, developing patriotism and courage, today tries bungee jumping. Extreme sports are a way to compensate for a life that has become dull. They are not only an escape from oneself, from one's own boredom. Devoid of any values, they are a quest for the self, a quest for a substitute sensation of existing, of experiencing something, of being the center of one's own attention. Emotions are experienced as self-worship. In themselves, the emotions are self-centered, but they lose their egocentrism when they are linked to a moral value, embraced in a personal choice. Emotions without value are deceptive because they claim to be true, while they are only true on a shallow level because they have lost contact with the spiritual dimension of the personality, where one adheres to truth and goodness.

Not that long ago, psychology as well as ethics were often characterized by a certain stoic distrust of emotions. The emotions seemed to be a threat because they led into the unknown and carried one beyond self-control. Now it is held that emotions have supreme value, that they are a way to express oneself and ostensibly to develop one's personality. The cult of emotions is associated with anti-intellectualism, which displaces the intellect. Certain trends in psychology promote the cult of the emotions: "Lose yourself; go to the level of the senses!" The influence of the left part of the brain, which is said to be analytical and logical, is to be replaced by the influence of the right part, which is more intuitive, emotional, and artistic. The West supposedly cultivated the development of the left part of the brain, while Asia cultivated the right part. It is hard to say whether these claims have a neurological foundation or are just mythical, but they communicate an escape from reflection and contemplative knowledge.

What is the place of self-knowledge and self-analysis in a world that cultivates emotional sensation? In Descartes's philosophy, the starting point was rational self-reflection. Descartes noted that he was thinking, that there was self-reflection in him, and this reflection led him to the certainty of cognition. In the cult of emotions, there is no self-reflection, no self-knowledge, and no analysis of one's own thoughts, beliefs, decisions, or actions. Turning to the self is concentrated on impressions, feelings, and sensations. More than

"I think, therefore I am," it is "I feel that I feel, therefore I am." The focus is on the exclusively pleasant experience of sensations. And what will happen when the experience of feeling is longer pleasant, when it becomes depressing in its dullness? There is a simple solution. Take a drug, big or small, that will restore that temporary but pleasant feeling! The Stoics of ancient philosophy treated emotions with suspicion, suggesting that one should not be moved by them. They believed that one should be cool, like a marble statue, because only then is a person mature. Biblical teaching and St. Thomas Aquinas rejected this approach because they saw it as inhuman. Elements of Stoic thinking, however, have infiltrated into Christian asceticism. Today, we can see that it is common to fall into the other extreme, although it does not place equal emphasis on all emotions. The emotion that is controlled the most is anger. A politician who displays his anger will be stigmatized as a fanatic. In professional life, anger should never be exhibited. Similarly, grief is concealed. External signs of mourning, which used to be part of culture, have disappeared. Widows no longer dress in black, which used to be the rule. Certain emotional reactions are denied, while others are exposed. In those cultures where there was a strong repression of sexuality, it has now become almost public. Sadness and mourning have become more taboo than sexuality.

In some religious currents advocating meditation and contemplation (these words have become fashionable again), the emphasis is on the experience itself. This is about the hedonistic search for rare, pure inner pleasures attainable through meditation, but not through the knowledge of truth, which would be binding due to its reality, or through an encounter with a personal God Who could make demands, Who must be worshipped, respected, thanked, and served. An understanding of meditation and contemplation revolving around sensation is egocentric. It does not foster the ability to love truly and, instead, leads to egoism. Claude Vorilhon, the founder of the Raëlian sect (which seeks to clone humans), proposes a sensual meditation designed to produce a "cosmic orgasm." This is an attempt to overcome the shallowness of emotional life — devoid of meaning and satisfaction — through an even more powerful sensation that will still be hedonistic and centered on self-satisfaction.

Are we not seeing a similar shift in attitudes toward emotional experiences in religiosity? Both in sects and church movements, there is a turn toward religious experience. Instead of placing an emphasis on churches, catechisms, and creeds, or community service undertaken in the name of the gospel, many movements seem to provide primarily religious experiences. The devotional practices of these movements emphasize the moving of the body in prayer, extended communal celebrations, displays of enthusiasm, and extraordinary states of consciousness. Should faith not be rooted in something more solid than the quicksand of sentimentalism? Should it not have its fundamental place in thinking, in study, in free choice, in decision-making, in perseverance, and in a generosity capable of sacrifice that may lack enthusiasm and passion? Is there a place for faith in normal rather than in excited states of consciousness and conscience?

Historians of culture have observed that the modern world struggles with the realm of emotions. The Middle Ages were much more humane in this respect. St. Dominic was remembered as a man who had a warm, humane personality. Before his death, he confessed that he found it more pleasant to talk to young women than to older ones. Many years after his death, the nuns he used to visit would recall details of his physique, his personality, and his friendly sharing of wine with them. The friars reminisced that St. Dominic would cover them with a blanket at night if they kicked it off in their sleep. Is there not a connection between contemporary affective difficulties and the kind of moral theology that was taught in the Church? Did not the overemphasis on moral obligation, dominant in the modern centuries, cause a deformation in the affective sphere? In the Middle Ages, there was more room for laughter, for hatred and anger, for sadness, and for sexuality. The explosion of the cult of emotions today is a reaction to the suppression of the emotional sphere that had been dominant in the Western culture for centuries.

In Victorian upbringing, which left a great mark on Protestant countries, the expression of the emotions was questioned. Emotions had to be hidden, pushed into the subconscious, in the name of outward elegant behavior. Manuals of etiquette recommended that one should not laugh too much, not display too much enthusiasm, but instead should maintain a polite, cold gentleness. This created an impression of psychological tension. In the second half of the twentieth century, expressions of affection started to be praised. Conversely, nowadays in the twenty-first century, because of the sex scandals in the Church, dioceses and religious orders in the United States are introducing strict codes of conduct. Altar servers are not allowed to vest in the sacristy; they are supposed to do it in front of the whole congregation, since they cannot be alone with the priest. Teachers, when they are applying a Band-Aid to the scraped knee of a crying child, must do so in such a way that they do not accidentally touch the knee, and they absolutely must not hug the child. The rules that are being imposed now are stricter than those that our great-grandmothers knew! Some fear that this icy coldness and this manner of approaching people marked by fear, which is becoming mandatory today, will damage the Church in the United States much more than the sexual abuse. Fortunately, Pope Francis is not concerned with such restrictions. He kisses and hugs children and the sick (but never young women!). He remembers that Jesus rejoiced when children came to Him. He laid His hands on them and blessed. Is not the world moving from one extreme to the other because it has no idea how to deal with the emotional sphere?

A lack of emotional maturity may manifest itself in emotional outbursts, anger, sexual arousal, or depression or sadness. Emotionally immature people who are insecure about their own self-worth easily fall into the pitfalls of emotional manipulation of others when they become overly dependent on parents, religious leaders, friends, or other dominant figures. The fear of losing a friend, of losing the emotional affirmation that comes from a prominent individual, leads to an abandonment of values and the dimming of the light of the conscience in the name of preserving the dependence that provides a sense of security. The inability to hold on to the judgment of conscience is often due to the fact that the emotional context of this judgment becomes decisive even though it is not an essential component of conscience. Action is then guided by the mood — good or bad as it may be — rather than by the light of reason. If this is accompanied by uncertainty about the spiritual life or ignorance of theological principles, manipulative situations can become even worse. The Dominican tradition, which clearly distinguishes between the interior life and the contact with one's confessor and governance in communities, aims to preserve inner freedom. The unity of the faith allows for differences of opinion and their expression in communities and in communal decision-making. When these rules are not observed and when that which belongs to the internal forum is confused with that which belongs to the external forum, then manipulations happen. The emotional life is as fragile as the spiritual life. It needs wise guidance along with clear and sound rules so that it does not become distorted.

Psychic difficulties arise from the repression into the subconscious of the emotions, which should have their rightful place in the personality, albeit under the guidance of the spiritual powers. When sexuality is viewed as a threat and is repressed, it is very difficult to live a pure and mature life. But the recognition of emotional repression by Freud led to the model of a society without moral restrictions. A genuine human emotionality is natural, unforced, but it is not left completely unrestrained. In normal psychic states, there has to be a place for the emotional sphere. Emotion, without being an idol, has the right to manifest itself in human relationships, in friendship, and in cordiality.

What was lacking in the inherited tradition of life and religiosity that such fluctuations in the treatment of feelings are now evident? Was not the traditional Catholic formation too rational, too dry and excessively focused on memorizing formulas, with insufficient room for joy, for the celebration of fraternity and friendship? Did not the religious symbols that in the past evoked religious feelings (the beauty of the liturgy, Marian devotion, pilgrimages, shrines, Baroque art) become devalued, and when they were rejected, was it not that nothing new was produced in their place? Was not the religious bond excessively obedience-based, without sufficient room in it for friendship, for human relationships? Perhaps these issues did not overly affect laypeople, who were living their own lives, but what was the emotional life of the clergy, religious, male and female, or students in schools or orphanages run by religious orders? Was it not that the atmosphere there was at times inhumane? Did the sexual abuses of the clergy, which are now being openly mentioned in a growing number of countries (although obviously they were not a mass phenomenon anywhere) not happen, above all, among those whose seminary or religious formation was too rigid, too voluntaristic, too lacking in humanity? When emotions are suppressed, they emerge in a distorted form. Was there room in the formation of religious and seminarians for the development of supernatural love, which first and foremost is a friendship with God and then a friendship with others for God's sake? Or rather, was the formation not built on obligation, obedience, and rigid reverence, coupled with the fear, as used to be said, of "particular friendships"? Was it sufficient to say that the human need for cordiality could be satisfied through devotion to Our Lady, when, at the same time, concern for people and friendly relationships in communities were missing? Deficiencies in the affective climate in church institutions are probably one of the reasons for the crash of vocations in many religious orders and seminaries. Today, whenever there is a rise in vocations, most young people entering religious orders are, above all, looking for a vibrant, authentic community life. And if they discover that the community life in the order is flawed and nonauthentic, they immediately leave, or even worse, they stay and seek affective satisfaction outside of the religious community, which should be their proper home.

What should we think about all this? How can we strike a balance between the exaggerated emphasis on emotional sensations and the negation of feelings? How should emotions be integrated into a healthy personality centered on true values, service, and virtue? How much room is there for emotional expression, and to what extent are emotions to be hidden in a mature personality? Is a harmonious integration of the emotional sphere with the spiritual powers possible, or are these two spheres bound to be in perpetual conflict? Do the virtues of temperance and fortitude reside in the emotions, or do they reside in the will, which dominates the emotions with its power? What part does human effort play in directing emotions, and what is the role of grace? Do we need God's supernatural help in caring for the emotional realm, or can we manage on our own? When emotional difficulties arise, do we need the help of a psychologist or a psychiatrist, or is it enough to pray and see a spiritual director? How far does our moral responsibility extend? Are we morally responsible for our emotions, or are they outside the realm of morality, being spontaneous and natural? How does one distinguish between wholesome control over one's emotions and neurotic control? Does the Christian vocation call us to be responsible but cold and without emotions? Or are emotions supposed to stir us and direct us into the unknown? If they are to stir us, how far should that go? Can a moralist provide a theoretical answer here, or are these matters to be worked out by trial and error as we go through life?

It seems that these questions have not been sufficiently addressed in the Church and that a serious psychological, philosophical, and theological reflection on the subject is missing. Or rather, it should be said that there was a time when these issues were reflected upon in the Church, but this medieval tradition has been forgotten and should be revived. Just as we have received the important encyclical *Fides et ratio*, providing us with a theology of cognition, in which St. John Paul II, starting from the mystery of the Faith, invites the philosophizing mind not to stop but to reach out further into the depths of truth, similarly, we need a study of *Fides et passio*, which would present the principles of the encounter between the supernatural life and the emotions. A serious reflection and robust profound theological study must be undertaken to revive this forgotten tradition. A precise grasp of its principles and a liberation from distrust of the affective sphere are needed so that, directed by grace, Christian life may acquire its full luster. Emotional maturity is not attained easily. The integration of affectivity into the moral life requires patience, wisdom, self-humility, a deep respect toward the goodness of our being in all its aspects, and, above all, a practical initiation into the spiritual life. Only when one affirms the ontological goodness of feelings in their natural proper orientation will the spiritual powers, open to supernatural support, be able to guide them.

The emotions of God made man

The Gospels show us Jesus as a fully humane, sensitive person, capable of warmth, joy, emotions, and tears. Although nowhere are we informed that Jesus laughed, we should not think that His joy was without a smile on His face. When we read in *Gaudium et spes* that Jesus "worked with human hands, He thought with a human mind, acted by human choice and loved with a human heart" (22), we are presented with a living person in all aspects. Moreover, although the Council is using the past tense here, our belief in the Resurrection means that Jesus continues to enjoy the fullness of humanity.

God so loves man that, for all eternity, He wanted to be human. The devotion to the Sacred Heart of Jesus and also the use in prayer of the image painted at the behest of St. Faustina Kowalska remind us that the gift of grace is given to us through the glorified humanity of Jesus. All that belongs to humanity, including corporality, the whole range of emotions, fascination, commitment, or sorrow, is an integral part of Christ even today. Receiving Him in the Eucharist, we receive not only His divinity but also His humanity. By forming a relationship with Him through faith and love, we reach the divinity through His human heart and emotions.

Coming to this conclusion took the Church centuries. The councils of antiquity clarified the doctrine of the simultaneous full divinity and humanity of Jesus. In Him, the two natures are found in one Person. In the seventh century, St. Maximus the Confessor defended the further conclusion that in Jesus there are simultaneously two wills, divine and human. Jesus' humanity is not fictitious; His personal human choices are not dwarfed by the power of His divinity. In the Middle Ages, theological reflection went even further. St. Thomas Aquinas, arguing against the position of St. Hilary of Poitiers, defended the authenticity of Jesus' emotions. St. Hilary held that Jesus' human emotions were somewhat anesthetized by His divinity. St. Thomas, although he did not venture to deliberate on all the emotions of Jesus one by one, nevertheless defended the claim that the full humanity of Jesus must encompass the whole range of emotions that are genuine and uninhibited,[120] even though they operate differently in Him than they do in us. As a result of Original Sin, emotions frequently steer us toward evil acts. They sometimes anticipate the judgment of reason, thereby coloring and distorting our thinking. Jesus' feelings are not tainted by this disorder, because He is free from Original Sin, and this increases rather than decreases His sensitivity.[121] (A

---

[120] Paul Gondreau, *The Passions of Christ's Soul in the Theology of St. Thomas Aquinas* (Muenster: Aschendorff, 2002).

[121] *ST*, IIIa, q. 15, art. 4: "Note however that these emotions were not quite the same in Christ as in us, on three counts. Firstly, as regards their object: in us, more often than not, these emotions reach out to things that are not lawful — which was not the case with Christ. Secondly, in their origin: in us these emotions often anticipate the judgment of reason, but in Christ all the

sensitive person is pained to perceive that someone else has been wronged. A thick-skinned, insensitive person does not care about the sorrow of others because he fails to notice it.)

The meditation of the fully integrated personality of Jesus, in which everything is in its proper place, helps us to understand in what lies our own fully integrated personality. We can try to specify psychic balance and health through sociological and psychological studies, but the end of such an enquiry will be the cognition of what people deem to be psychic health, or in which moods and attitudes people feel best. Such studies cannot grasp the fullness of humanity. Only Christology allows for a precise formulation of theological anthropology that explains humanity. That is why the Church has taken such a long time to clarify precisely the dogmatic teaching about Christ, God made man. At the core of these reflections lay the search for an answer to the questions of who man is and how the encounter of the natural psychic and spiritual powers with the supernatural gift of grace takes place in him.

The encounter between grace and the sphere of emotions

The raising this question as part of the study of Christian morality is crucial. If we are looking for God's fecundity in human actions, we must consider how this divine fruitfulness manifests itself in the human personality and how it integrates and orders it. It is true that psychic equilibrium is not the end of either the spiritual or the moral life. If somebody were only to seek psychic maturity, then such an individual would constantly remain stuck in being concerned about the self. The essence of the Christian life consists in transcending oneself, in reaching out toward God, and then, as a consequence of loving God, in reaching out toward neighbors whom one is called to serve. The concentration on oneself blocks the development of the spiritual life because such a person makes an idol of himself. One should not, therefore, be concerned exclusively with the analysis one's psychic states, even when

---

impulses of the sense appetite arose under the control of reason.... Thirdly, in their effect: sometimes in us these feelings do not confine themselves to the sense appetite but take reason in tow. This did not happen in Christ" (trans. L. G. Walsh, vol. 49, 1974).

disorder in the psyche sometimes manifests itself and generates moments of anxiety and confusion. Sanctity consists in the meeting of our own weakness with God's power and love and not in being psychologically composed. One of the main themes of the message of St. Thérèse of Lisieux — which, incidentally, is fully in line with the teachings of St. Paul — is the conviction that we are not to wait until we are morally perfect to enter the path of communion with God. The deification of man by grace does not require pure perfection or full psychic equilibrium; God gives Himself already now, if only one engages in contact with Him, responding with trust and love to the offered mercy. And current moral or psychic imperfections will in time be flushed out on their own, as long as the relationship with God grows in love.

Probably the main reason St. Paul fell in conflict with the Jewish world was his discovery that the moral law is insufficient for salvation. The moral law — both the natural law, and therefore the basic moral intuition of which the Gentiles are capable, since "they show that what the law requires is written on their hearts" (Rom. 2:15), as well as revealed law, which confirms the natural moral intuition with divine authority — in itself is unable to lead man to holiness. If moral teaching is reduced to the presentation of the moral law along with a description of true values, inevitably it will lead to the experience of moral incapability. One is then faced with three possibilities. One option is that of clinging desperately to the moral law with one's strength (while inhibiting one's emotions), which will produce a sense of righteousness and superiority with concomitant frequent lapses that are meticulously concealed. Alternatively, one may despair and hold that it is impossible to live according to the requirements of the moral law, and so there is no point in exerting oneself, and therefore it is best to treat moral teaching as some questionable fiction. Or finally, one may follow the third path, which consists in placing one's hope in Christ. St. Paul very vividly shows the hypocrisy of the Jewish way grounded in the Law: "You then who teach others, will you not teach yourself? While you preach against stealing, do you steal? You who say that one must not commit adultery, do you commit adultery?" (Rom. 2:21–22). And similarly, he points to the despair of the pagan world: "Since they did not see fit to acknowledge God, God gave them up to a base mind and to improper conduct"; "for this reason ... their women exchanged natural relations for unnatural, and the men likewise gave up natural relations with women and were consumed with passion for one another, men committing shameless acts with men and receiving in their own persons the due penalty for their error" (Rom. 1:26–27, 28). Finally, St. Paul shows the prospect of justification accomplished by the power of God. When a person recognizes his moral helplessness and relies on the power of the grace of God Himself, "the righteousness of God has been manifested apart from law ... the righteousness of God through faith in Jesus Christ for all who believe. For there is no distinction; since all have sinned and fall short of the glory of God, they are justified by his grace as a gift, through the redemption which is in Christ Jesus" (Rom. 3:21–24). This redemption in Christ leaves space for the emotions, which, incorporated into supernatural love, do not need to be suppressed rigidly, nor do they run rampant.

St. Paul's description of the hypocrisy of some and the moral despair of others is extremely convincing. It resonates perfectly with our times, since moral teaching that inadequately leads to a true communion with Christ is interpreted by the world as a display of hypocrisy. To many, the Church appears more as a moralistic institution whose task is to denounce all kinds of evil, rather than as the Body of Christ bringing about a liberating spiritual life. That is why we witness the constant interpretation of every Church pronouncement as a condemnation, and the simultaneous pursuit, with ill-disguised schadenfreude, of any evidence of weakness on the part of the people of the Church. Moral failures of the clergy, especially in the sexual sphere, are immediately publicized. At the same time, those same people who express outrage at the misconduct of the clergy often lack the conviction that it is possible to know moral principles and to abide by them. With genuine intellectual despair, they regard skeptically the possibility of recognizing the moral good and they are not perturbed by the ever-deepening moral imbalance and promotion of all kinds of corruption.

The answer to this paradoxical combination of exposing alleged hypocrisy with an actual desperate rejection of moral orientation is not an increase in moralization but an introduction into the genuine justification accomplished by the power of the grace of the Savior Himself. In so doing, justification is not to be reduced to God's merely treating us externally as righteous.

When God justifies, He really makes us just. His grace becomes incarnate in human life, effecting an inner transformation, and making something of His power manifest in it. Therefore, theology has to be confronted with a number of important questions: How is this accomplished? What are the laws of development of grace, not only in the essence of the human soul, but also in corporeality, in feelings, in angry indignation, in sorrow, joy, and in sexuality? If God's fecundity is manifested in human acts, as it is manifested in Christ's incorrupt humanity, which encompasses human emotions, how is it accomplished in our lives, the lives of ordinary people who nevertheless are transformed by grace? What can we know about the interplay of grace with emotions and carnality, and the development of grace in the whole personality? How can this be seen without simultaneously falling into the common mistake of adolescence, where grace is confused for emotions and moods? Emotional sensations are not at the forefront of the spiritual life, and so the intensity of the supernatural life should not be measured by them, but it is also necessary to examine whether and how it may be possible to have such an encounter with the supernatural life that it will radiate throughout the entire personality, and therefore also through the emotions.

Dealing with these theological questions that are at the intersection of ethics and psychology is not easy. The temptation to focus on moralization criticized by St. Paul has always been present in the Church. Whenever the initiation into the supernatural life was missing, with the primacy of theological virtues being forgotten and replaced either by the formation of moral virtues ("First of all be human! Take control over yourself, and the time for mysticism will come later!") or by mere obedience to the commandments, in practice this amounted to the heresy of Pelagianism. Grace was not denied, but it remained an empty external platitude, whereas the moral life was pursued by willpower alone. In theological instruction, the teaching of grace was separated from moral theology and transferred to dogmatic theology, where it was treated in a sterile, speculative way. This meant that moral teaching, devoid of initiation into grace, remained at the level of practical moralization. Overconfidence in natural willpower turned out to be unreliable, and it led to austere rigorism. Practically speaking, this led to the confusion of the will (which is a spiritual power that allows itself to be attracted to the good) with the emotions of the irascible appetite, whose overstimulation led to neurotic reactions. Over time, a healthy psychic reflex sensed that there was some error in this approach, and so some liberation was sought, often leading to the other extreme — despair. In many countries, the rejection of the straitjacket of unhealthy moralization led to a total rejection of the Church and in particular of the Sacrament of Reconciliation.

Unraveling the accrued misrepresentations requires a precise determination of what are the emotions. What is their role, and what is the difference between the healthy integration of the emotions and their unhealthy repression, however well-intentioned?

Emotions are highly delicate. When they harmonize with the choice of the good, they add human expression to the personality and facilitate contact with others. When they are misaligned, they create confusion, and moreover, they become accustomed to reactions from which it is then difficult to liberate oneself. The emotional sphere includes the sexual drive, which has its own powerful dynamics. Since human life is a fundamental good, the sexual drive, oriented toward the transmission of life, engages all the powers with extraordinary force. We may discern multiple levels in the human being: there is the purely corporal, physiological level, the emotional level, the volitional level, the intellectual level, and, in a person immersed in divine life, there is also the supernatural level. At each of these levels of life, there is movement. Where there is life, there is transformation, there is dynamism, there is the reception of sustenance, there is the growth of life or its dying, and there is the tendency to transmit that life. This may be termed the dynamism of the fundamental love — *amor*, which inclines toward giving. The sexual drive seeks to transmit life by begetting offspring. Emotional life draws others into the orbit of one's feelings and moods. The willing of the volitional life directs the free choice to the good, which also triggers in others the capacity for a personal gift. The intellectual life seeks to share the known truth with others. And finally, the spiritual life, which consists in the participation in the fecundity of God Himself, works toward the birth and development of that same supernatural gift in others.

At each of these levels, it is most appropriate that there is movement. A human being is like water in a lake or river. If the water is moving, it is clear.

If the water is stagnant, it becomes putrid. Since the waters of the Dead Sea have no outflow, they have become saline through evaporation, and, as a result, all life has disappeared in it. It is thus normal and desirable that there is movement at every level of human life. The bringing together of all these levels of life does not mean their denial or the suppression of their inherent movement. A peaceful and harmonious integration of the whole is possible, but only when the dynamism of the highest level is developed. The supernatural life given by grace but consciously received, sustained, and nurtured has such an internal potency that it may involve in its movement all the dynamics of the other levels, without repression, without excluding their dynamics introducing suitable order into them at the same time. The deepest integration of the personality occurs when primacy is given to communion with God that comes about through faith and the practical taking up of the call of grace. The highest fecundity of grace manifests itself in spiritual paternity or maternity, which, through human contact with a person trying to lead the spiritual life, generates in the other a fascination with God and also contributes to the development of the divine life.

When the impact of grace within the emotional realm was discussed, classical theology spoke about moral virtues infused by grace that is not acquired through natural human effort. The fact that these infused virtues are not "felt" does not mean that they do not exist. Guided by faith and love toward God, we can rely on divine power. This takes place in the darkness of faith, but it is real and conscious, because trust in God is deliberate. If this trust occurs also in the context of responding to external and internal stimuli, faith lets grace enter specific dimensions of life, and, over time, this causes a real transformation of the entire ethos. The infused virtues are nascent, but they are to be developed consciously, believing in their influence and eliciting their acts. The alignment of the dynamics of the emotions with reason, undertaken within the entrustment, does not ever entail the denial of the power of the emotions. That is why the cardinal virtues of temperance and fortitude and their derivatives are located within the emotions themselves, which cooperate with reason enlightened by faith. Virtue causes the emotions to be restrained on certain occasions and expressed freely on other occasions. A musician playing an instrument will play well only if he allows himself to be carried away by his feelings, and this submission to these feelings is judged by his reason to be proper. Moreover, the virtues do not stop the movement of the emotions toward their proper objects; they only regulate adherence to this movement so that it is not disproportionate. The fact that somebody experiences pleasure in drinking good wine is not a bad thing, and this pleasure may be infinite, resulting from a cultivated taste. The virtue of temperance merely regulates the dispensing of this pleasure, taking into account broader circumstances and considerations. Furthermore, the virtue ensures that the focus is on the proper object of the emotion, as recognized by right reason, and not just on some aspect to which excessive significance would be accorded. Just as, on the natural level, the virtue of prudence or creative resourcefulness provokes the acts of the other virtues, so at the level of grace the virtue of charity infiltrates prudence and, through it, activates the operations of the infused moral virtues.

The impact of grace engaging and transforming the emotional dynamic may be grasped more clearly by considering the important distinction introduced by St. Thomas in his discussion of the virtue of infused chastity. This virtue integrates the sexual desire, ensuring that it is lived out with respect for the human dignity of the other. Chastity safeguards against the isolation and disordered indulging of the urge, but it does not negate the urge as such, since it is natural and therefore good, having its natural finality. Human beings are not structured like the mythical centaur, with the animal part set beside the human part. That which is proper to humans intersects with that which is shared with animals. This integration, however, is not always accomplished seamlessly, and hence there are temptations to grant full autonomy to those forces that are shared with animals, including the sexual desire. Grace infused into the soul heals the entire person, and so the virtue of chastity protects sexuality from being impoverished and deprived of its human dimension. It enables a person to experience the bodily dynamics in a way that corresponds to the natural finality of sexuality, the actual intentions of life, one's own vocation, and the full integral dignity of others. In the conjugal act, chastity accords an appropriate rank to sexual pleasure, so that it will not obscure other deeper values that have to be preserved if love is to be true. The stirrings of sensuality are then affirmed, directed, and elevated to a fully human and simultaneously divine dimension. The virtue of chastity differs from another moral reflex that is not a full virtue and that St. Thomas called *continentia*. Unlike chastity, *continentia* resides in the will and not in the concupiscence itself. This means that when the urge is restrained by the will through this *continentia*, it behaves in exactly the same way as when it is not directed at all.[122] The urge is characterized by a strong impetus, and *continentia* restrains it by sheer willpower, keeping it in check; but under the grip of this spiritual power, the urge continues to spiral out of control on its own. For this reason, St. Thomas does not consider *continentia* a virtue but only an emergency defense mechanism, useful in situations of sudden danger but not actually conducive to psychosexual equilibrium. The difference between the virtue of chastity and *continentia* stems from the fact that chastity moderates the drive, which then is inclined from within and by itself by means of a permanent capacity toward the recognized true good,[123] while *continentia* sets itself in resistance to the drive, coming to it from without — that is, from the will. The one who employs *continentia* appeals to his reason, and this reason then triggers the will, which restrains the drive, but the sexual appetite continues to rebel, resisting the reason and the will, although temporarily, willy-nilly, it surrenders to it.[124] In contrast, when the drive is directed virtuously, it is permanently, as it were, domesticated in the light of reason and cooperates with it willingly. The virtue of chastity

---

[122] *ST*, IIa-IIae, q. 155, art. 3: "Now the desirous sensory appetite has the same disposition both in a continent and an incontinent person; with each it breaks out into strong and unruly desires. Clearly, then, the desireous sensory appetite is not the seat of continence.... Continence must needs dwell in that faculty of the soul of which the act is choice. And this, as we have shown, is the will" (trans. T. Gilby, vol. 44, 1972).

[123] *ST*, IIa-IIae, q. 155, art. 4, ad 3: "Hence the values of being reasonable, for which virtues are admirable, are more amply displayed when they reach past the will to the emotions, as in the temperate man, than when they stay with the will, as in the continent man" (trans. T. Gilby, vol. 44, 1972).

[124] *ST*, IIa-IIae, q. 155, art. 4: "Now intelligence burgeons more in the temperate than in the continent, because by temperance the sensory appetite itself is subordinated and as it were wholly possessed by mind, whereas with continence its low desires remain rebellious" (trans. T. Gilby, vol. 44, 1972).

is an expression of the full cooperation from within of the sexual drive with reason. Thanks to the virtue infused by grace, the drive within the conjugal act expresses the highest kind of love, that love which God plants in the human heart. This love is responsible, consonant with the nature of the drive and therefore open to the gift of life, and free from selfishness.

Recognizing the essence of the interaction of bodily sensuality with grace is extremely important. For there are people who desperately implore God, begging for His help in regulating their sexual sphere, but do not trust their urge, do not recognize it as a good, and they constantly apply *continentia* against it. As a result, they do not grow in the virtue of chastity and in psychosexual freedom. They constantly apply the brake, and as soon as they experience the urge, they immediately activate the prohibitive will, failing to acquire balance, even if this is accompanied by fervent prayer. They lack the initiation into the virtue of chastity, which demands a different psychic mechanism involving not only a rational but also an emotional recognition of the fundamental goodness of sexuality, along with a responsible loving steering of this urge in a way that considers its nature and does not prune anything out of it. Whenever the procreative finality is excluded from sexuality, even if only mentally, stopping solely at the moment of sensation, the isolation of only this aspect attributes to it an exaggerated importance that is impossible to satiate, and this makes the integration of sexuality through chastity difficult. Chastity includes respect for the potential parenthood of oneself and the other person. Also, those who are unmarried or celibate have to affirm the full goodness and finality of sexuality, with its procreative purpose, in order for the virtue of chastity to guide from within their drive. A moral upbringing that fails to distinguish the various psychological mechanisms at play will turn out to be flawed and deficient. A lack of clarity in this sphere, and, even more, a lack of the step-by-step initiation into the virtuous life flowing from grace that allows one to depend on God and not just on the power of one's own will, is the root cause of many of life's difficulties.

Continentia is not a permanent element of the supernatural organism functioning in the soul, which is composed of the theological and moral virtues infused by grace and the gifts of the Holy Spirit. *Continentia* serves as a substitute in moments of emergency, thereby protecting against sin, and that is why St. Thomas mentioned it, but moral maturity, in keeping with the image of God that is elicited in man and gives psychosexual balance, needs more than that. It requires, above all, "faith working through love" (Gal. 5:6), and that, for its authenticity, necessitates the virtue of chastity in the sexual sphere. Since St. Thomas was focused on the good and he primarily described the fecundity of grace working throughout the human psyche and ethos, he mainly dealt with the virtues, and that is why he did not mention in his moral theology yet another mental mechanism that also occurs, maybe more so nowadays than in his times, which is like a lower extension of the mechanism that he termed *continentia*. This is a neurotic attempt to control the sexuality purely by emotional force. When this is not just a sudden temporary endeavor but a permanent way of dealing with the power of unwanted emotions, it does not lead to a psychosexual balance but leads instead to emotional disorders that have nothing to do with virtue and generate a psychic ground for various perversions. As the interface between grace and the emotional sphere is described precisely, it is necessary to distinguish three possible and entirely different psychological mechanisms: (1) the moral virtues infused by grace, located in the emotions themselves; (2) the occasional application of the quasi-virtue of *continentia*, located in the will rather than in the emotions, which remain unabsorbed by the dynamism of grace; and (3) the neurotic attempt to exclude certain emotions through the power of other emotions.

The experience of the Church shows what a great treasure it is to integrate the dynamism of the entire bodily-emotional endowment with the spiritual life. Multiple extant sources that have allowed the study of the personality of St. Thérèse of Lisieux show that the development of the spiritual life — that is, communing with God through faith and love — was so advanced in her while she was still a child that, when she entered puberty, she did not experience the mental and emotional turmoil that usually accompanies this stage. This does not mean that she did not have a sex drive. But the power of grace turned out to be so deeply rooted in her personality that the integration of the drive took place calmly and without problems. Thus, her charming femininity and sensitivity, united with recurring acts of generosity undertaken out of the love for God blossomed in a wonderful way in her into spiritual motherhood. The lack of arousal of the sexual desire in chaste virginity is cherished in the Church, not out of some Manichaean notion about the sordid nature of sexuality but due to the fact that it facilitates the preservation of the orientation toward God. This does not mean that the development of the spiritual life is impossible in those who have a history of sexual experiences, whether integrated into sacrificial love as in marriage or lived out in selfish and manipulative ways. The example of the Samaritan woman who talked to Jesus at the well is a reminder that God may be found even after a turbulent sexual life. But an inappropriate stimulation of sexuality and the emotional life results in the development of habits that take root in the psyche, and then it is difficult to break free from them. These habits may become a real obstacle to the spiritual life.

The absence of a favorable atmosphere where emotional life can develop and find its proper place in the personality leads to wounds, and this creates fertile ground for the development of addictions and sexual deviations. Whether it be an addiction to alcoholism or drugs, or any other addiction, including a clinging dependence on a single person due to a lack of self-reliance and personal courage, this stems most often from an underdeveloped or distorted emotional life. Similarly, a neurotic approach to sexuality makes it fertile ground for degenerations, including that of homosexuality. The restoring of trust in feelings and their harmonization with the spiritual and supernatural life allows one to break free from such addictions and to integrate sexuality into a mature life, in which any potential inclinations to misuse sexuality selfishly will be corrected by the dynamics of charity oriented toward the true good. Whatever may be the causes of homosexuality or other sexual deviations, which may originate in a somatic condition or have been acquired as a result of initiation and an overload of external stimuli, the Church believes that divine grace is powerful enough to allow for a life of chastity. The assimilation of grace, however, requires, as it were, "letting it into" all the spheres of the personality, including the emotional life. Neurotic disorders, resulting from a distrust of the emotions, make the process of liberation extremely difficult, because a mechanism of natural self-defense is developed, in which there is no place for grace. The undoing of these habituations takes time, patience, and trust in God, which does not allow for a spiritual paralysis induced by chronic guilt.

The prime stress placed on obligation that was prevalent in modern moral theology introduced a distrust of the emotional sphere. When the main emphasis was placed on obedience to the law rather than on the life of grace, the feelings that carry a person, unleash fascination, and drive toward that which is beautiful and good appeared as a threat. The equating of moral rectitude with stoic insensitivity led to distortions. These excesses appeared not only in Catholic theology. They were even more pronounced in traditions originating from the Reformation. The setting of human causality in a rival position in respect to divine causality led to the negation of the possibility of the operation of grace within the human personality, its actions, and its choices. Since there was no place for sacramentality or infused virtues, the only response to disorder in concupiscence had to be rigorism. Over time, the Puritanism of the Protestant world, which lacked the imagination and splendor of the Baroque, led to harsh reactions. Today, in those countries in which there used to prevail a cold distrust of feelings and of sexuality and where moral formation was extremely obligation-oriented, the sexual revolution with all its dysfunctions is most apparent. On the one hand, there is concern for the affirmation of friendships, including friendships between people of the same sex, which are immediately given a sexual context; and on the other hand, all emotional contacts are viewed with malicious suspicion. Confusion caused by the distrust of emotions will probably last a long time before societies find their equilibrium. The teaching of St. Thomas, who places friendship at the center of charity, directed both to God and to one's neighbor for God's sake, has fallen into oblivion, even in the Catholic world. This friendship, while not limited to the emotions, contains an emotional component through which grace is made manifest. This means that chastity, undertaken as a vow for the sake of the kingdom of Heaven, while excluding sexual activity, does not exclude friendship in all of its dimensions, including the emotional. Restoring a proper place for feelings in life is essential for the fullness of the Christian life.

The nature of the emotions

St. Thomas's theological synthesis, which looks for the image of God in man sanctified by grace, contains an important and forgotten treatise on the emotions. The theological perspective, focused primarily on God and therefore on the fecundity of His grace operating in man, does not negate the natural perspective. Indeed, the higher theological threshold provokes and simultaneously rectifies the philosophical insight. With the horizon of faith in sight, one can appreciate nature better. Therefore, the disposition of the treatise on emotions is optimistic. St. Thomas does not see emotions primarily as a threat to the eliciting of a moral act; on the contrary, he views them as a necessary element for fully human actions that are simultaneously transformed by grace. The saint's intuitions, even though dating from medieval times and developed within the framework of a theological synthesis, have preserved their value. They furnish us with a description of the psychology of emotions that is useful also in the interpretation of emotional disorders. More importantly, in the treatment of neuroses, Thomistic terminology based on commonsense observations turns out to be much more serviceable than the psychiatric terminology of Freud.[125] It is important that the theological description of the psyche's collaboration with grace corresponds with the psychological description, and even with the psychiatric description, especially when help is needed in dealing with neurotic disorders. If each discipline were to use completely different and incompatible terminology, an inaccurate initiation into religious and moral life could result in neuroses, and attempts to be delivered from them could sometimes seem like a negation of religious life.

In addition to the physiological dimension, which is common to all living beings, including plants, animals and humans have a sensory dimension. It enables them to go beyond themselves toward objects that are cognizable through the senses. In animals, the senses are autonomous because animals neither think nor have a spiritual will, whereas in humans, the spiritual level reaches out beyond the sensory dimension. The intellect is capable of grasping the nonmaterial, universal meaning of things abstracted from concrete

---

[125] See Anna A. Terruwe and Conrad W. Baars, *Psychic Wholeness and Healing* (New York: Alba House, 1981). In the remainder of the chapter, I present the work of these two Dutch psychiatrists who discovered the value of the Thomistic theory of emotions in treating neuroses. Their books reflect their clinical experience, which included the treatment of many clerics who suffered emotional wounds as a result of unwholesome upbringing.

objects. Both sensory cognition and experience can thus be integrated into mental apprehension and willing of a wider good. In addition, the level of grace leaning out toward God through faith and hope, if it is cultivated, imparts to emotional reactions a reference to friendship with God and with people for God's sake. Then the emotional contribution to good action is the plane in which something of God's goodness is made manifest.

At the sensory level, we distinguish between sensory cognition and the sensory appetite. Traditionally, five external sensory cognitive faculties are mentioned: sight, hearing, smell, taste, and touch. Of course, today's physiology provides more extensive information regarding these senses, the functioning of their relevant bodily organs, and their complexity. This does not, however, change the value of the traditional view. In sensory cognition, four internal senses are also involved: the common sense (*sensus communis*), which collates various impressions together, imagination, memory, and the sensory usefulness judgment (*vis aestimativa* in animals and *vis cogitativa* in humans). The usefulness judgment delivers an instinctive response to an object that appears to be useful or dangerous. Animals instinctively recognize that a particular type of grass will be useful in the building of a nest or that a certain other animal poses a threat. Sensory memory allows for the acquisition of experience. Based on sensory memory, animals can be trained. And thanks to the imagination, which is an active memory that extracts stored accumulated impressions, absent objects can be made present in the psyche.

Since man has spiritual powers, his sensory cognition is connected with mental cognition. The mind penetrates sensory cognition and perceives the object cognized by the senses in the context of general knowledge. The imagination, under the influence of the mind, may separate individual impressions and assemble them in new and creative ways. Also, the sensory usefulness judgment is subject to the influence of the mind. When sensory cognition is accompanied by the sensory usefulness judgment, followed by a stirring of the sensory appetite, the mind supplies wider knowledge, which, in turn, directs the spiritual appetite of the will, and then the free choice leads the sensory appetite — that is, the emotions — toward a higher level in which universal values are considered. Sight, taste, memory, and imagination, along with the usefulness judgment may stimulate the desire to drink alcohol, but the mind, realizing that at a given moment this would not be appropriate, due to a scheduled car ride, will influence the usefulness judgment to assess that drinking in this moment is not suitable. Not only will the free choice refuse the drinking of beer, but the sensory usefulness judgment about its being inappropriate will facilitate in the restraint of the sensual desire. The proper functioning of the usefulness judgment is therefore important in the guiding of the emotions.

When the sensory cognitive faculties know their respective objects, they trigger the corresponding appetite — that is, a stirring to or from the recognized object. These stirrings are called *feelings* or *emotions*. It is in their nature to be passive. Emotions allow themselves to be moved; they are passions. When we experience emotions, we experience a stirring that absorbs us. We distinguish two sets of emotions that react to sense cognition. The external cognitive senses, the common sense, and the imagination recognize in an object its goodness or evil. In turn, the usefulness judgment and the sensory memory or experience recognize the usefulness or harmfulness of an object. Depending on this sensory assessment, two types of emotional response are generated: emotions grouped in the pleasure appetite; and utility emotions grouped in the irascible appetite, reacting to the usefulness or nonusefulness of the object.

Pleasure appetite		Irascible appetite	
Appetitus concupiscibilis		*Appetitus irascibilis*	
Love	Hate	Hope-ambition	Courage
Amor	*Odium*	*Spes*	*Audacia*
Desire	Aversion	Despair	Fear
Desiderium	*Fuga*	*Desperatio*	*Timor*
Joy	Sadness		Anger
Delectatio	*Tristitia*		*Ira*

This inventory of the passions captures the basic emotional reactions. Poetic language, of course, provides many more terms to describe different kinds of emotional sensations. All of them, however, fall under one of the eleven emotions. The Latin terms are included here to show the wealth of meaning in each of these emotions. It is not easy to find the right terms to designate them, as some words carry also moral connotations, good or bad. In this description, love and hope do not signify a virtue, either natural or theological. They denote an emotional response, which, as such, is devoid of any moral value. Only the using of these feelings as a resource may serve virtue or sin. Therefore, *spes* may be rendered not only as hope, but also as ambition, or emotional eagerness that confers the strength to take on challenging tasks. Likewise, anger, or to put it differently, the capacity to be indignant at evil, does not mean sin. One must be able to be indignant at evil in order to engage in the good. All the emotions are psychosomatic reactions to sensory perception. Since they belong to the natural endowment of both man and beast, they are all fundamentally good and necessary. The emotional reactions include a bodily agitation, which adds a corporeal element to virtues or vices. Sadness caused by the suffering of others is the emotion of pity, an important human expression that enhances the virtue of love. Sadness caused by the success of others is an act of envy. Sadness in response to the call of grace is the vice of *acedia* — that is, spiritual sloth.

The intensity of emotional reactions varies from person to person because it is influenced by each individual's somatic constitution. One man may be easily excitable, while another may be slower. The development of emotions is influenced by the power of other people's emotions. The person's ability to feel, to respond with warmth and cordiality to directed affection, grows from infancy. The development of the emotional life begins even before birth. Prenatal psychology studies the impact of the emotional milieu on an unborn child. If an expectant mother places her hand on her womb every day and directs her loving affection toward the child, the child will move closer to her hand. If she forgets this gesture one day, the baby will start kicking because he craves love! It is vital that children experience emotional contact long before they acquire the ability to reason. If it is not only the mother but also the father who touches and caresses the infant, then the child will develop the capacity for emotional involvement, which is a mark not of being infantile but of a fully human response. Then an emotional sensation is developed in the child, which in time will contribute to the child's conviction that he is loved not for what he does (the child as yet is not capable of doing anything) but simply because he exists. When people love one another, they express their emotions; they do not have to put on masks, and their interpersonal contact is deeper. If there were no freedom to express emotions, interpersonal contact would be cold and rigid.

It is important for the emotions of the pleasure appetite to develop before the ability to reason is formed. These emotions react to that which is or is not pleasurable. In turn, the feelings of the irascible appetite provide emotional eagerness, making it possible to achieve that toward which the emotions of the pleasure appetite are striving. They are distinguished by a certain assertiveness and optimism, or its lack. Therefore, the emotions of the irascible appetites are subservient toward the emotions of the pleasure appetite. When one is thirsty in the desert, the emotions of hope and fear spur eagerness to hurry to the oasis, where water will be found. Since the emotions of the irascible appetite serve the other ones, the main emphasis in emotional life should be on the emotions of the pleasure appetite. When the emotions of the irascible appetite become dominant in a person, this leads to an inhibition of the emotional life.

In animals, autonomous emotions supply the energy for acquiring food and for reproduction. In humans, the emotions interact with the spiritual level, the mind and the will, which guide them. It is normal for the emotions to submit to the guidance of the spiritual powers. St. Thomas notes that the sensitive appetite is structured in such a way that it tends to obey reason.[126] In the structure of the emotions, there is a receptivity to the light of reason. Reason recognizes the object of sensory cognition in its subordination to the universal good, and as such, this object is then willed by the free choice, which allows for the expression of the emotions of desire or love. Thus, the emotions have a natural disposition toward the guiding light of reason. This claim may at first appear to defy experience. We do not live in primordial justice, and often we witness discord within ourselves. The emotions do not always willingly submit to the guidance of reason and will. We experience

---

[126] "Appetitus sensitivus natus est obedire rationi." *ST*, Ia-IIae, q. 74, art. 3, ad 1.

emotional stirrings whose instant gratification would defy common sense, and yet they are compelling. When nonetheless, the emotion submits to the guidance of reason, it does not experience this as a deformity. Sometimes reason prompts a person to deny himself some appealing objects, and while habituating the emotions to respond to the light of reason may involve hardship and a gradual education in virtue, this guidance of reason is natural to emotions because inherently they are receptive to it. Denying oneself the expression of emotions, when it is done in a rational manner, does not lead to mental aberrations. When the desire inclines one to eat a large piece of cake, and reason denies this, whether for health reasons, or because some cake must be left for others to enjoy, or because the cake happens to be in the store and one would have to pay for it, the refusal of the desire made by reason is a healthy phenomenon that does not lead to repression. But, if the emotion allows itself to be carried away against the guidance of reason, it feels uncomfortable, generating a feeling of guilt. The sense of guilt is not the voice of conscience, because conscience is an act of the practical reason, but in a healthy person, it is an emotional reaction that supports the judgment of conscience. The feeling of guilt makes it known that something was missing in the act. The missing element was a reference to the judgment of reason, toward which the emotion by its very nature tends.

When discussing the gifts of the Holy Spirit, St. Thomas shares with us another intuition that is analogous to his observation about the compliance of the emotions to the light of reason. The gifts of the Holy Spirit express God's direct intervention in human actions. Working by way of counsel, they offer wise promptings of the Holy Spirit that expect a generous response. This divine influence will never be crippling to the psyche, because all the human powers have such a construction that they are amenable to being moved by the divine instinct.[127] This means that the entire human personality, including the body, all the drives, nerves, emotions, memory, imagination, recollections, as well as the reason and the will possess within themselves a receptivity to the direct influence of the grace of the Holy Spirit. Openness

---

[127] "Omnes vires humanae natae sunt moveri per instinctum Dei." *ST*, Ia-IIae, q. 68, art. 4.

to divine life not only does not cause inhibitions, but it also contributes to the flourishing of the personality. Many internal anxieties, which also occasionally cause somatic infirmity, have their origin not so much in external corruption as in a lack of surrender to God. When one is united with God, communing with Him in trust, giving oneself generously to Him in the small daily situations of life, the presence of the grace of the Holy Spirit increases psychic resilience and inner balance. The working of grace on the emotions, which is a supernatural action, does not occur alongside or even in competition with the reason and the will. Grace works through nature, and therefore through the reason and the will. Thus, it can be correctly said that the emotions are both *natae obedire rationi* and *natae moveri per instinctum Dei*. The integration of the emotions will involve not just the light of reason and the following of the free choice, but also a receptivity to grace. This, in turn, may radiate most fully in the soul, so long as there is a recognition of the limits of the capacities of the natural powers and a reliance on supernatural help. Difficulties in the integration of emotions frequently stem from a lack of such reliance on grace. In some instances, grace is theoretically accepted, but it remains only at the level of declaration, and in practice there is an attempt to deal with oneself through one's own efforts, which ends in failure. The difficulty lies in that one has to allow God to be God and, through faith, introduce divine action into the very center of the psyche.

In men, emotions tend to be more penetrated by reason. In women, emotions tend to be more autonomous. In men, the various levels of personality, the physical, emotional, volitional, intellectual, and spiritual, are more separated, whereas in women they are more integrated. A woman can help a man to view things more holistically, and not see just a single dimension in her, such as her being for him a cook, an intellectual, a lover, a prostitute, or a companion in the spiritual adventure of life. Children are more sensitive to emotions than adults. Therefore, the person teaching children must not only instruct them but also captivate them with her personality. In adults, the emotions are either aligned with free choice by virtue or hidden under a mask, while in children, the emotions are not yet subordinated to the habit. Children, therefore, easily fluctuate in their emotional states, going from tears to laughter. They are very sensitive to the emotional states of others.

They immediately sense the falsehood of emotional masks. They sense that adults feel uncomfortable when a thorny topic is being raised. They prefer contact with a mother, who can get angry, to meeting an excessively sweet aunt whose kisses lack authenticity.

The word *mortification* appears frequently in spiritual and ascetical literature. This term does not adequately capture the process of acquiring emotional and moral maturity. To mortify means to make dead, that is, to kill (from the Latin *mortificare*, "to kill"). Meanwhile, the emotions should not be killed but directed with the help of the light of reason and free choice. All the emotions are fundamentally good, but in accordance with their nature, they need direction from the spiritual powers. Sometimes, it is not the emotions of the pleasure appetite that should be restrained, but the emotions of the irascible appetite, including those of energy (hope-ambition and courage combined) or fear, as their excessive prevalence generates confusion in the psychic life. The old adage "*in medio virtus*" does not mean that virtue is in the middle, as if there should be neither too much nor too little of it. One should grow as much as possible in all the virtues, but in the virtues of temperance and fortitude, prudence finds the right measure for the emotional stirrings, stimulating or restraining them and habituating them to cooperation with the spiritual powers. In the virtues there is room for creativity, and the emotional dynamic provides the necessary zeal encouraging virtuous action.

In animals, the stirring of the emotions is basically egocentric (although they exhibit emotional contact and generosity toward their offspring). In a healthy human being, since the spiritual powers recognize the sensual good in the context of the universal good and the good of other people, the emotional stirring loses its egocentric character. Then the emotions are elevated to a higher level, in which they are transformed into an expression of true love. In contrast, in a healthy but sinful person, the emotion is directed to its object, but in the moment of sin, the emotion ignores the light of reason.

In the personality of the psychopath, there is a fundamental, constitutive disruption between the emotional and the rational spheres. The psychopath's emotions function independently, without collaboration with reason. The psychopath's emotional reactions are therefore irrational, responding immediately to stimuli. Since his emotions are not subject to rational guidance, he has no feeling of guilt. This is what healthy people find so disturbing about the psychopath's behavior. He may understand that he has done something wrong, but he does not show any remorse because his emotions do not cooperate with reason and so they do not lend their dynamism to the spiritual realm. This is a disorder of the mental composition that is basically incurable.

In a neurotic personality, the emotions are fundamentally healthy. They have the intrinsic need to submit to the guidance of reason, but due to a flawed upbringing, they experience a mutual interlocking, resulting in tension and a temporary incapability of being guided by reason, either in one sphere of life or in all. Since a neurotic's emotions are fundamentally sound, they can be properly directed, and the neurotic will return to emotional equilibrium.

Thus, it is important to understand the difference between a healthy direction of the emotions and a neurotic attempt to repress them. If the requirements of the Christian life are misunderstood, if their reception is not rational but emotional, fearful, or forced, this will produce neurosis. Growth in virtue, including the infused virtues, needs as its foundation the recognition and feeling of the basic goodness of emotional reactions, even when they have to be guided. The sensations provided by emotions are neither virtuous nor sinful; it is only their guidance by the spiritual powers that gives them a moral qualification. It is worth remembering that the Church's teaching places trust in feelings.[128]

The repression of the emotions

Sigmund Freud had the brilliant intuition that in a neurotic person a repression of the emotions takes place, causing the repressed feeling to be pushed into the subconscious. There it cannot function normally and therefore

---

[128] In the face of the negation of the emotions preached by the Reformation, the Council of Trent explicitly confirmed the natural goodness of concupiscence: "There remains in the baptized concupiscence.... Although this is left to be wrestled with, it cannot harm those who do not consent, but manfully resist by the grace of Jesus Christ.... This concupiscence, which at times the Apostle calls sin [Rom. 6:12ff.] the holy Synod declares that the Catholic Church has never understood to be called sin, as truly and properly sin in those born again, but because it is from sin and inclines to sin" (DS 792).

it resurfaces in an enslaved manner. Freud held that responsibility for the repression is to be attributed to the superego, which, in his understanding, was a combination of social and moral requirements, upbringing, and one's own psychic powers. He concluded that for relief from neurosis, the superego had to be unblocked, which meant questioning the role of social pressure in moral upbringing. Giving up moral standards, however, does not lead to psychic equilibrium but only breeds further psychic disorders.

Freud was not the first to observe unhealthy outbursts of repressed emotions. We find similar observations already in St. Thomas.[129] The precise psychology of the passions outlined by Aquinas provides tools for a convincing description of the phenomenon of repression of the emotions. In neurosis, the repressive conflict occurs not between the emotions and the moral teaching but between the emotions themselves. The recognition that in a person's emotional endowment, there are two distinct groups of emotions — the emotions of the pleasure appetite and the serving emotions of the irascible appetite — allows for the explanation of emotional disorders, especially when emotions from the two groups are in conflict.

The conflict arises when two contradictory emotions are directed simultaneously toward the same object. This is not the same thing as when one emotion follows another. The phenomenon of mixed emotions (sadness and joy, such as after the death of a mother-in-law) does not represent a conflict of emotions, and thus it is not a disorder. A classic case of repression occurs when an emotion of the pleasure appetite is experienced (e.g., sexual feeling) and immediately an emotion of the irascible appetite (e.g., a feeling of fear) represses the desire that has arisen. This repression occurs under the influence of the sensory usefulness judgment, which assesses the

---

[129] *Ad Rom.*, c. 5, l. 6 (454): "Internal affections, when they are kept within and permitted no outlet, burn the more strongly within. This is clear in sorrow and anger which, when they are kept within, continually increase; but if they are given any kind of release outwardly, their vigor is dissipated. But a prohibition, since it threatens a penalty, compels man not to give outward expression to his desire, so that, being kept within, it burns more vigorously." *Commentary on the Letter of Saint Paul to the Romans*, trans. F. R. Larcher (Lander, WY: Aquinas Institute for the Study of Sacred Doctrine, 2012).

sexual desire as being fundamentally wrong, and then fear seeks to push out the experienced desire from the consciousness. Reason may know and judge sexuality as being necessary and good, while the emotions of the irascible appetite may feel that it is bad. Similarly, an overly zealous novice may feel hunger accompanied with a simultaneous feeling of guilt about that sensation, because he has told himself that sanctity requires of him not to experience the desire for food.

Self-denial of a desire through the power of the free choice is a healthy reaction. A diabetic who follows the doctor's orders and avoids sugar is acting rationally, and so his feelings of desire will accept the directions of the reason and the will. It may take some time and effort to become used to obeying the precept of reason before one acquires the ability to deny oneself sweet treats, but there will be no conflict among the emotions here. There is no psychic conflict when one adheres to the requirements of the natural law. The natural law corresponds to the basic structures of being, and so the rational execution of that which is right does not cause psychic disturbances. Since the emotions of the irascible appetite serve the emotions of the pleasure appetite, when reason prompts them to influence the remaining emotions, this is a perfectly normal phenomenon.

It may happen, however, that the true and just precepts of the moral law are received not rationally but emotionally, and this causes neurotic reactions. Since the moral law is sapiential, offering wise guidance to reason, its reception should be rational. When the moral law is received emotionally, an emotional feeling follows that challenges another feeling. In the process of emotional repression, the emotions of both groups are directed toward the same object. The emotions of the irascible appetite, most commonly the feelings of fear or energy, are then used to eliminate the emotions of the pleasure appetite. The result is that the repressed emotion of the pleasure appetite does not find its natural fulfillment and remains in a state of tension. The repressed emotion is as if buried alive. It continues to operate, striving toward an object it cannot achieve. It does not follow the guidance of reason, because the repressing emotion has been driven like a wedge between the repressed emotion and reason. The repressed emotion, therefore, reacts in an irrational way (like someone buried alive) because it is completely beyond the control of the reason and the will. Obsessive-compulsive symptoms then occur, which are completely beyond the control of the reason and the will. A man whose sex drive has been repressed will experience an obsessive-compulsive desire for pornography. If the sexual desire has been repressed by the emotions of energy, all effort to restrain the sexual urges will not generate the virtue of chastity. The building up of energy against the sexual feelings will only aggravate the repression of the drive, which will then resurface in an enslaved and irrational manner. A neurotic may be free in most of his actions and decisions, but, in this one field, he experiences enslavement, which means that, in this area, his moral culpability is negligible or nonexistent. Even though his action is disordered and, given a different psychic setting, it would be a sin, in the case of his neurotic enslavement, it entails moral fault. (This distinction is not only a tenet of modern psychiatry; it has a foundation in the teachings of St. Thomas.[130])

In neurosis, the repressed emotions cannot submit to the guidance of the reason and the will. In a healthy situation, when reason guides the emotions, it does not negate the sensations that the feeling provides. A chaste person does not repress the sexual desires. The movements of sexuality are accepted as good, and then they are focused on the good of persons. In neurosis, as soon as the first impression appears, it is repressed. Entering as a foreign entity into the psychic life, the repressing emotion precludes the intervention of reason in the repressed sphere. The reestablishment of the direction of reason is possible only when the repressing emotion is alleviated and normal psychic conditions return. The presence of the repressed emotion may be more or less conscious. The process of emotional repression is usually involuntary, but it can be conscious to some extent. The intensity of repression may increase. Repression that initially is mild may become more intense in time. The emotions of the irascible appetite that are most

---

[130] *Ad Rom.*, c. 8, l. 1 (599): "For it is not true that any act proceeding from the habit of a damnable sin is itself damnable, but only when it is an act perfected by the consent of reason. For if the habit of adultery is present in a person, the stirring of adulterous desire, which is an imperfect act, is not a mortal sin for that person, but only the perfect motion that exists by the consent of reason."

commonly responsible for repression are the emotion of fear, sometimes joined with the emotion of despair, and the emotion of energy, composed of the emotions of hope-ambition and courage. Depending on which emotion causes repression, there are different types of neuroses, fear neurosis or energy neurosis.

It may happen that each one of the emotions of the pleasure appetite will be repressed, not just the emotions of love, desire, and joy. Also, there may be a repression of sadness when a child is told never to cry, even in the face of real suffering. Similarly, the emotions of the irascible appetite may be repressed. Some people do not want to expose their fears, and they repress them with energy. One may also repress anger in the false conviction that indignation is always sinful. In addition, it may happen that someone represses an emotion with the same emotion, being afraid of his own fear! St. Thérèse of Lisieux, during a period of emotional disturbance in childhood, first would cry and then would cry because she had cried!

Emotions tend toward various objects. The emotions of the pleasure appetite are oriented toward listening to music, consuming delicious food, interacting with people, learning, and so forth. It is only when emotions that are directed to the most important dynamisms of life are repressed that a serious neurosis will develop. Often neurosis is caused by the repression of sexual feelings stemming from an inadequate upbringing, suggesting that there is something vile in the very emergence of this desire. Another type of neurosis is caused by the repression of the assertive emotions when the feelings of energy and personal initiative had been repressed by an upbringing that preferred immaturity. Sometimes formation in seminaries and religious houses that seemed to follow the model of military barracks left no room for the development of personal initiative, and this made people puerile. If parents cling to their adult children in a possessive way, not allowing them to be independent, this leads to a neurotic permanent adolescence. Communism that had inhibited the development of personal initiatives in social, economic, or political fields produced people with a sad, stunted personality, and this most frequently led to alcoholism. When in June 1979, at Victory Square in Warsaw, St. John Paul II said that there is no dimension of our lives into which Christ has no right to enter, the crowd interrupted the Holy

Father's homily and applauded for fourteen minutes! The pope could have shortened the applause and continued his homily, but he preferred to wait until the crowd had expressed its joy. Up to that point, people were afraid of their faith, afraid of their own initiatives, and they would repress their healthy aspirations with fear. The psychological shock that was the first visit of the Polish pope to a communist country contributed to the unblocking of fear and the liberation of suppressed aspirations. The following year, the Solidarity movement was born.

The repression of the assertive feelings renders individuals submissive, lacking any initiative of their own, and incapable of making personal free choices. In some countries, women are raised to have no opinion of their own and always to appear complacent. Such submissiveness, in which one's own initiatives have been extinguished, makes one incapable of deciding for oneself, of living one's own life, and of assuming the challenges of a virtuous life. There are multiple causes for the repression of the assertive emotions. One of them is an upbringing that claims that feeling anger is sinful. The moral judgment of children's quarrels should refer only to unjust actions, and not to feelings of indignation. People who are unable to get angry should be advised to go to a forest and shout out the words of Jesus: "Woe to you, scribes and Pharisees, hypocrites! for you are like whitewashed tombs, which outwardly appear beautiful, but within they are full of dead men's bones and all uncleanness" (Matt. 23:27). Another cause for the repression of assertive emotions is an upbringing that is not grounded in the good shown in the moral law but only in the emotions and reactions of other people. Such people then lack confidence in their own actions. When a boy had witnessed many angry quarrels of his parents, or when he himself had caused serious harm to another during a childish fight, he may then react by trying to repress his feeling of anger completely. Such an attitude leads to the repression of one's own assertiveness. Also, a woman who loves her children more than her husband may attempt to force her adult children to stay with her, being afraid that she will be left alone with a husband whom she does not love. The repression of the assertive emotions leads to bad moods, self-centeredness, lack of joy, depression, and then severe outbursts of anger, followed by strong feelings of guilt, and in many cases by alcoholism.

The repression of emotions that are directed to objects less important than the sexual drive or assertiveness will not cause neurosis. If a religious superior in an arbitrary and emotional way bans watching TV, this will not cause neurosis. But, if neurosis is already present in a person, then it may also shift to less important objects.

Neurotic repression occurs only when the denial of a desire or a feeling is based not on rational motives but on feelings. A repressed emotion may either have the occasion to develop to a certain degree before repression occurs, or its first appearance in the consciousness meets with immediate repression. The exclusion of the natural physiological manifestations of an emotion caused by repression prevents the person from giving a natural impression. Over time, this will become outwardly visible. The repression of emotions may become habitual, causing a withdrawal from everything that can be associated with the repressed emotion. Such a person becomes cold and expressionless. If the neurotic individual is highly intelligent and possesses a strong capacity for introspection, the awareness of the constant recurrence of the repressed emotion may lead to a deepening of the neurosis. Repression tends to deepen in intensity and to expand onto other objects.

The repressed emotion cannot accept the guidance of reason, and it acquires an autonomous obsessive feverishness. This prompts actions that shame the neurotic, and this, in turn, fuels the repression, and so the vicious circle continues. Instead of the person becoming increasingly free to act virtuously, he becomes increasingly enslaved by neurotic reactions. If it is the sexual desire that has been repressed by the emotion of fear, it manifests itself in an obsessive and compulsive pursuit of sexual gratification together with a concurrent moral disapproval. This results in a rising fear and renewed repression. Over time, a psychic mechanism called *transference* may ensue. A certain image replaces the forbidden feeling. Somebody who is unable to cope with a dislike for his father will begin to hate all authority. A repressed sex drive may manifest itself in compulsive eating of sweets or seeking gratification in religious experiences. The suppression of the emotions causes psychic disorders. The neurotic becomes nervous, overexcited, and has a heightened sensitivity. Somatic symptoms such as fatigue, headaches, insomnia, or back pain can also develop.

a. Fear neurosis

Traditional manuals of moral theology have always had a chapter on the scrupulous conscience. Confessors are often tormented by penitents who are afraid of everything: themselves, their sins, past and future, their sexuality, and God. Scrupulous penitents come to Confession frequently, sometimes several times a week. They can be easily recognized by the way they speak and present their problems. Basically, their difficulty is psychological rather than spiritual, but this is usually due to a false introduction into the spiritual and moral life. Scrupulosity is a neurosis in which the emotion of fear has become dominant and replaces the conscience. The fear is born not only of real threats but also of those that are imagined and anticipated. Fear neurotics are afraid of any sign of sexuality, and they seek to defend themselves against the danger of sin through fear. The symptoms of fear may become chronic, causing insomnia and occasional speech difficulties, such as stuttering. Fear neurotics are uncertain about everything they do. They will check several times to make sure the gas in the kitchen has been turned off. They are afraid that they have sinned even when it is clear that they did not commit a sin. They are unable to distinguish between temptation and sin, and so, just in case, they blame themselves every time they have been tempted. They fear that they are guilty of the remote consequences of their actions. As soon as a doubt arises regarding whether they may have committed a sin, they immediately feel guilty and condemned.

They are afraid that they have forgotten to mention something in a previous confession; thus, they easily conclude that the previous confession was invalid or sacrilegious, because they failed to mention something, or failed to recount all the circumstances accurately, or the priest could not hear them clearly during the confession because the organ was playing. They keep making promises to God to make amends for their sins, but because they are unable to fulfill these promises, they feel even more guilty. For such people, Confession is not an encounter with the merciful God; it is a magical practice that brings them peace for a while, but shortly thereafter they are overcome by fear all over again. What guides their lives is neither their own reason nor love but fear. Fear neurosis prevents them from trusting the judgment of their own consciences. Any attempt to help them is interpreted as a threat. If a priest tells them, "Don't worry about these things," they think the priest is lax, and they do not trust him. If they encounter a confessor who himself has difficulties with fear neurosis, their psychic state will deteriorate considerably. After some time, the excessive fear takes over their entire lives. The constant doubts and difficulties in making decisions are a source of never-ending suffering and pain. Severe anxiety affects the imagination, which becomes overstimulated. The sleep of fear neurotics is light, and their dreams are vivid. In more severe cases, fear neurosis may cause phobias, sometimes outbursts of anger, and eventually depression and despair. Fear neurosis is more common in women, although it is more difficult to cure men from it.

To heal such a person, the fear has to be defused. If the word *mortification* is mentioned, it has to be explained that the only emotion that needs to be mortified is that of fear. This can happen only if such an individual meets with trust and care. It is necessary to explain to this person the essence of the problem (the commonsense diagram of the two groups of emotions provided by St. Thomas is helpful in this), but a mere rational explanation of the nature of the neurosis is not enough to free from this emotional turmoil. The neurotic has to enter into the orbit of the human, affective concern of the one who tries to help him. If it is a priest who is helping in the liberation, the neurotic has to have confidence in his doctrinal preparation and feel his concern. Since fear neurotics are usually intelligent people, it can be explained to them that their fear is irrational and excessive. These issues are explained better outside the confessional because some people who suffer from scrupulosity are so terrified that they may have accidentally forgotten something from their long list of sins that they do not listen to what the priest is telling them. Outside the confessional, in a calmer atmosphere, it may be explained that the fundamental problems are only fear and a lack of trust in God. But that God is merciful they must discern from the demeanor and sensitivity of the one who explains the neurotic mechanism to them.

It is good to look into the origin of the excessive fear. It may be that the scrupulous person received a faulty moral upbringing, which drove him to fear. Sometimes, disproportionate emphasis was placed on moral obligation, on religious duties, or on sins against the sixth commandment. Occasionally, overly strict parents had drummed into the consciousness the notion that God is only a punishing judge. If it is a case of fear of the sexual drive, the neurotic has to accept that experiencing sexual feelings is not wrong in itself, and it is not to be feared. Sexuality is a good gift from God, and it is to be experienced as such. It includes not just the physical and physiological dimensions of sexuality but also the feelings and desires, which are likewise good. A fear neurotic will usually understand that sexuality is essentially good but may still perceive it as a threat. Psychoanalytic methods should not be used in the treatment of fear neurosis because they bring out the repressed feeling instead of the repressing one. This will only intensify the fear rather than diminish it. The repressed feeling should not be stimulated to emerge. Emotions should develop spontaneously, step by step, so that the transformation of the personality will occur gradually. It is good for the penitent to recognize that he also has some good qualities. Sometimes people can name very quickly a long list of their faults, yet they are unable to find anything good in themselves! To love one's neighbor, one has to love oneself, being convinced that one has some qualities that may serve others.

In the confessional, the scrupulous penitent is to be shown the beauty of God. He needs to be guided to treat Confession not as a magical procedure but rather as an opportunity to encounter a forgiving God, "in whom we have boldness and confidence of access through our faith in him" (Eph. 3:12) because Christ took upon Himself the fault and consequences of our sins. Each time we encounter Christ in faith, especially in the Sacrament of Reconciliation, His grace eradicates our sins, and since this takes place, there is no point in dwelling on past sins. It is not that, above all, we are to strive to be flawless. Precisely because we are weak, we need divine grace, and this grace invites goodness. It is possible to do good even when traces of various bad habits are still present in the personality. It is important that the scrupulous person stops considering as a sin that which is not a sin (and is only an occasion for sin or is just a temptation). He must be forbidden from confessing sins that have been previously confessed. If he has even the slightest doubt as to whether he has committed a sin, it is imperative that he does not mention it in the confessional. A scrupulous person always exaggerates in favor of his own fault, so he must be freed from unhealthy scruples. Let him confess only mortal sins. When he finishes listing his sins, he should be forbidden from adding anything. He should be taught to keep his confession short and to the point — not because an excessive recitation of fictitious sins annoys the confessor but for his own good. He should be instructed to confess no more frequently than once every three weeks. The assigned penance should be simple and easy. The old manuals of moral theology mentioned special privileges of scrupulous people: they are exempt from having to make a careful examination of conscience; they are exempt from guarding themselves against falling into sin; and they are exempt from having to go to Confession before Holy Communion in the case of grave sin. It is enough if the scrupulous penitent makes an act of contrition, based on the authority of the confessor. These rules were developed to free the penitent who has become entangled in a fearful living out of his moral life and relationship with God. They prudently aim at liberating from a paralyzing fear. Of course, these principles should not be proclaimed from the pulpit, because they apply only to those suffering from scrupulosity!

It is not possible that somebody suffering from fear neurosis will change after just one encounter. The misalignment of the emotions in neurosis operates like a permanent habit, and therefore it takes time and patience before equilibrium can be restored. Such a person will find great help in a kind friend, provided that the friend understands the nature of the erroneous emotional mechanism and, through explanation, kindness, and patience, can help the person attain psychic maturity. Since neurotics' emotions are fundamentally healthy, even though they are misdirected, when the influence of the repressing emotion ceases, after an initial period of restlessness when the person feels helpless, the repressed emotion will submit to the guidance of the reason and the will, and the person will acquire psychic equilibrium.

b. Energy neurosis

Another type of neurosis, analogous to fear neurosis, is energy neurosis. Theology has been familiar with this phenomenon for a long time, although there has been less pastoral sensitivity to the problem. In fact, energy neurosis may be identified with the heresy of Pelagianism. Because it was generally discussed within the framework of dogmatic theology, the practical implications of this ancient heresy, whose errors were demonstrated by St. Augustine, were not always recognized, and the teaching of moral theology lacked the initiation into the life of grace. The heresy of Pelagianism boils down to the claim that grace may at best play some external role in stimulating sensitivity to God, but it is unnecessary in the practical moral life. The failure to invite grace into the guiding of the emotions results in placing too much hope in the directive capacities of the will. The most common consequence of this error is confusion between the will and the emotions of the irascible appetite. The will is a spiritual power that allows itself to be drawn by the good. The emotions of the irascible appetite are corporeal, related to the physiology of the body. When, in the absence of faith in the power of grace working in the will and also in the emotions, the emotions of the irascible appetite are stimulated against other emotions, energy neurosis follows.

In energy neurosis, there is a similar repression as in fear neurosis, except that here the cause are the emotions of hope-ambition and courage, which together may be called *life energy*. In neurosis, this energy is used to repress an undesirable feeling away from the consciousness. While those with scrupulosity are always fearful, energy neurotics seem to be strong people. Not all human energy causes neurosis, and not all people with enthusiasm and vital energy are neurotic. When energy is not used to repress the sexual drive or the assertive emotions, it plays a useful role in life. Somebody who is full of energy, dedicated to work, even to some extent a "workaholic," may be completely balanced, although sometimes an excessively strong energy may make it difficult for such an individual to show tenderness and empathize with what others are feeling. A person with a life energy that is too strong, while not being neurotic himself, may cause emotional difficulties in others, who try to defend themselves from his strength. In particular, if a woman is overly expansive psychologically with an underdevelopment of the emotions of the pleasure appetite, she will become less feminine, and ultimately less happy.

Energy neurosis occurs only when the assertive emotions or the sexual drive are repressed with energy. If a resolute child is told that all expressions of sexuality are bad, or if he or she senses in childhood that any conversation about these topics is emotionally unpleasant because adults give the impression that engaging in it is a dirty and sensitive matter, the child will acquire the habit of vigorously repressing any feelings tied with sexuality. As the child will grow into adolescence, the sexual drive will surface and will immediately be repressed. This practice will contribute to psychic tension, to which the psyche will respond with increased repression, taken up by the power of the emotions of energy. Over time, the emotions may be so effectively repressed that the neurotic person will seem to be balanced. Repression undertaken by the emotion of fear leads to insecurity and irritability. Repression executed by energy gives the impression of self-confidence, efficiency, and self-control. This, however, is a different kind of self-mastery from the virtuous cooperation of the emotions with the free choice of reason and will, flowing from infused grace. In an energy neurotic, spontaneity disappears and is replaced by a deliberately programmed mask. Such people are unnaturally inflexible and inhibited. It is difficult to establish emotional contact with them because their reactions are cold. When somebody reveals feelings to them, there is the impression of being up against a wall. The energy neurotic is lonely in his self-control, but he is unaware of his loneliness. He has no need of contact with others because he is self-sufficient. But between him and others there is a cold chasm. The energy neurotic controls his imagination. He does not dream much. He usually sleeps like a rock. The repression of the emotions, however, causes general tension that sometimes erupts into aggression. The constant repression of the emotions through energy often makes the neurotic exhausted, and he has low blood pressure. The energy neurotic is proud. He is convinced of the value of his path to perfection. He considers that all passions should be repressed, and therefore, over time, he gives up fascination with music and nature. He is a stranger to the delight over a beautiful mountain view. He does not accept situations in which he would have to limit his energy and allow the emotions of pleasure to direct themselves freely to their objects.

From time to time, repression of emotions causes the emergence of obsessive-compulsive symptoms, resulting in strong feelings of guilt. If it is the sexual drive that is repressed, this incites compulsive masturbation, the search for pornography, or other sexual activities. After such acts, strong feelings of guilt provoke further repression, and so the vicious cycle continues. Instead of increased freedom of the virtue of chastity, the obsessive search for sexual gratification intensifies, and this leads to a streak of lapses, strong feelings of guilt, and renewed repression. In the healthy control of emotions, the spiritual powers of reason and will accept the passive nature of the emotions that allow themselves to be drawn. There is always a certain unknowable in the operation of the emotions, as they take us outside of ourselves. Thus, the harmonization of the spiritual and sensory powers involves a certain moment of risk. Such a situation is normal and brings fancy and vividness to life. Controlling the emotions does not mean extinguishing them so that they are as cold as marble. The presence of grace in the spiritual powers and in the senses does not deprive them of their warmth and dynamism. The recognition of the primacy of grace over mere human effort instills trust in divine help and trust in oneself, and this allows for unconstrained feelings. True saints are always open-minded, charming, dynamic people, with personalities that are captivating in their warmth and cordiality.

The energy neurotic will not seek the grace of Christ in the confessional. His greatest emphasis will be on the firm purpose of amendment. While, for the fear neurotic, Confession is often a magical procedure that provides a moment of respite and peace until the next bout of anxiety, for the energy neurotic, Confession is often a release from a strong sense of guilt and an opportunity to intensify willpower (or rather, emotional energy). He will promise that this is the last time, that he will change this time, that the decision to amend his life has been made, but, in essence, this will be another instance of repression. Encountering Christ includes trusting in His saving power. Encountering only one's own resolve to improve comprises a decision to reform, a decision that has no need of Christ and His grace. Since, in the neurotic approach to Confession, there is hardly any trust in God through faith, it is not surprising that such an approach to the sacrament is not fruitful. The sacrament is a meeting point between human misery and God's power and mercy. If, in the experience of Confession, there is no reference to this mercy, and in its place there is only an increase of repressing emotions, such Confession does not bring deliverance.

In therapy, patients suffering from energy neurosis have to be convinced that they need to reduce their own energy. It is not the sex drive that has to be mortified but the energy itself. They need to relax, but the problem is that they do not want to do this. They are usually intelligent people, so it is possible to explain to them the false mechanism of their emotional lives. Their understanding of the nature of religious duties and moral obligation needs to be corrected. It is not moral obligation that is at the center of the Christian life, but the grace of Christ. The trouble, however, is that while energy neurotics can quickly grasp where the problem lies, they then want to repress their excessive energy with further energy. Instead, they should let their repressed emotions return to consciousness on their own, especially the emotion of love, if the neurotics have become cold and hard. They should develop that modicum of feelings that remains in their psyche. They should give themselves the time and freedom selflessly to cultivate those things that still engage them, such as an interest in music or travel. The emotional life is passive and is to remain such. Repressed feelings are not to be forced to return. Their restoration has to be a spontaneous process.

Relief from energy neurosis brings with it a transformation of the understanding of Christian morality. The moral law is basically sapiential and not volitional. It shows the wise light of God, which is to be received by reason and not by the emotions. Thus, the manner of reception of the moral law will change. The energy neurotic is usually more interested in the obligation that is contained in the law than an indication that leads to happiness. It is necessary that, within the moral life, the spiritual life, which is a relationship with God in grace, will appear. Jesus said, "Apart from me you can do nothing" (John 15:5), and this truth needs to reach not just the reason but also the psyche and the emotions. Thus, the experience of one's own weakness, which is manifested in obsessive-compulsive actions, may be used not to stimulate energy once again but to place greater hope in divine power. A transformation of the kind experienced by St. Paul must therefore take place. He wrote:

> And to keep me from being too elated by the abundance of revelations, a thorn was given me in the flesh, a messenger of Satan, to harass me, to keep me from being too elated. Three times I besought the Lord about this, that it should leave me; but he said to me, "My grace is sufficient for you, for my power is made perfect in weakness." I will all the more gladly boast of my weaknesses, that the power of Christ may rest upon me. (2 Cor. 12:7–9)

We do not know what the difficulty that St. Paul experienced was, but he repeatedly asked Christ for deliverance. Christ's response does not mean that St. Paul was denied grace. God's help is infinite, but it has to be applied in life. Only the acknowledgment of one's own helplessness may bring about the deep faith and trust that breaks through the pride of self-sufficiency and allows the divine life to enter into the very interface of the spiritual and sensual powers. The transformation from a self-reliant, hubristic efficiency to a tender affectivity is slow, but in time it produces the experience foretold by God through the prophet Ezekiel:

> I will sprinkle clean water upon you, and you shall be clean from all your uncleannesses, and from all your idols I will cleanse you. A new heart I will give you, and a new spirit I will put within you; and I will take out of your flesh the heart of stone and give you a heart of flesh. And I will put my spirit within you, and cause you to walk in my statutes and be careful to observe my ordinances. (Ezek. 36:25–27)

This is a foretelling of life in the fullness of the New Covenant, in which the dominant role is played by the grace of the Holy Spirit.

c. Deprivation neurosis

Anna. A. Terruwe and Conrad Baars, who applied Thomistic principles to the clinical practice of treating neuroses, identified yet another type of neurosis that is not the result of emotional repression.[131] Deprivation neurosis is an inhibition of the emotional life caused by a lack of affection in childhood. It may be called *hospitalism*, an affliction experienced by those raised in orphanages or in families where parents did not show affection to their children. Deprivation neurotics find it difficult to establish emotional contact. They experience their emotions like children, in an egocentric way. When someone shows them affection, they are capable of establishing a bond, but they will not take the initiative themselves. They are often misunderstood and remain on the sidelines. Sometimes they attempt to make

---

[131] See Anna. A. Terruwe and Conrad Baars, *Healing the Unaffirmed: Recognizing Deprivation Neurosis*, (New York: Alba House, 1981).

emotional contact by willpower, but this does not build real friendships. They have acquaintances, but no close friends. Some of them do not think there is anything wrong in this. When they marry, they struggle because the husband is looking for a mother in his wife or the wife is looking for a father in the husband. In marriage, one needs to empathize with the other person's emotional state and respond with a gift, whereas the deprivation neurotic is unable to do this because he himself is starved for affection. Sometimes women having this problem do not want to have children because they find it difficult to be emotionally invested in a child's needs. A teacher will be better at teaching adults than children. A priest will feel better working as an archivist or a librarian because he will not have to interact with people. People are more attracted to warm personalities than to cold arguments. Some deprivation neurotics react to their predicament with fear, withdrawing from human contact, while others react with energy, sometimes achieving great efficiency and success at work, but, deep in their souls, there is constantly a strong desire for affirmation ("Appreciate me, appreciate me!"). They are very sensitive to the opinions of others. They constantly want to be praised. Some do not object to anyone, even considering it a virtue, because they find it hard to accept that some people praise and others respond with reserve, and that this is normal. They find it hard to distinguish between things said in seriousness and those said in jest. Deprivation neurotics have an inferiority complex, and they feel maladjusted. They do not feel that they are loved or worthy of love. They lack confidence in their own strength. Some end up reacting with aggression, while others become depressed.

 To cure somebody of deprivation neurosis, it is essential that he or she feels affirmed. A child is loved regardless of what he does. Deprivation neurotics seek affirmation through action, whereas they need to grasp that action is not a necessary requirement because they are loved for what they are. Such a person needs to find a place in the safety of the emotional orbit of other people. It is not enough to be treated coldly and officially. The neurotic has to feel that he matters to somebody. When the deprivation neurotic finally feels loved, there is an experience of a certain emotional rebirth. Sometimes people do not understand what is happening with the deprivation neurotic. They want him to behave like an adult, and when he finally tries to gain psychic independence and emotional self-reliance, he is misunderstood because all are accustomed to his soft personality.

The deepest affirmation comes from spiritual affirmation. God loves us the way He created us. He chose us even before the foundation of the world to become His adopted children (Eph. 1:4–5). The awareness of being beloved by God will not, however, come about through mere theological knowledge. One needs to see the reflection of God's goodness in the hearts, gestures, and feelings of living people. The fecundity of divine grace within human action enables the transmission of God's love to others. This communication of charity is not tied to the Sacrament of Holy Orders; any baptized person who is open to divine love may transmit it to others through personal contact. But the spiritual affirmation given through the sacraments will be more convincing and fruitful when it passes through the cordial personality of a priest.

The liberation of emotionality in the spiritual life

There is a fundamental difference between spiritual direction and the therapy of neuroses. A severely neurotic person will sometimes need psychiatric help and not just spiritual assistance. These two spheres, the psychic and the spiritual, are different but are deeply intertwined, and that is why their confusion results in so much misunderstanding. A great deal depends on whether a person has been truly introduced into the spiritual life. It is important, therefore, that a spiritual director is capable of distinguishing the basic types of neuroses, so that he does not fuel them with his poorly articulated teaching and so that he leads a person toward a trusting communion with God that frees that person from psychic difficulties.

Basically there are two cures for neuroses. The first is the practice of the theological virtues. A neurotic is focused on his own problems. The eliciting of faith, hope, and charity means the shifting of these problems onto the shoulders of God. When we rely on God, we allow God to be God; we allow Him to heal us with His grace. The influence of grace then permeates the spiritual and psychic life. Faith and hope, if they are not merely declared but develop into a true trust in God, protect from an unhealthy short-circuiting, in which the neurosis-generating emotions of the irascible appetites take over. A relationship with God frees a person from inner fears and from attempts to control himself "by force" and helps the person not to be discouraged by his weaknesses. Relying on grace does not mean giving up one's effort. It means placing one's effort within a reliance on God, in which one believes that the will and the feelings are subject to the healing power of the Almighty. In directing the emotions, above all one must trust in divine help, without fear that the emotions will carry him away toward their objects, and one must take small steps, counting entirely on the Savior, Who, in His goodness, makes everything work toward the good. "We know that in everything God works for good with those who love him" (Rom. 8:28). This, then, allows one to accept the natural movement of the emotions toward the unknown. The recognition that in failures there is a possibility to return to God frees one from an excessive preoccupation with his own falls, a preoccupation that is typical of the self-centered neurotic. Commenting on St. Paul's discovery that the thorn in the flesh that tormented him was a means of bringing him closer to God, St. Thomas states:

> Therefore, because the matter of this vice, that is, pride, is mainly found in things that are good, because its matter is something good, God sometimes permits his elect to be prevented by something on their part, e.g., infirmity or some other defect, and sometimes even mortal sin, from obtaining such a good, in order that they be so humbled on this account that they will not take pride in it, and that being thus humiliated, they may recognize that they cannot stand by their own powers.[132]

Bringing God into the center of emotional life does not mean giving up asceticism. Reigning over selfish pleasure-seeking as well as persisting in chastity facilitates sensitivity to others, allows one to be generous and to embrace the call of grace. Asceticism however must not be prideful and brought about uniquely by natural forces. It has to take place within the recognition of the primacy of the theological virtues that unite one with

---

[132] *Super II ad Cor.*, c. 12, l. 3 (472), trans. F. R. Larcher, B. Mortensen, and D. Keating (Lander, WY: Aquinas Institute for the Study of Sacred Doctrine, 2012).

God, and therefore for the pleasure of God Himself. It is not a question of repressing the emotions and enjoying one's own perfection. The point is to let God into one's personality, into the psyche, so that God may delight in giving Himself through the goodness, charm, and passion of a living person. The Holy Trinity rejoices most when He encounters transparent souls, ready to transmit with their whole selves the radiance of God Himself (Luke 10:21).

The emotions, when they are guided by free choice, and even more so when virtue has developed permanently, preparing them to respond creatively to the truth of the situation, are still, and even more so, characterized by their sensitivity. They are susceptible to stimuli; they react with all their vividness, allowing themselves to be moved and drawn to the limits shown by the free choice, open to the truth. This gives the personality prone to be moved emotionally a heartfelt, human dimension. Virtue denotes the ability to adhere to the truth, including the truth about the other person, in a way that makes room for creative choice, commitment, sensitivity, charm, joy, outrage, or even tears. Healthy emotions deliver not only joy but also pain when they encounter lies, dishonesty, or harm toward others or toward oneself. "Hurt feelings" are a signal of a humane reaction to evil, not only that of the reason and the will but also of the heart.

A mature spiritual life, in which the theological virtues and trust in God are at the forefront, releasing the emotions so that they play their role fully, allows for excitement or fervor for a good cause. Similarly, it does not shy away from the prospect of hurt feelings when the good is attacked, which really hurts. When the emotions have not been liberated due to a lack of trust in God or because there is a neurotic inability to feel one's emotions as fundamentally good, or else when they are underdeveloped, their enslavement may easily increase, and they may even be manipulated by powerful individuals. Immature people are led to an even greater confusion when their emotions are aroused by unwanted stimuli, such as provocative fashion or advertising. Young people who live their entire lives in emotional turmoil caused by wars, fear, humiliation, or helplessness easily fall into despair, into drugs, or into dependence on criminal groups that keep them hooked by reward, threat, or fear.

The decisive issue for the liberation of the emotions, therefore, is the cultivation of theological virtues through contemplative prayer. Communion with God takes place at the level of the spiritual powers, although, by liberating the emotions, it also enables them to have religious experiences. But this is neither essential nor central in the spiritual life. The beauty of religious art or the elated atmosphere at crowded liturgical celebrations evokes an echo in religious emotions, and this may dispose to the adherence to God through faith, hope, and charity, but it may also create the appearance of adhering to God when the spiritual life is confused with experiences of an emotional or artistic nature. A mature spiritual life takes place through "faith working through love" (Gal. 5:6), and therefore, it does not attach critical importance to religious feelings — nor does it care too much that someone may, at times even maliciously, want to "offend religious feelings" through blasphemous gestures or words, questioning symbols that, in a given culture and religiosity, function as vehicles of religious experience. Since faith is primarily located in the reason and not in the emotions, the hurting of religious feelings is not the worst type of harm. A deeper harm is the confusing of reason when the mystery of faith is expelled from the life of the intellect, whether through half-truths and ideologies that block faith or by anchoring faith solely at the level of emotions and sentiments.

The second important remedy for neuroses that repress the emotions is a sense of humor. A neurotic is very serious; he leaves no room for humor. When we can laugh at ourselves, at our own blunders, this has a healing effect. Blessed are those who know how to laugh at themselves, for they will have good fun throughout their entire lives!

9

Faith Holds on to the Holy Spirit, Who Then Leads

The message of St. Thérèse

ST. THÉRÈSE OF LISIEUX wrote in one of her poems, "Alas I am nothing but my very weakness. You know it, oh my God! I have no virtues."[133] However, the experience of moral limitations did not terrify her. She wrote to her biological sister:

> I feel that ... what pleases him [the Good Lord] is to see me love my littleness and my poverty, it is the blind hope that I have in his mercy.... Understand that to love Jesus, to be his victim of love, the weaker one is, without desires or virtues, the more fit one is for the operations of this consuming and transforming Love.... You have to agree to remain poor and without strength and that is the difficult thing.[134]

Clearly, St. Thérèse's spiritual path is not based primarily on goodness, recognized theoretically by philosophical reason, nor on values or virtues to be acquired, much less on norms that would impose obligation through their solemnity, but it is rooted in the Person of the Savior, Whom Thérèse came to love and Whose love she learned to cherish beyond measure. A reliance

---

[133] Poem 53.
[134] Letter 197, to Céline (with my correction).

on Jesus brings with it a total surrender to Him in faith and in practical love lived out in detail, but without constant self-control, without a proud locating of hope in one's own perfection.

> If I said to myself, for example: I have acquired such a virtue, I am certain of being able to practice it … then it would be relying on one's own strength, and when one is there, one risks falling into the abyss. But I will have the right, without offending God, to do little stupid things until my death, if I am humble, if I remain very small.[135]

The very ability to engage in acts of love flows from the love that is granted by God.

> Indeed spiritual directors make people advance towards perfection by performing a great number of acts of virtue, and they are right, but my director, who is Jesus does not teach me to count on my own acts; He teaches me to do *everything* out of love, to refuse Him nothing, to be content, when He gives me an occasion to prove to Him that I love Him, but this is done in peace, in *surrender*, and it is Jesus who does everything and I do nothing.[136]

St. Thérèse is familiar with the concept of virtue, which was more prevalent in religious literature and in preaching in her time than it is today, but her unwavering Christocentrism compels her to declare:

> To be small is still not to attribute to oneself the virtues that one practices, believing oneself capable of something, but to recognize that the good Lord places this treasure in the hand of his little child so that he uses it when needed; but it is still God's treasure.[137]

This distancing from the way in which the role of virtues in the moral life was understood gives St. Thérèse a tranquility that frees her from the

---

[135] Yellow Notebook, CJ August 7, 1897.

[136] Letter 142, my translation from *Oeuvres complètes* (Paris: Cerf, Desclée de Brouwer, 1992), 464–465.

[137] Yellow Notebook, CJ August 6, 1897, no. 8, https://archives.carmeldelisieux.fr/en/archive/cj-aout-1897/#le-6-aout.

dread with which one's own sinfulness, whether actual or merely imminent, paralyzes many on their spiritual journey. In a letter to her sister, who was struggling with her challenging personality, St. Thérèse writes:

> The little child ... sleeps on the Heart of the Great General.... Close to this Heart, we learn courage, and above all confidence. Grapeshot, the sound of cannon, what is all that when you are carried by the General?[138]

Could it be that St. Thérèse did not recognize the need to valiantly reject threatening temptations and to build up moral virtues within herself? And yet she writes:

> Since it was given to me to also understand the love of the Heart of Jesus, I confess to you that it has banished all fear from my heart. The memory of my faults humbles me, leads me never to lean on my strength which is only weakness, but even more this memory speaks to me of mercy and love.... I try not to worry about myself in anything anymore, and what Jesus deigns to do in my soul I leave it to him.[139]

And elsewhere she says:

> We would like never to fall? ... What does it matter, my Jesus, if I fall every moment, I see my weakness there, and it is a great gain for me.[140]

St. Thérèse's writings have a different tone from that which prevailed in common moral teaching in the modern Church. This freshness of spirit and

---

[138] Letter 200, to Sr. Marie of St. Joseph, October (?) 1896, Archives du Carmel de Lisieux, https://archives.carmeldelisieux.fr/en/correspondance/lt-200-a-soeur-marie-de-saint-joseph-fin-octobre-1896/.

[139] Letter 247, to Abbé Bellière, June 21, 1897, Archives du Carmel de Lisieux, https://archives.carmeldelisieux.fr/en/correspondance/lt-247-a-labbe-belliere-21-juin-1897/.

[140] Letter 89, to Céline, April 26, 1889, Archives du Carmel de Lisieux, https://archives.carmeldelisieux.fr/en/correspondance/lt-89-a-celine-26-avril-1889/.

unlimited trust in God's mercy meant that the faithful very quickly recognized in her writings a light for our times that delivers from distortions and a moralistic narrow-mindedness. A superficial exposure to her teachings might suggest that here we have a cheap quietism that tells us not to worry about anything and to leave the solicitude for one's spiritual and moral growth entirely to Jesus. The truth is that trust in God's love frees one from anxiety and produces spiritual fervor. Just as, in neurotic entanglement, the emotions become inwardly blocked, and just as, in ideological captivity of the mind, the impulse of the intellect toward the truth is occasionally stunted, so too, in the spiritual life, the impulse of love for God is occasionally stunted, whether by false doctrine that clips its wings by focusing on sin, by discouraging external social pressure, or by spiritual laziness. This spiritual captivity, more dangerous than the captivity of emotion or intellect, is truly a spiritual malady. The writings of St. Thérèse, the youngest and most recent Doctor of the Church, with their freshness and grace, show the way of deliverance from this spiritual captivity. One should not think, however, that St. Thérèse offers spiritual and moral easy riding. Her path is one of concrete generosity, of daily practical love that is demanding. She writes:

> It was not necessary to do dazzling works but to hide and practice virtue so that the left hand does not know what the right is doing.[141]

Her advice to those who struggle with discouragement is as follows:

> Many souls say: But I do not have the strength to perform such a sacrifice. So let them do what I did: a great effort. The good Lord never refuses this first grace which gives the courage to act; after that the heart is strengthened and we go from victory to victory.[142]

> What the good Lord asks of us is not to dwell on the fatigues of the struggle, it is not to be discouraged.[143]

---

[141] Manuscript A 32r.
[142] Yellow Notebook, CJ August 8, 1987, no. 3, Archives du Carmel de Lisieux, https://archives.carmeldelisieux.fr/en/archive/cj-aout-1897/#le-8-aout.
[143] Yellow Notebook, CJ April 6, 1897, no. 2, Archives du Carmel de Lisieux, https://archives.carmeldelisieux.fr/en/archive/cj-avril-1897/.

The minimalistic vision of life, based only on the commandments that exclude the wrong paths, is rather simple, though not very joyful. A life in which the love of God is nurtured in an attempt to respond creatively to that love at every moment is extremely demanding. St. Thérèse, while bringing liberation from Pelagianism, does not preach the other extreme, which is quietism. She teaches active love, realized in a deep trust in the goodness of God, and for the sheer pleasure of God, Who can give Himself through human generosity.

> Merit does not consist in doing or giving much, but rather in receiving, in loving much.... It is said that it is much sweeter to give than to receive, and it is true, but then, when Jesus wants to take for Himself the sweetness of giving, it would not be gracious to refuse.[144]

St. Paul

St. Thérèse's teaching, full of confidence in divine power, can be viewed as a wonderful commentary on the teaching of St. Paul, who writes, upon having recognized his weakness, "I will all the more gladly boast of my weaknesses, that the power of Christ may rest upon me" (2 Cor. 12:9). While preaching freedom before the Law, St. Paul points to the inner workings of the Holy Spirit, which transform man. St. Paul treats his weakness (of which we do not know whether it was physical, mental, or moral) as a gift from God, delivering him from spiritual pride. The experience of this weakness, combined with trust in divine power, generates transparency for the operation of grace, "When I am weak, then I am strong" (2 Cor. 12:10). A phrase that appears frequently in Paul's letters is "in Christ," which signifies an inward orientation, centered on the Savior, liberating from sinfulness and from being focused on it and enabling the Spirit of Jesus to be accorded a primary role in a person's life: "There is therefore now no condemnation for those who are in Christ Jesus. For the law of the Spirit of life in Christ Jesus has set me free from the law of sin and death" (Rom. 8:1–2). The Christian living by the grace of the Risen One does not measure his life through an externally formulated moral

---

[144] Letter 142, to Céline.

law but by the Person of the Holy Spirit, Who, working within the soul, becomes like a personal law. Like St. Thérèse of Lisieux, aware of her childlike relationship to her Heavenly Father, St. Paul declares that "all who are led by the Spirit of God are sons of God" (Rom. 8:14). The attitude of a child of God entails the reception of the inspirations of the Holy Spirit, who guides through life, inviting one to a trusting love and to a direct response to His stirrings. The recognition of the primacy of the Holy Spirit's work in one's life must transform the entire human ethos, provided that the connection with the Holy Spirit is cultivated. This is not so obvious, however, because it is possible to lose the receptivity to the Holy Spirit, either through indifference or by clinging to a more comfortable, seemingly easier and reassuring external principle. St. Paul issues a resounding rebuke to the Galatians who fell into this trap: "You are severed from Christ, you who would be justified by the law; you have fallen away from grace" (Gal. 5:4).

The freeing of oneself from a life perspective based upon an external law is demanding. "You were called to freedom, brethren; only do not use your freedom as an opportunity for the flesh, but through love be servants of one another" (Gal. 5:13). The love of God, "poured into our hearts through the Holy Spirit who has been given us" (Rom. 5:5), becomes an internal drive, shaping one's attitudes toward others and provoking generous action. "But the fruit of the Spirit is love, joy, peace, patience, kindness, goodness, faithfulness, gentleness, self-control" (Gal. 5:22–23). St. Paul's listing of the fruits of the Spirit is not exhaustive. St. Paul merely wishes to highlight the spiritual dynamics that combat evil inclinations and unleash a wealth of attitudes and actions through which the fecundity of God Himself is manifested. There is no reason not to expand this list and not to recognize how communing with the soul's inner visitor — the Holy Spirit — spills over into all other possible dimensions of human life and action and into various callings. Therefore, St. Paul proclaims, "If by the Spirit you put to death the deeds of the body you will live" (Rom. 8:13).

Lessons for Christian morality

In light of the teachings of both St. Paul and St. Thérèse, it is clear that the essence of sanctity is not moral perfection. Nor is it some psychic equilibrium.

The essence of sanctity is the encounter of human sinfulness with the power and love of God. The one who mistakes sanctity for moral perfection will be self-centered and will be constantly struggling to free himself from his own sinfulness. The one who mistakes sanctity for psychic equilibrium will also be focused on his own psychic or spiritual state. The clear recognition that this is not the point is liberating. St. Thérèse knew that "little stupid things" could happen to her, but she was not concerned about them. Her attention was focused on the goodness of God. Most of our time and life is spent doing good, doing things in which there is room for creativity, and tackling various life challenges. Why, in thinking about the religious component of life, is the attention so often fixated on sinfulness, whether sins that have been committed or sins that loom as a threatening temptation? What kind of transformation of religious perception needs to happen so that life according to the Holy Spirit will be brought to the center, so that the good to which the Spirit prompts us will be the subject of reflection, thought, prayer, and, above all, action? Has Christian religiosity not perhaps lost the optimistic vision of St. Paul, and instead unnecessarily moralized religiosity to such an extent that the power of the Holy Spirit has been forgotten? It is no wonder that, when Christian formation was centered on morality (understood in terms of obligation), forgetting communion with the Holy Spirit, or, at best, relegating that communion to the realm of the rare and extraordinary, this resulted, in some people, in fatigue and frustration (for how may one deal with evil if there was no initiation into this struggle "with the help of the Spirit"?), and in others, it even led to an outright rejection of Christianity. The strong, yet simple, girlish voice of St. Thérèse of Lisieux was needed to place things where they belong.[145] We are still a long way from profiting appropriately from her message.

The primacy of grace in the Christian moral life should be the central theme of evangelical preaching. Although moral perfection is not the end,

---

[145] St. Faustina's message, directing the faith toward the glorified humanity of Jesus, may be interpreted in a similar way. The merciful love of the Risen One liberates from sin. This message of the saints is a departure from exaggerated moralization.

communion with the Holy Spirit does bring life-changing repercussions and generates attitudes and actions in which moral goodness is manifested. Theologians are faced with the challenge of explaining the supernatural dynamic of grace in transforming the human psyche from within and the practice of moral decision-making — and in the context of the real moral dilemmas that life brings. Precisely because of this latter point, moral theology cannot be satisfied with merely repeating old formulations. Life situations change. The social context is sometimes very different, depending on the country and era in which one lives. Additionally, today we are faced with new technical, economic, and political opportunities. If it is true that the Holy Spirit transforms the human ethos from within, one must consider how, in practice, openness to the grace of the Holy Spirit manifests itself in the professional life of a civil servant, a judge, a blue-collar worker, a doctor, or an economist doing stock market transactions. Individual lives, married life, family life, and social and political life in all their dimensions are amenable to mysterious transformations originating in the grace of the Holy Spirit. Since moral teaching has often been restricted to preaching the theme of obligation, with reference to the moral law as it is formulated in the Decalogue and supplemented by canon law, it has necessarily been limited to the issuing of prohibitions and commands by an ecclesiastical or divine authority. And what happened to the teaching of life in the Spirit? Should not the divine gift be shown first, followed by a practical demonstration of how this gift may be lived out, thus explaining the "instruction manual" of the grace of the Holy Spirit, and only at the end be a warning against erroneous paths that poison the receptivity to the divine gifts?

 This shift in emphasis is not just a necessary requirement for those who are spiritually and morally advanced. It is necessary precisely for those who deplore their mistakes and failures. Those who are caught up in sin, even if they are so exhausted that they have lost the sensitivity of their conscience and easily absolve themselves of their failures, most of all need an initiation into communion with the Holy Spirit. And even more, they need a discourse that is related to their real moral dilemmas and questions. The initiation into communion with the Holy Spirit is necessary when embarking on any human endeavor. St. Paul VI knew this when, in his encyclical on contraception,

Humanae vitae, he addressed priests, writing, "So speak with full confidence, beloved sons, convinced that the Holy Spirit of God ... also illumines from within the hearts of the faithful and invites their assent" (29). He knew, of course, that it is within conjugal love that the love coming from the Holy Spirit has its pride of place. Purifying it from the taint of selfishness, the Holy Spirit, in the likeness of natural fertility, endows all love with spiritual fecundity. A total gift of self, free from egoism and manipulation, empowers further generosity and becomes an opportunity to renew and to further that immersion in divine love that is promised in all the sacraments, beginning with Baptism.

Concern for life permeated by the power of grace has provoked theological thought to seek a language that will describe this mysterious reality. This is not easy, of course, because the mystery cannot be completely enclosed in simple formulas, but theology cannot eschew this task. And when it turns out that certain terms have been worn out because they trigger wrong connotations or do not evoke a social response, it is permissible to look for other terms that will perhaps resonate better in the soul. If there are people in a given society who wonder about the spiritual life and seek to name it somehow, then formulations, including the classical ones, have meaning. If there are no people in a society who ponder about living a life of grace, then words such as *virtue* either mean nothing or evoke distorted connotations. In addition, when the clergy limit moral instruction merely to recounting a catalogue of obligations, and the legal order hinders all social grassroots initiatives by subjecting them to the meticulous control of state officials who enforce ideologies that are currently being promoted, most people descend into passivism, into an attitude of entitlement, and they lead shallow lives focused on "bread and circuses," and no one is interested in "virtue." On the other hand, in countries such as the United States, where the sphere of freedom is still defended and where it is possible to establish schools and universities independent of the state, with their own funding, their own curricula, and their own ethos, just as it is also possible to initiate autonomous associations, businesses, independent insurance systems, and a private health-care sector with a specific ethos, the term *virtue* is present both in ethical discourse and in public debate because the widespread social generosity demands a term that will describe it. Diffidence regarding attempts to describe the fecundity of grace within human generosity has, moreover, an additional source in the legacy of the philosophy of positivism that is present in culture. It then becomes easier to speak of the concept of virtue rather than of virtue as such because the philosophical connotation suggests that virtue is, at most, a philosophical or poetic concept rather than an actual reality embedded in the powers of the soul. A mind formed by positivism and recognizing only empirical methods does not want to acknowledge the fact that grace may take root in the psychic powers of man, in the will or in the emotions, generating permanent dispositions. This rejection is, of course, a consequence of the enslavement of the mind, which does not recognize the existence of a spiritual structure of the soul that cannot be measured and therefore wants to dictate what reality should be! Theological discourse, however, does not have to yield to these biases and may boldly proclaim the presence of grace in human life and actions.

Today, personalistic terms are being sought. God does not grant gifts that simply drop down from above. It is God Who grants Himself to us, accomplishing a profound transformation within us. But this transformation has to be described in some way. Sometimes, at the root of personalistic language lies an understanding of divine transcendence that emphasizes God's otherness to such an extent that His participation in creation seems impossible. Failure to accept the truth that grace is both a divine and human reality leads to the Protestant *solus Deus*, which separates nature and all natural gifts from grace and from responsibility in grace. Catholicism accepts the difference between God and us but not their mutual inaccessibility. Divine transcendence is not such that God Himself cannot bridge the distance. If one negates divine fecundity in a natural human being, one falls into the trap of post-Tridentine manuals of moral theology: grace seems to be too distant to be of any use, and nature cannot reach grace on its own.

In attempting to describe the operation of grace, different starting points may be adopted. One may begin with specific challenges that emerge in different vocations and professions, reflecting how the action of the grace of the Holy Spirit is manifested within the life tasks of a soldier, a doctor, a farmer, or a politician. Such a theology of the various professions will be more than a rational professional ethics, as long as the primary focus of reflection seeks light (in the Word of God, in the experience of the saints, in theological reflection and in the teaching of the Magisterium) on the fecundity of grace in the context of a given professional life. Alternatively, one may begin with specific vocations in the Church, considering how the work of grace is manifested within family life, religious life, the priesthood, or the life of the laity. Such a theology will refer to the theology of Baptism, the theology of marriage, of the priesthood, or of consecrated life. One may also begin the search from the most rudimentary threshold, pondering on the fecundity of grace in the life of each person, starting from the basic faculties found in the human psyche and analyzing how the natural finality of these faculties is supernaturally transformed by grace.

The fundamental analogue of this search will be the glorified humanity of Christ, in which the entire natural endowment of human nature was transformed and enriched through the hypostatic union, uniting divinity and humanity in such a way that nothing of Jesus' human nature was destroyed or called into question. Just as the divinity became visible in the glorified humanity of Jesus, so the image — or rather, icon — of God, inscribed in the soul of every person transformed by the grace of the Holy Spirit, will somehow be recognizable through faith. By focusing on the light shining within the image of God that is the holy person, or by focusing on his or her good actions undertaken in such a way that — even spontaneously — a desire to "give glory to your Father who is in heaven" (Matt. 5:16) is born, something of the fecundity of grace will be recognized. The intuition that compels one to perceive a reflection of God in the wrinkled and fatigued face of St. Mother Teresa of Calcutta suggests that in the analysis of communion with God, of the reactions, generosity, and trustful faith of saints, a light may be discerned for the description of the outpouring of the grace of the Holy Spirit in human souls. Of course, the working out of a discourse that describes the supernatural reality in broken human language is not easy. However, the wisdom of the saints accrued over the centuries provides material for such an attempt. Theological effort seeking not only a phenomenological description of religious experience but the reality itself strives to define it with clear concepts and precise definitions.

Terminological challenges and escalating miscomprehensions

During the first millennium of the Church, the Fathers sought to describe the reality of grace using the language of dialogue, derived from the Greek culture. They wrote about divinization, the restoration of God's image, the vision of God, the *admirabile commercium*, and participation in divine life. St. Augustine wrote about the supernatural love — *caritas* — that God has for us and about our exaltation, which allows us to respond properly to God. St. Augustine, aware that he was introducing a certain novelty, was the first to apply the messianic text from Isaiah to every Christian. The prophet announces the gifting of the future Messiah: "There shall come forth a shoot from the stump of Jesse, and a branch shall grow out of his roots. And the spirit of the LORD shall rest upon him, the spirit of wisdom and understanding, the spirit of counsel and might, the spirit of knowledge and the fear of the LORD. And his delight shall be in the fear of the LORD" (Isa. 11:1–3).[146] These six or seven "spirits" that cannot be precisely named or measured express the gifting of the Holy Spirit that accompanies Christian existence, thus prompting the kind of life in which God's power is manifested. Starting in the twelfth century, medieval theology attempted to explain the mystery of God's presence in human action using the term *habitus*.[147] This word, which is the Latin translation of the Greek *hexis*, was introduced to describe the real and profound transformation wrought in man by God when He offers Himself to man. When the term was understood in the context of God's interpersonal relationship with man, it expressed the theological anthropology of the believer. It appeared in the context of the theology of Baptism and the virtues infused by grace. The reality of the Faith was expressed by a term that has its roots in the philosophy of Aristotle. *Habitus* denotes the dynamic principle of sanctification, which transforms a person's way of living and his

---

[146] Most likely for stylistic reasons, both the Septuagint and the Vulgate translated the repeated "fear" of the Lord as "piety," thus bringing the number of the gifts of the Holy Spirit to seven.

[147] Gianni Colzani, "Dalla grazia creata alla libertà donata: Per una diversa comprensione della tesi sull' *habitus*," *Scuola Cattolica* 112 (1984): 399–434.

actions. It describes the profundity of the new life that God grants in such a way that man loses nothing of his natural dignity, while he becomes capable of actions that are marked from within by God's power. Underlying the use of this term in theology is the conviction that the gift of grace requires a new way of being, a new personality. Grace is not limited to a new external layer superimposed on a person, nor is it manifested exclusively in certain actions. An inner change takes place in the person, and this change is precisely what theology strives to convey with this term.

Peter Abelard argued that God creates in us by grace new dispositions, which are a created gift, but there is no personal participation and presence of God in them. This theory amounted to essentialism. It reified grace, treating it as a created thing that God supposedly deposits in the human soul (or pours like a liquid into the soul). Peter Lombard objected to this theory, showing that it is God who sanctifies us, rather than a reality that is distinct from God. Lombard thus identified charity with the Person of the Holy Spirit. Charity enjoys a unique status because, through it, the Holy Spirit imparts Himself. In positing this claim, Lombard pushed the anti-Pelagian logic of St. Augustine to the extreme.

St. Thomas Aquinas rejected this theory because it leads to pantheism. If charity is equated with the Person of the Holy Spirit, that would mean that the Holy Spirit is merged with the human person, depriving him of his proper dignity. If charity were the Holy Spirit Himself, this would mean that the human person would be reduced to the status of a passive puppet manipulated by the Holy Spirit. The solution proposed by Aquinas leaves room for God's power and for human action, neither of which competes with the other. The grace of the Holy Spirit pours into the soul gifts that are both supernatural and created. The term *habitus* expresses qualities emerging from grace that transform the human faculties, rendering them capable of supernatural functions, but they continue to benefit from their own natural dynamics. Among these supernatural habitus, Aquinas mentions the gifts of the Holy Spirit and the infused virtues, theological and moral. These supernatural transformations of human faculties are not identified with God, although they come from God. They are the fruit of the invisible but real mission of the Divine Person, Who embraces the sanctified human being with His power. The interpretation that Aquinas gave is both personalistic and dynamic. St. Thomas Aquinas does not attribute to man a union with God similar to the hypostatic union that is in Christ, nor does he reify grace. In the supernatural life, we are elevated to a new level in which God moves us, but we experience this new life as something that is ours, not as something that has been imposed upon us from above. In order to be divine, the good that we undertake by grace must be fully human — that is, it must flow from mature, transformed human faculties that are also our own, human, and that recognize the primacy of God. Grace does not wield a person like an inanimate tool; it does not descend onto a block of wood. Grace works within mature, personal human choices. The theological use of the term *habitus* is intended to describe the capacity for conscious self-giving that flows from the stirrings of grace. In the great Scholastic theology, the connection between the habitus and the Holy Spirit was so obvious that it did not need to be constantly mentioned. Difficulties with the term, however, began in the late Middle Ages.

William of Ockham, who lived in the fourteenth century, held that God's freedom is so great (in order to be divine) that God is indifferent to values and, with His arbitrary will, He can condemn the righteous and save the sinner. In this perspective, the transformation of the human ethos by grace had no sense. Luther, in turn, viewed grace as being given to man externally. Grace covers the sinner as a cloak but does not transform him from within. Under the cloak of grace, man remains a sinner. Thus, in Luther's logic, there was no place for the infused virtues. Meanwhile, the personalistic and spiritual dimension of the habitus was forgotten in post-Tridentine Catholic theology. Suárez understood the habitus as an external help that facilitates action but has no effect on the one acting, somewhat like oil that improves the functioning of a machine but in no way determines its nature. In modern theology, the term *habitus* came to be construed in a reified and natural way. When the authors of manuals of moral theology wrote about virtues, it is not clear whether they meant infused virtues or virtues acquired by natural effort. Most often, these manuals first described moral action from a natural perspective and only later mentioned grace. Moral virtues in this description seemed to be a crypto-Pelagian expression of human perfection that establishes for itself a space of freedom that is autonomous from God. Such a presentation is a misunderstanding and deformation of the medieval doctrine.

The German theologian Otto Hermann Pesch,[148] sensitive to Lutheran reactions to Catholic moral theology, raises several objections to the modern doctrine of virtues. If the habitus is conceived first and foremost as a capacity that is acquired through careful conscious practice, just as one acquires proficiency in playing the piano, and this understanding is then transferred to virtue, then the conviction arises that the Christian moral life — that is, the life of faith — is primarily a matter of practice. This view leads to a "moralization of grace," implying that openness to the reality of grace and abiding in it is a matter of practice, in which willpower plays the dominant role. If the life of faith is a matter of practice, then grace is necessary only to sustain man's natural faculties, and not simply to enable faith and the Christian life. One then forgets that faith is a matter of grace and falls into semi-Pelagianism, claiming that the supernatural life originates from human effort rather than being a gift from God. When faith is made into an obligation to be exercised, various objections and questions arise regarding the salvation of unbelievers. Since the word *habitus* is derived from the Latin *habere*, or *se habere*, one often understands capacities, and therefore both virtues and gifts of the Holy Spirit, as something one has or as the possessed ability to command oneself, one's personality, and one's affections. Grace, which is a divine gift, given according to God's generosity and pleasure, is then viewed in the category of "having" rather than in the category of "being." The received gift becomes, in a way, an appropriated gift, in which the reference to the Giver of the gift vanishes. When the naturalistic understanding of the habitus prevailed in the description of the work of grace, the personal dimension of the divine gift was forgotten. The doctrine of virtues, conceived as habits, possessed and developed by practice, tacitly assumed that the prerequisite for the growth of virtues is the permanent rejection of sin. This is at odds with human experience, in which moral weakness accompanies the whole of life. St. Paul painfully experienced that which was a "thorn in the flesh," and St. Thérèse

---

[148] *Thomas d'Aquin: Grandeur et limites de la théologie médiévale* (Paris: Cerf, 1994), 294–295.

knew that "little stupid things" would happen to her. Yet St. Paul with courage proclaimed life through the grace of the Resurrection. The suggestion that sin must first be eliminated before the entire discourse of Catholic theology on grace and the virtues could gain meaning practically dismissed the life of supernatural virtue *ad kalendas Graecas*! This understanding reaffirmed the erroneous conviction that first many years of ascetical life are needed, and the mystical life is left for a future, distant day. The understanding of the virtues, therefore, is the knot in which all the errors of modern moral theology converge. In order to grasp the liberating role of grace in life, it is also necessary to free oneself from the Kantian understanding of virtue as an exercise of character in view of ethical conduct or as conformity of the will to obligation.

The habitus

In Polish neo-Scholastic literature, Aquinas's *habitus* was translated as *sprawność* — meaning "prowess." Fr. Jacek Woroniecki, O.P., rightly distinguished between a custom or a habit, which can be mechanical and become a manifestation of routine, and prowess, in which the spiritual powers are involved.[149] In habitus, there is a moment of a conscious choice of the good, a creative moment. The one who has acquired the habitus, although he acts efficiently and lightly, is sensitive to all the richness and multidimensionality of his action. A skilled pianist gives the impression of playing quickly and effortlessly, moving his fingers over the keyboard with ease. However, every movement of the muscles of his fingers and his entire body, his artistic sensitivity, and the force of impact or the subtlety of his movements are the result of work. That which appears to be a purely mechanical and painless movement is, in fact, the result of conscious schooling and effort that stressed the invisible and seemingly imperceptible features of the performance. Thus, each movement is consciously chosen and executed with precision. The understanding of *habitus* as a property that is fundamentally acquired, prevalent in neo-Scholastic Thomism, found its echo in the Polish scouting movement. When the foundations of the movement were laid at the beginning of the

---

[149] *Katolicka Etyka Wychowawcza* (Lublin: KUL, 1986), vol. 1, 334.

twentieth century, priests trained in neo-Thomism were involved. Among them were Cardinal Mercier's disciple Fr. Kazimierz Lutosławski and Fr. Woroniecki. Are they not to be credited with introducing into the scouting formation program the "earning of proficiency," certified by merit badges sewn onto the uniform? While it is possible to gain technical or artistic capacity through deliberate exercise, is it not an error to simply transfer this understanding of prowess to the moral realm? Although one may spend a certain amount of time every day practicing the piano or studying a foreign language, this is not how one grows in the moral virtues of patience, chastity, and fortitude. An understanding of a natural capacity, including a certain natural moral perfection designated as an "acquired virtue," must therefore go through a process of purification and adaptation if it is to be applied to the description of the reality of grace. This is not surprising because we do not have a language to describe a supernatural reality. A natural habitus, acquired through practice and effort, may be an analogue for the fecundity of grace in the ethos, but it is a distant analogue, since the difference has to be grasped, lest grace be naturalized. (One should not, of course, fall into the other extreme and propose to abandon the term altogether because then the need to nurture generous self-giving will be forgotten, leading to a quietistic understanding of grace. Since the risk of Pelagian extremism in the formation programs of the scouting movement has been mentioned, it is also necessary to bring up the risk of a quietistic search for only religious experiences, which may characterize the Light-Life and the Charismatic movements. Finding in education an appropriate middle ground, in which the primacy of communion with God is situated in the context of real life, duties, and generosity, is not easy.)

By introducing the term *habitus* into his theology of agency, Aquinas expanded the meaning of the term to some extent. Originally used to describe technical or artistic abilities, when it was applied to ethics, the word also included for Aquinas innate, constant qualities and dispositions, such as health and the habit of first principles of cognition, or synderesis, which is defined as an innate habit, located in the practical reason, that directs one to pursue good and avoid evil. The use of the term *habitus* to describe these entitative proficiencies means applying it also to innate qualities that do not require practice but are in conformity with the metaphysical structure of the human being. These qualities are grounded not in practice but in something that is more primordial and deeper in man. Since Aquinas did not hesitate to apply the term *habitus* to the innate qualities of the faculties inherent in the human being, it is not surprising that he also used this term to describe the transformation of the faculties by grace.

Although the stirrings come from grace, the ease of creatively choosing the good is accomplished through human faculties that have been marked by grace. Christian life does not happen apart from or above natural powers but precisely through them. Man is sanctified completely by the grace that is manifested in him. Introducing the theory of the habitus into the theology of grace, medieval theologians wanted to raise a bulwark against Pelagianism, which implied that grace has no influence on moral action, which takes place uniquely through the natural powers. The theory of the habitus seeks to demonstrate how making a free choice may come from man and yet simultaneously originate from a movement of grace. Grace and infused virtue precede the free choice, just as rain precedes the fruitfulness of trees. This is so because justification accomplished freely by grace precedes moral effort, rather than being subsequent to it. Otto Herman Pesch wryly notes that the habitus theory was accepted in the Middle Ages for the very same reason for which Luther rejected it later. Luther was also struggling against Pelagianism, and he viewed the habitus theory, already conceived in an overly naturalistic manner, as a contestation of grace.[150]

It is not enough to know the rules of good conduct. The inner disposition has also to be properly oriented. An immature person finds it difficult to act purposefully. The term *habitus* implies possessing oneself in a specified way in view of an end. In mechanical action, there is no rational reflection, no conscious choice. In mature action, there is a creative choice, which expresses the dignity of the acting person. Habitus, which defines a constant disposition in action and in being, means, as it were, a "second nature." It expresses the subjectivity of man, who is the master of his actions, and not merely a cog moved by the social machine. Not all people who act well are truly virtuous.

---

[150] *Katolicka Etyka Wychowawcza*, 310.

Likewise, not all those who act badly have an ingrained evil habitus, i.e., a true vice. It happens that people are moved by social demands or by situations that push them to act, but they never cross the threshold of virtue or vice. When they act well, they do so because there was no other choice and they had to act that way, but their action lacks a conscious commitment and choice. A truly virtuous person is always unpredictable because he does not automatically act in accordance with acquired habituations but is creative, constantly reinventing ways to react and act that correspond to the situation, which is always unique.[151] Likewise, someone who has a true vice, that is, a person who is creative and thoughtful in the evil he commits, will be creative in the good when he converts. Someone who has not matured to be creative in the good will be monotonous and mundane, even when he cannot be reproached for anything. Habitus ensures that the action is undertaken easily, efficiently, quickly, and with pleasure. All the talents, gifts, personal charm, and appropriate faculties are creatively harnessed into action. Since the inner spiritual powers are fully engaged, the action is then authentic. This does not mean spontaneity, which may be characterized by a lack of forethought and planning. Solidarity and resistance, as opposed to conformity and avoidance, are authentic attitudes in which there is a moment of creative free choice.[152] Mature action confers inner joy, which is different from fleeting pleasure. Since creative action entails a certain fecundity, the begetting of something new, it includes the joy of accomplishing a good work.

Habitus may exist only in those beings in which there is potentiality. The intellectual habits of knowledge or science may become more and more

---

[151] When my father was in a German POW camp, he received letters from my mother, which were censored by the Nazis. If the censor decided that a certain part of a sentence should be banned, he would cut it out with scissors. The letters would arrive cut up, with holes in the text. Even in the last months of the war, when the Allied offensive was drawing near, some German official would be sitting at his desk and cutting out suspicious sentences with scissors! Undoubtedly, this man must have been distinguished by his conscientiousness, but he lacked imagination and creativity in life! Although he was thorough in his work, and basically harmless, he was not a virtuous man!

[152] Karol Wojtyła, *Person and Act and Related Essays*, trans. Grzegorz Ignatik (Washington, D.C.: Catholic University of America Press, 2021), 400–407.

deeply rooted in the mind and may encompass an ever-growing spectrum. Moral or theological virtues may become increasingly embedded in the subject, but in order to be true, they cannot be limited in scope. True justice has to apply to all people, not just to some. Animals do not have habitus; they may have only quasi abilities, cultivated not by the animal itself but by a trainer who, by playing on the animal's emotions, forces a certain action. In a human person, the habitus may be located in the body or in the emotions, insofar as the body or emotion is subject to the influence of the reason and the will. Aquinas, drawing from this understanding of the habitus, will say that grace subsists in the essence of the human soul as an "entitative habit," elevating it to participation in the divine nature. In contrast, the infused virtues and the gifts of the Holy Spirit are like "operative habits" rooted in the faculties of the soul.

Since the habitus makes action easy, quick, creative, and enjoyable, one should not think that only such action that is difficult and requires effort represents value. The habitus theory attempts to show how faith, hope, and charity, being gifts from God, can be obvious, spontaneous, joyful, and come effortlessly. Why is joy lacking in Christian life today? Does it not strike us as naive? Have we not convinced ourselves that in Christian life the emphasis must be on trial, on hardship, and on humorless tension? The joy of God's children seems suspicious. There was a time when people in the Church thought otherwise. The virtuous person is not the one who struggles hard against temptations, even if he manages not to succumb to them, but the one in whom temptations do not arise at all, who easily, obviously, and spontaneously grasps what is worth being involved in and immediately does that. Joyful and creative spontaneity in goodness is a quality of all Christians who live by grace. Introducing the theory of the habitus into the theology of grace was intended to demonstrate how a sanctified person becomes natural and fully human. The ease of undertaking creatively the good in grace is not acquired through arduous practice or effort. But it is not connatural to man, since undertaking goodness must sometimes contend with discouragement, fatigue, or laziness. This ease, which comes from trusting in the power of grace and from the freedom to respond to God in love, is a gift from God. While a person who is diligent and conscientious but does not have a relationship with God may undertake a good action that will have something of the serious precision of art, he who lives by grace will be characterized in his good action by a childlike playfulness that immediately responds to love with love.

The gifts of the Holy Spirit

The classic text from Isaiah (11:1–3) is not the only one that describes the working of the Holy Spirit in men. The Word of God repeatedly forecasts the presence of the Holy Spirit within human action itself. "When they deliver you up, do not be anxious how you are to speak or what you are to say; for what you are to say will be given to you in that hour; for it is not you who speak, but the Spirit of your Father speaking through you" (Matt 10:19–20). "But the Counselor, the Holy Spirit, whom the Father will send in my name, he will teach you all things, and bring to your remembrance all that I have said to you" (John 14:26). This reminding sometimes comes about at the very moment of undertaking an action. A text from the Word of God that was heard or read comes to mind at some point, and one is then faced with a choice. The call to a greater love, to forgiveness, or simply to remain silent in a difficult situation: Will it be heeded — or not? Recalling the quarrel of the Chosen People with God, as they refused to recognize Him in the hardship of the desert pilgrimage, the psalmist exhorts, and this is echoed daily in the liturgy, "O that today you would hearken to his voice! Harden not your hearts" (Ps. 95:7–8). The expectation of being prompted by the Holy Spirit during the day prepares for a surprise and liberates from a wrathful hardness of heart, in which one's own designs screen God's plans. Although the text of Isaiah, merely due to an inaccurate translation, heralds seven rather than six "spirits," other texts speak explicitly of seven gifts. "I saw a Lamb standing, as though it had been slain, with seven horns and with seven eyes, which are the seven spirits of God sent out into all the earth" (Rev. 5:6). The number seven, in the language of the Bible, denotes plenitude. In the Hebrew version, the enumeration of six spirits in Isaiah does not, in fact, permit a precise differentiation of the Holy Spirit's actions. The meaning of the words used partially overlaps. The biblical text primarily draws attention to the guidance of the Holy Spirit, without offering a basis for a strict distinction of individual "spirits." The more one is drawn into the mystery, the more that which can be said of it becomes hazy. Actions can be precisely defined, and virtues may be distinguished exactly, but the breath of the Holy Spirit does not lend itself to such a detailed analysis.

Being led by the Holy Spirit has been a topic of theological reflection for centuries. The Fathers of the Church used many terms to describe the action of the Holy Spirit. It was not until Scholasticism that an attempt was made to clarify the terminology. In the liturgy, the term *munus* (*Tu septiformis munere*) has been preserved, a word that means an offering, a bribe, an obligation, and a task assigned with trust. Most often the action of the Holy Spirit is described as a *donum*, as opposed to the Latin *datum*. The gifts of the Holy Spirit are not merely given; they are the fruit of a generous endowment. The term suggests the bestowal of a precious gift. This gifting is done freely, without the expectation of a necessary recompense.

A precise determination of what the gifts of the Holy Spirit are within the supernatural organism of the Christian took a long time. Aquinas himself vacillated in fine-tuning the details of his doctrine. Certain Scholastics (Peter Lombard, Duns Scotus) held that the gifts were not different from the virtues. Other authors equated the gifts with some virtues or held that they are used only in extraordinary and rare vocations. Aquinas states clearly that the gifts are not the fruit of an extraordinary charismatic grace. They belong to the basic spiritual endowment of every baptized person, and they are necessary so as to confer a supernatural dimension to all action.

When viewed from God's perspective, the gifts of the Holy Spirit do not differ from actual graces. Seen, however, from our experience, we distinguish them as a supernatural habitus, that is, as an enduring quality that allows for a continuous receptivity to the stirrings of the Holy Spirit. The gifts may be imagined by comparing them to an antenna that receives radio waves, or to a funnel that allows one to pour liquid easily into a bottle. They denote a constant disposition, open to the stirrings of the Holy Spirit and triggering an immediate response to the divine call.[153] When these "spiritual antennae"

---

[153] *ST*, Ia-IIae, q. 68, art. 3: "The gifts of the Holy Spirit are likewise *habitus* by which man is perfected so as to obey the Holy Spirit readily" (trans. E. D. O'Connor, vol. 24, 1974).

are activated, when receptivity to the guidance of the Holy Spirit is awakened, this means that the interior suggestions and promptings of the Holy Spirit appear in the very midst of human action. In his exposition, Aquinas posed a seemingly logical objection that, since the gifts cause perfect responsiveness to the stirrings of the Holy Spirit, they should be a perfection of the Holy Spirit Himself rather than of the human person, just as the skill of the musician who plays a guitar is his attribute, not that of the instrument. Such reasoning would be true if man were a passive instrument in the hand of the Holy Spirit. Man, however, possesses spiritual faculties. When he acts under the influence of the Holy Spirit, he does not lose his own faculties and dignity. The Holy Spirit acts within the human free choice. The more the Holy Spirit is at work, the more He bestows freedom, because this spiritual stirring frees man from inner resistances, and action is then in conformity with the deepest finality of the faculties. When man is under the influence of the Holy Spirit, he is increasingly in accord with the deepest dimension of the will and the reason, which strive toward goodness and truth, and therefore he is free. The enslavement of the will consists either in one's acting against his will because he is drawn by the senses or sin, or in his acting well, in conformity with his deepest willing, but this is experienced as a burden and not as a dimension of personal love.[154] When someone inspires us to good action, he does not order us what we are to do, or how in detail we are to do it, nor does he take away our freedom. The suggestion and the willingness of the will come from without, but the creativity, talents, experience, and the execution itself are ours. And this involvement of the whole personality is liberating. A drug addict, who, enslaved by addiction, chooses to take a drug to get high, is not free. St. Maximilian Kolbe in Auschwitz, where, at the prompting of the Holy Spirit, he gave his life, was free. The stirring of

---

[154] *Summa contra gentiles*, l. 4, c. 22 (3589): "When the Holy Spirit by love inclines the will to the true good to which it is naturally directed, he removes both the servitude whereby a man, the slave of passion and sin, acts against the order of the will, and the servitude whereby a man acts against the inclination of his will, and in obedience to the law, as the slave and not the friend of the law" (trans. L. Shapcote, Books II–IV [Green Bay, WI: Aquinas Institute, Emmaus Academic, 2018]).

the Holy Spirit, prompting him to the generous gift of self did not deprive him of his freedom or the dignity of his human faculties, or of his personal contribution and choice regarding his own conduct.

When, in his youth, Aquinas was wrote his *Commentary on the Sentences of Peter Lombard*, he taught that the gifts enable a higher way of acting than the virtues. The virtues, including the infused virtues, perfect a person to act in a fully human way. Meanwhile, receptivity to the gifts of the Holy Spirit makes an action superhuman. The ultimate measure of action transcends the limits of rationality and accepts the direct divine light. In theological effort, man learns about divine matters through a rational reflection conducted in faith. The gift of understanding, however, gives a foretaste of the knowledge that is to come in Heaven, and the gift of counsel gives the certainty, coming from the Holy Spirit, that one should act in such and such a way. At that stage in the development of his thought, Aquinas held that the infused virtues are supernatural, but their way of functioning is human. Through the receptivity of the soul, however, the gifts allow for the guidance of the Holy Spirit, and consequently, the way in which acts of the virtues are elicited is divine. Being familiar with the traditional enumeration of the seven gifts as well as the three theological virtues and the four cardinal virtues, Aquinas sought to associate each virtue with a specific gift. This somewhat artificial association does not seem to be convincing.

When Aquinas proceeded to write part Ia-IIae of the *Summa theologiae*, he developed a new approach to understanding the gifts. Since the underlying theme of this entire work is God, viewed through the *motus*, the movement of man, or rather the moving of man by God and toward God, the concept of movement emerged in the reflection on the gifts. He who is led by the Holy Spirit is moved by Him. Although the traditional account, informed by the biblical tradition, speaks of the breath of the Holy Spirit, Aquinas introduced the term *instinctus* in place of *inspiratio*. The one who is moved by the Holy Spirit has a new instinct within him that guides him. Inspiration suggests an idea coming from without and directed to the reason. The introduction of the term *instinctus* stratifies the understanding of the Holy Spirit's action, which also extends to the human will. The Holy Spirit instigates, offers an impetus, invites, enlightens, and fortifies. While, in the earlier work, Aquinas compared the human and divine modes of action, in the *Summa theologiae*, he compares the human and divine principle of action. In the earlier work, he spoke more as a psychologist. In the later one, he speaks as a metaphysician and a theologian. He views the gifts as a permanent disposition, a habitus that allows the Holy Spirit to draw one in. All the gifts of the Holy Spirit act similarly, in the manner of a counsel,[155] affecting action.

When Aquinas embarked on the task of writing part IIa-IIae, he abandoned the idea of treating the seven gifts as a coherent system. Medieval writers, whether for catechetical reasons or in order to work out something of a rebus, endeavored to correlate the various occurrences of the number seven (seven sacraments, seven gifts, seven days of Creation, seven capital sins, seven penitential psalms, seven appearances of Jesus after the Resurrection, seven instances of "The Lord be with you" in the liturgy, etc.). In this section of his moral doctrine that deals with particular morals, Aquinas considers the gifts together with the virtues, which he discusses one by one, assigning individual gifts to individual virtues according to how they best fit together, but he does not try to convince us that to each virtue corresponds a particular gift. The individual gifts should not be understood as specific endowments that animate only a certain sector of the moral life. It is more important to grasp their essence. The Holy Spirit permeates the entire Christian life, while the number and specific differences of the individual gifts — which, incidentally, are not so easy to grasp — are not so important. While working on the second part of the *Summa*, Aquinas was simultaneously writing a commentary on St. Paul's Letter to the Romans. In his discussion of chapter 8, where St. Paul most thoroughly develops his teaching on the guidance of the Holy Spirit, Aquinas merely states that the Holy Spirit enlightens the mind and moves the will, and he no longer refers to the traditional scheme of the seven gifts. It must be said, therefore, that Aquinas liberated the teaching on the gifts of the Holy Spirit from the restrictive scheme into which it had been forced. Unfortunately, Aquinas's successors failed to recognize his freedom in the face of the established

---

[155] *ST*, IIa-IIae, q. 52, art. 1: "The Holy Spirit moves rational creatures by way of counsel" (my translation).

tradition and repeated the scheme linking specific gifts to specific virtues, making this teaching incomprehensible.[156] The traditional teaching on the gifts of the Holy Spirit, therefore, should not be construed as a mere speculative exercise based on a mistranslation of the text of Isaiah. The traditional presentation incorporates a true spiritual experience of generations of saints. However critical one may be of the individual elements of this tradition, the religious experience that underlies this doctrine should be approached with respect and in faith.

St. Paul's affirmation that "all who are moved by the Spirit of God are sons of God" (Rom. 8:14) implies a childlike trust in God that opens one up to the guidance of the Holy Spirit. This means that primacy is to be attributed to the theological virtues. They also are a divine gift that allows one to establish a relationship with God. Faith, which is the humility of the intellect, grants first place to God. It is followed by hope and charity, in which trust in God is expressed. Even though faith is a divine gift, given according to God's pleasure, the actual eliciting of an act of faith depends on the human decision. This is what happens in contemplative prayer. It is standing in the face of the mystery and abiding in it in an attitude of trust. Beautiful ideas, let alone images, do not need to pass through the mind. It is even better if there are none. Similarly, the emotions may be fervent, but they may also be cool and disengaged. This is not the most significant part. What is vital is the contact with God, expressed through actualized faith. We need to believe in the supernatural power of faith. Faith, given by God, and infused in the reason and the will, allows one to break through concepts about God to the living God Himself. Whenever that moment of humility of reason that reaches out toward God arises in the soul, there is a union of the human soul with God. Only good may come out of this encounter. The encounter with the living God in the act of faith precedes the cognitive content that the reason of the believer accepts. The cognitive content in the act of faith, handed down in the Church and delivered to reason, is a certain mental structure that helps sustain the act of faith. But the very act of trusting God and opening

---

[156] See Edward D. O'Connor, "English Translation, Notes and Appendices," *ST*, vol. 24, 1974.

oneself to His power may be very simple, drawing on very meager content. "Whoever would draw near to God must believe that he exists and that he rewards those who seek him" (Heb. 11:6). Faith inclined toward God and trusting in His goodness opens the soul to the gift of grace, which will bear fruit in the entire moral ethos. (This also pertains to those people who have not heard the name of Jesus but who trust in God, whatever they call Him, and give themselves generously to Him.)

If there is anything to be learned at the start, it is that one must learn to struggle for God so that there is time in the daily rhythm of life to meet with Him alone. Half an hour, offered daily and generously to God, in an attitude of trustful abiding before the mystery, generates deep trust and disposes one to the impulse of invoking God and to the development of grace. Although faith is to be trusting and childlike, it has to be the faith of an adult — that is, there must be daily moments of a conscious abiding in faith with God that are planned in a mature way. By ensuring a contact with God, contemplative prayer enables the transformation of life, making it supernatural. One may even say that the act of faith makes one "grasp" God, or "seize God by the heart." God's inner need is such that, touched by one's trusting faith, He has to give Himself because such is the nature of the merciful God. When the woman suffering from a hemorrhage touched with her finger the fringe of Jesus' cloak — and, even more, touched with her faith His heart — Jesus' reaction was immediate. "Some one touched me; for I perceive that power has gone forth from me" (Luke 8:46). When faith is expressed, it establishes a contact with God, through which intimacy between God and man develops.

The gifts of the Holy Spirit, which are a permanent element of contact with God, constitute that reality in the soul that allows one to detect divine suggestions coming from within a living faith. The Holy Spirit prompts actions that transcend human reasoning and natural cunning or prudence. He suggests a course of action that, like instinct, previously did not even come to mind. For growth in faith, some people do not need new and more persuasive arguments but need to stop relying on such arguments and trust God directly. Faith imbued by the gifts of the Holy Spirit reaches deeper than human arguments and opens a person to divine promptings. An important moment in the acquisition of spiritual experience is the recognition of these stirrings of the Holy Spirit in order to respond to them. They should not be confused with psychic states or the imagination or with one's own laziness or one's own ideas that one would like to impose upon God. An important indication of the Holy Spirit's work is that His guidance is invariably unexpected in its novelty and surprise. A childlike attitude toward God allows one to enjoy this surprising guidance, whereas the imposition of one's ideas or ideologies upon God closes off the childlike trust.

Receptivity to the gifts of the Holy Spirit is tied to the generosity of one's response. If, instead of self-centeredness, there is a generous willingness to serve others and a frequently renewed total gift of self, to the delight of the God Whom one loves, the Holy Spirit captivates, suggesting an ever more demanding generosity. There is a certain humility or timidity of the Holy Spirit in this, as if He were afraid of offering His promptings to those who do not respond to them. The Holy Spirit does not want to put us in the uncomfortable position of having received His suggestions and then refusing them. That is why He patiently waits for generosity to be born in response to the divine instinct. (Sanctity, therefore, is ultimately measured not by inspirations one may have received from the Holy Spirit but by virtues that testify to the constant availability to respond to God creatively with generosity.) True communion with God in faith and practical charity brings an increasingly supernatural transformation of life. This is not accompanied by an easy feeling of being carried away by a wave of spiritual exaltation. On the contrary, spiritual growth is accompanied by a realization of one's poverty, to the point where one is even forced by necessity to call upon the help of the Holy Spirit at every moment. But in generosity flowing from love of God there is joy. Aquinas's emphasis on ease, promptness, and pleasure in the virtues expresses that inner joy that flows from creativity, which is a response to the stirrings of the Holy Spirit.

Sensitivity to the guidance of the Holy Spirit presupposes that it is possible to recognize this stirring. How is this done? Can we recognize grace or experience it in our psyche? If we answer this question in the affirmative, will it not contradict the Faith? But since the gifts of the Holy Spirit involve a certain stirring, generating a generous response that must be conscious in order to be true, somehow we must be able to recognize that it is God Who is prompting us. There must therefore be some echo of the Holy Spirit's stirring in our spirit. Distinguishing between the authentic prompting of the Holy Spirit and our own ambition and personal desire is necessary so that we can give ourselves completely to God, rather than pushing our way through. Can we have the certitude that it is indeed the Holy Spirit Who is urging us on a particular matter? One should not conceive the stirrings of the Holy Spirit in a nominalist way, assuming that, by His divine authority, God keeps sending us His personal decrees, imposing specific and immediate obligatory tasks (as it is often imagined by the Pentecostals). The guidance of the Holy Spirit, which releases in us a spiritual infancy, takes place within our faculties, our mature thinking and willing. But this cannot take place entirely outside our consciousness and generosity, or else it would be a fiction. So how does it occur?

St. Thomas attempts to fathom this mystery with two phrases. One is *quasi experimentalis cognitio Dei*, and the other is *instinctus Spiritus Sancti*. The former appears in the context of the divine indwelling of the soul, and the latter in the context of the gifts of the Holy Spirit. The divine indwelling of the soul is accomplished through two created but supernatural gifts: wisdom and love. Through these gifts, a personal relationship with the Persons of the Holy Trinity is attained. In supernatural wisdom, located in the reason, the believer recognizes the divine promptings as wise and transcending purely human calculations. In this wise intuition that is born in the mind, there is the recognition of something of the personal characteristics of the eternal and incarnate Word — that is, Jesus. A discernment is born that Jesus would have acted in such and such a way in a given situation. A joyful impulse of love is born in the will, and this charity is marked by the personal qualities of the Holy Spirit. The mission of the Divine Persons in the human soul is accomplished through these two gifts of wisdom and love, which are attributed to the Son, sent by the Father, and to the Holy Spirit, sent by both of Them. In the recognition of these gifts occurs a quasi-experimental cognition of God.[157]

---

[157] *In Sent.*, I, dist. 14, q. 2, art. 2, ad 3: "Not every cognition is attributed to the mission, but only that which is received from some gift that is proper to the person, through which results our joining with God, according to the mode

This does not mean that God imposes some individually applied norm through these two gifts, but it does mean that a personal encounter with God has taken place in the soul, and this necessarily impacts the response that takes place both in prayer and in action. Of course, the grasping of the wisdom of God, characterized by the personal mark of the Son of God and of the liberating supernatural charity in which there is something of the fire of the Holy Spirit, requires advanced practice in recognizing divine promptings and constant readiness never to refuse God. No education is needed for this; even children respond in this way to initiatives that come from God.

But what can Aquinas's mysterious formula "quasi-experimental knowledge of God" mean? Scholars studying his teaching have proposed various theories.[158] One should not look here for sensual, emotional, or purely intellectual cognition. Normally, the word *experimental* refers to cognition through the senses, but Aquinas here carries out an analogous transfer of the term to spiritual cognition. For this reason, this cognition is called *quasi-experimental*. The cognition that divine wisdom suggests is permeated by love. What appears as a suggestion coming from God immediately evokes a certain delight, a joy in the will, and this overflow into the affective sphere is expressed by the word *experimental*. On the basis of an admittedly false etymology, Aquinas holds that wisdom means a knowledge that is tasty.[159] So this is simply a cognition that is accompanied by love.[160] It is not any

---

that is proper for the given person — that is, through love, when the Holy Spirit is given. And so this cognition is quasi-experimental" (my translation).

[158] John F. Dedek demonstrated that certain theologians, disregarding the historical study of Aquinas's thought, had arrived at erroneous conclusions, looking here for some extraordinary intellectual cognition of God ("*Quasi experimentalis cognitio*: A Historical Approach to the Meaning of St. Thomas," *Theological Studies* 22 [1961]: 357–390). There are no grounds to seek here a "direct super-intentional perception" (A. Gardeil) or "direct super-discursive knowledge" (R. Garrigou-Lagrange) or a "discursive knowledge" (P. Galtier).

[159] The word *sapientia* supposedly was derived from *sapida scientia*.

[160] *ST*, IIa-IIae, q. 97, art. 2, ad 2: "There are two kinds of knowledge about God's goodness and will. One of them is theoretic.... The other is affective and experimental knowledge of divine goodness and loving-kindness, whereby a person experiences within himself the test of God's sweetness and the delight in his loving" (trans. T. F. O'Meara and M. J. Duffy, vol. 40, 1968).

sophisticated or extraordinary experience. An intuition coming from God, which triggers fascination and provokes good actions, belongs to the ordinary experience of Christians. It is necessary to grant this intuition a place in moral agency if one seeks to specify the essence of the Christian dimension of life.

The second term introduced by Aquinas is the *instinct* of the Holy Spirit. This phrase appears repeatedly in the *Summa theologiae*, Ia-IIae, q. 16, which deals with the gifts of the Holy Spirit. Aquinas seems to have adopted it from a faulty translation of Aristotle's work *De bona fortuna*. (This is yet another example of Aquinas's profiting from terminology developed by pagan philosophy so as to describe the deepest mysteries of the Faith.) The term itself does not establish whether the stirring of the Holy Spirit falls into the category of an impulse, enlightenment, invitation and call to repentance, or assent in faith. The grace of the Holy Spirit becomes the measure of works when man is led by this divine instinct, which is somehow analogous to the similar instinct of reason. The natural inclinations in human nature make it possible to recognize instinctively that which is in accord with human nature. Similarly, a direct prompting of the Holy Spirit instinctively triggers an action of the will.[161] God alone may work in the human will in such a way that the human will is not enslaved by this but, instead, is liberated from its limitations. And when the Holy Spirit invites with His instinct, man without hesitation should respond with his generosity,[162] even though this prompting of God is sometimes anonymous, embodied in a stirring that is also natural. A suggestion that comes from the Holy Spirit may be expressed unknowingly by someone else. It is not accompanied by any special signs or sensations. Sensitivity to this divine guidance is an ordinary experience of people who persist in union with God.

---

[161] *Ad Rom.*, c. 8, l. 3 (635): "The spiritual man is inclined to do something not as though by a movement of his own will chiefly, but by the prompting of the Holy Spirit."

[162] *Contra pestiferam doctrinam retrahentium homines a religionis ingressu*, c. 9 (797): "When, therefore, a man is moved by the instinct of the Holy Spirit … immediately he should follow the impetus of the Holy Spirit" (my translation).

It is possible to attempt to describe this encounter with the guidance of the Holy Spirit using language that is less speculative. Karl Rahner, asking questions, finally concludes:

> Have we ever kept quiet, even though we wanted to defend ourselves when we had been unfairly treated? Have we ever forgiven someone even though we got no thanks for it and our silent forgiveness was taken for granted?... Have we ever tried to love God when we seemed to be calling out into emptiness and our cry seemed to fall on deaf ears, when it looked as if we were taking a terrifying jump into the bottomless abyss, when everything seemed to become incomprehensible and apparently senseless?... Once we experience the spirit in this way, we (at least, we as Christians who live in faith) have also already in fact experienced the supernatural.... The chalice of the Holy Spirit is identical in this life with the chalice of Christ. This chalice is drunk only by those who have slowly learned in little ways to taste the fullness in emptiness, the ascent in the fall, life in death, the finding in renunciation.[163]

Similarly, Bl. Marie-Eugène of the Infant Jesus perceives a working of the Holy Spirit's gifts through a counterexperience:

> The action of God through the gifts is clearly distinct from the experience that we can have of it.... The direct communications of God are not, then, always accompanied by awareness of them. Consequently, one could not affirm that there is no mystical life without mystical experience.... This suffering from emptiness which has been preceded by divine communications, seems to be a kind of experience of the capacity of the gifts of the Holy Spirit, which bears painfully their privation.... In this quasi-experience, there is one central impression. Most of the time, this is the dominant one and the strongest; sometimes even the only one, exclusive of any other:

---

[163] Karl Rahner, "Reflections on the Experience of Grace," *Theological Investigations*, vol. 3, 87–89.

namely, the perception or the experience of the contrary of what is given by the divine communication, an experience that we might call negative.... His dazzling light produces darkness in the intellect not adapted to receive it; His strength overwhelms human weakness. The very sweetness that comes from the gift of wisdom makes the soul rejoice in its littleness.... The negative experience explains those antinomies often pointed out as characteristic effects of the gifts, and is the basis for the relations of the gifts with the beatitudes.... The littleness of the creature and the transcendence of God, man's sin and God's mercy, must become more and more manifest in the proportion that God reveals His action and His truth in the soul.... At times the gift of understanding fills the soul only with darkness; and again, it throws penetrating light on a truth of faith.... The gift of counsel sheds light on a decision to be made — or it leaves the soul hesitant until some event sets it, as it were in spite of itself, in the direction it should take.... Under the impact, so to speak, of the power or the light of God, the reactions of one will differ from those of another; in the same grouping of impressions, the optimist will lay stress on those that are pleasant; the pessimist, indicate only the painful.... Spiritual fecundity always accompanies the action of the Holy Spirit.... Yet the discernment of the fruits of the Spirit of God will not in every case be easy; for, even in the holy man, good works are accompanied by defects and faults; and their fecundity is manifest only at a long date.[164]

This teaching of this great expert in Carmelite spirituality highlights the importance of faith in recognizing the gifts of the Holy Spirit. It is important to commune with God, and this is accomplished in the darkness of faith, in which trust toward God increases. Passive purifications, in which God deprives one of the experience of His presence, and in which one persists in loving God and doing the good without feeling anything, ensure that

---

[164] *I Want to See God: A Practical Synthesis of Carmelite Spirituality* (Chicago: Fides, 1953) 351–356.

it is God Who is loved rather than mystical experiences. If these religious experiences were to become an idol, they would obscure God.

So, in spiritual experience, the practice of the theological virtues comes first. Faith establishes contact with God. Although faith is born in the soul as a gift of God, the practice of the faith always comes from a conscious human choice. The promptings of grace may not be consciously recognized. But trusting God and acting on the strength of that trust are conscious. When one persists in faith, sensitivity to divine impulses is born. By virtue of these impulses, acts of the moral virtues are elicited. When the sole motivation for action is the love of God, toward which one is inwardly urged, then such action is marked by divine fecundity. Thus, it is possible to distinguish the following order: First comes the act of faith, followed by charity. Within this faith, the "spiritual antennae" are activated, as it were, and a sensitivity to divine prompting is born. The call of grace, in turn, provokes acts of the moral virtues, infused by grace.[165] In this process, which may seem arbitrary, there is room for the Church's teaching. It is not primary, since the grace of the Holy Spirit stimulates man more than external instruction. But the Church's teaching, participating in the law of the Spirit, excludes in a general way those acts that are intrinsically evil. It does not specify so closely which good acts are worth performing. The corrective influence of the Church's teaching and the mandates of superiors, in the case of religious, or the remarks of a spouse guard against the danger of subjectivism. This does not mean, however, that before responding to the call of the Holy Spirit, one must consult a confessor or another person regarding every issue. The conscience of the acting individual, open to the gifts of the Holy Spirit, has its own dignity, on the basis of which it governs action.

The taking up of the light and promptings of the Holy Spirit not only through free choice, in which the reason and the will act together, but also through the senses, which surrender to this action, is not in any way an

---

[165] *ST*, Ia-IIae, q. 68, art. 8: "The theological virtues are superior to the Gifts of the Holy Spirit and regulate them.... But in comparison with the other virtues, both intellectual and moral, the Gifts are higher" (trans. E. D. O'Connor, vol. 24, 1974).

inhibition of the natural finality of the faculties. Man was created by God in such a way that he is receptive to divine interventions, which, in no way, are a limitation for him. Just as the light of reason poses no threat to the emotions when they submit to it in moral virtue, so the stirring of the gifts of the Holy Spirit permeates the entire human personality without producing inhibitions or neurosis. Not only the spiritual powers but also the senses and the body are susceptible to the divine supernatural influence.[166] This is an important truth, not only for moral theology but also for psychology, pedagogy, and medicine. There are difficulties that people experience that are reflected in their psychic and physical state that have their deepest cause in the lack of complete trust in God. When resistance to God continues, it affects the entire personality. The physical, psychic, intellectual, and spiritual dimensions of a person are interconnected. A spiritual person, generously given to God is distinguished not only by a psychic and spiritual balance but also by a certain external beauty. People who are fully given over to God are captivating due to the warmth of their personalities. This is the essence of spiritual fatherhood and motherhood. Those who are sensitive to divine promptings and respond to them, contribute by their very personality to the emergence in others of a readiness to give themselves to God. Thus, it is clear that the deepest and most spiritually fertile dimension of evangelization has its origin here. The Church grows from within, not through actions and extensive evangelization plans but through the radiation of God's goodness in people who have become sensitive to the stirrings of the Holy Spirit.

It is possible to grow in the spiritual life by giving oneself more and more to God. This requires a generous application of faith and the stirrings of the Holy Spirit to all dimensions of life. We need to accept that the Holy Spirit is wise, that He knows where He is leading us. We need also to accept, without becoming discouraged or disheartened by falls, that the infiltration of the personality by the Spirit of God will be gradual. We read about this

---

[166] *ST*, Ia-IIae, q. 68, art. 4: "Just as the appetitive powers are 'born' (that is inclined by nature) to be moved by the command of reason, so all human powers are 'born' to be moved by the instinct of God, as by a higher power" (my translation).

gradual learning of the receptivity to the Holy Spirit in the New Testament. The apostles knew Jesus; they were sent by Him on apostolic missions. They participated in the Last Supper. They saw Jesus' total gift of self in His Passion and death, which was incomprehensible to them. They met Jesus after the Resurrection when He breathed the Holy Spirit on them. And yet Jesus instructed them to wait for Pentecost. Openness to the Holy Spirit is gradual, dependent on the human response in which there is a generous and total gift of self.

The infused virtues

In many European languages, the word *virtue* has disappeared from Christian reflection and preaching. Some associate it with endearing incompetence or puritanical perfectionism. Thus, attempts have recently been made to replace the term *virtue* with such terms as *attitude, characteristic, good moral quality, moral character,* or *moral excellence*. It is not that important which word we use; what matters is that it helps grow the reality in question. Theological reflection on the transformation of the ethos by the power of grace, which used the term *virtue*, although it may have implied strength, presupposed that the source of this strength is grace, not one's own vital energy. Sensitivity to the stirrings of the Holy Spirit results in a capacity for good action that reveals something of God's supernatural power.

Aquinas, repeating Peter Lombard's compilation of St. Augustine's texts, defines *virtue* as a good quality of mind through which one lives righteously, which no one can use improperly, and which God causes in us without us.[167]

There is no doubt that what is discussed here is virtue that is the fruit of the action of grace in the soul and the psyche. Traditional Catholic theology, following Aquinas, always spoke about moral virtues, infused by grace and distinct from the acquired virtues. The pronouncements of the Church's Magisterium on this issue, however, are sparse. *The Catechism of the Council of Trent* in the context of Baptism mentions the "most splendid train of all

---

[167] *ST*, Ia-IIae, q. 55, art. 4: "Virtue is a good quality of mind by which one lives righteously, of which no one can make bad use, which God works in us without us" (trans. W. D. Hughes, vol. 23, 1969).

virtues," the *omnium virtutum comitatus*, belonging to the order of sanctifying grace.[168] Presently, the *Catechism of the Catholic Church* mentions only the theological virtues as being infused by grace, while it presents the moral virtues as natural, acquired by human effort, although they are sometimes "purified and elevated by divine grace" and are "rooted in the theological virtues, which adapt man's faculties for participation in the divine nature" (see 1804, 1810, 1812, 1813). Is there not in this reserved approach toward the teachings of Aquinas a certain echo of Pelagianism, of a disbelief that grace can indeed prove fruitful in the moral life? It is true that the person in the state of grace does not "feel" the moral virtues infused in him, but it is important that he believes that grace has been given to him and that it extends all the way to his moral life because without this faith he will become either helplessly passive or rigoristic with himself. It is precisely when engaging in all actions with a simultaneous trusting in the power of grace, which always is and will be mysterious, that one truly lives by faith, and then grace may turn out to be fruitful. A spouse who does not believe in the graces of the Sacrament of Marriage or a priest who does not believe in the reality of the graces received during his ordination will constantly falter and fall.

The mentioning of the role of the mind in virtue, even in a virtue that is located in the emotions (such as fortitude or temperance) confirms that virtue is a good habitus — i.e., that the spiritual powers of the reason and the will are creatively engaged in acts of virtue.[169] In every virtue, the virtue of prudence is involved, as it brings in the spiritual faculties and ensures the transition from intention to decision, sometimes to deliberation, to actual execution. Grace does not operate passively in a person. It engages that which is best and most human in him. St. Augustine referred to virtue as *ordo amoris*, which means "order in loving," or the order that charity brings into the soul and to the faculties.

---

[168] *The Catechism of the Council of Trent for Parish Priests*, trans. J. A. McHugh and C. J. Callan (New York: Joseph Warner, 1956), 1988 (pt. 2, chap. 2, q. 5).

[169] *ST*, Ia-IIae, q. 56, art. 4: "A virtue in either the irascible or the concupiscible powers is nothing else but a certain habitual conformity of these powers to reason" (trans. W. D. Hughes, vol. 23, 1969).

The study of the virtues, comprehensively undertaken by Aquinas in his *Summa of Theology* should be interpreted in union with the intent of his entire work. The in-depth analysis of more than fifty virtues that we find in part IIa-IIae of the *Summa* can be interpreted in a purely natural way. Numerous philosophers have read Aquinas in this way, abstracted from the dynamics of grace. This, however, is a limited interpretation. It is true that we do not have a special language to describe the reality of the divine, and so we use human language to express the ineffable. Thus, one can use Aquinas's analysis to describe the natural acquired virtues, although such an analysis is overall of little use in their education, since the consequences of Original Sin manifest themselves too readily for purely natural efforts to achieve moral perfection, even if one were rationally to study aretaics, the science of virtue. Aquinas embarks on the description of the virtues because he is interested in God, in particular as He is seen through the prism of a sanctified human being. It is therefore necessary to interpret his aretaics theologically in conjunction with what he wrote in the prologue to the second part of the *Summa* about the image of God in man, as well as with his explanation of the dynamics of the gifts of the Holy Spirit, which imbue the human capacity for proper moral action with the power and wisdom of the Holy Spirit Himself. The placement of the study of the virtues in the structure of Aquinas's work is significant. The description of the virtues that shape the human interior precedes the study of the moral law. In the virtues, prudence and charity, reinforced by the direct intervention of the Holy Spirit, inspire the creativity and novelty of good action. The precept of the moral law is not the factor that confers the essential movement. In fact, it would be correct to say that eliciting virtuous action in a creative way is possible only when the moral law has been allocated its proper, secondary place. The moral law, like a signpost, provides instruction and, above all, points out the wrong paths that are to be avoided, but it is not the source of action. What animates the traveler is not the signpost but the end of the journey and the inner will to achieve it. A virtuous man does not constantly look at the moral law but at the good that is worth pursuing for its own sake. Excessive legalism stifles personal initiative and creative recognition of situations in which one is confronted with an inner moral call and contrives a novel way of responding to challenges.

Therefore, when Aquinas mentions the divine commandments, after having extensively discussed each virtue and the gifts that stimulate it, and after having discussed the sins opposed to the virtue, he does so very succinctly, indicating only the relevance of the external instruction contained in the commandment. Thus, it is not so much the content of the divine commandments that he is exposing as their pedagogical function. It is clear that the dynamics of good action have their source within the person more than in an external instruction.

Aquinas's description of the virtues serves to demonstrate that which God offers us, that which grace may accomplish in each one of us. It presents the divine ideal of a sanctified and happy man. The divine view taught by the gifts of the Holy Spirit reaches beyond the immediate reality toward that which each of us may become. "See what love the Father has given us, that we should be called children of God; and so we are. The reason why the world does not know us is that it did not know him. Beloved, we are God's children now; it does not yet appear what we shall be, but we know that when he appears we shall be like him, for we shall see him as he is. And every one who thus hopes in him purifies himself as he is pure" (1 John 3:1–3). God does not want us all to be identical, replicating one pattern, one mold. The first cause leaves room for further causes, so that the richness of the individuality and personal creativity of each person may express itself. Aquinas rejects the opinion of the Stoics, who held that virtues are identical in all people. In one person, virtue may be more deeply entrenched than in another. Over the course of a lifetime, a virtue may grow, but it may also regress. This growth is uneven, though proportional, just like the growth of the fingers of the hand. Over time, the goodness of one who sincerely gives himself to God will spread to other dimensions of his life.

Studying each virtue one by one, Aquinas sought the *ratio* of the virtue — that is, the value at the heart of the virtue. He looked into the good that is appropriate for every human faculty, toward which it gravitates by its objective nature, finding in it not just stability and direction but also its proper fulfillment. Thus, the description of each virtue provides us only with a generic picture of it. When it is said that moderation in eating means finding the right measure between binge eating and anorexia, Aquinas does not say precisely what that measure will be. The measure is different for a man, a woman, and a child. Similarly, the measure of wine drinking is different in the Mediterranean culture and different in other places. Moreover, in the virtuous life, which includes moderation regarding food and drink, there are also the culinary arts, with all their creativity and cultural richness, that are not a manifestation of a purely arbitrary fantasy but are oriented toward an actual good. The virtuous action of each person has a particular measure that has to be creatively found by each individual while searching for the appropriate *verum bonum* (true good). In moral teaching, including that of the Church, we receive only a general description of the virtuous life. Neither God nor the Church gives us strict instructions sent individually to each one of us. It is up to each person to determine for himself the proper measure of his conduct. Through the divine indwelling in the soul of the Christian, the human faculties are enriched with a supernatural habitus. Communion with God frees these faculties from woundedness and disorder and leads them out toward a spiritual adventure. The determination of each act, however, is the fruit of the creative invention of each virtuous person. When charity poured out into the soul influences the entire ethos, the good deeds one elicits are both a sign of God's fecundity and the thoughtfulness and generosity of the individual person.

When a personal and total gift of self is undertaken often, in a creative way, out of love for God and in response to the prompting of the Holy Spirit, this develops the capacity to act well, which we call *virtue*. The motto *in medio virtus* does not mean that one should not be excessively virtuous or insufficiently virtuous. In virtues that order the sensitive sphere, it draws attention to the need to adjust one's adherence to the object of movement to that measure that reason determines. The sensitive response itself depends on the individual's body, and it may be extremely intense, having its legitimate place within the virtue. As for the reason, it ensures that the sensitive involvement does not become an idol, eclipsing other values. It determines, for example, to what extent indignation at evil should be manifested and to what extent anger should be restrained, in such a way that justice is preserved in the manifestation of fortitude; or to what extent one should allow oneself the pleasure of tasting wine and to what extent the sensation should be restrained for the sake of other important reasons. In the virtue of justice, reason aligns the will to the factual measure, which is external and objective (in settling a debt, the exact amount owed should be returned). In the theological virtues, reason perceives that there is no end to growth in trusting and loving God, although the outward expression of faith or love of God is subject to the judgment of prudence. Since reason has a decisive and creative role in the eliciting of acts of virtue, it follows that the mature formation of a believer's personality is not like the formatting of a computer disk. Personal talents and predilections, one's own viewpoint and experience play a decisive role in virtuous action. A mature individual perceives himself and his place in the world personally. The more sensitive he is to the promptings of the Holy Spirit, the more he notices the moral obligation in various situations and responds with generosity and creativity, sometimes surprising others with his inventiveness and richness of response. That is why Christian maturity is not to be dull but full of inventiveness.

Analyzing the virtues that are located in the emotional sphere, Aquinas places them within the senses. The virtue of temperance is found among the emotions of the pleasure appetite, and the virtue of fortitude among those of the irascible appetite. It is the emotion that directs itself to its proper object, granting dynamism to the action, and reason merely determines the proper measure of that dynamism. Since both emotions and the light of reason are compatible with human nature, there is no inevitable conflict here, even when the consequences of Original Sin are considered. The harmonious cooperation between the rational and sensitive spheres, especially in the context of grace, is possible and necessary. Reason affirms the sensitive movements and knows that sensual goods are to be loved as such. The attractiveness of the object of sensitive movements lies in the fact that it is concrete, present here and now. The emotions interact with the light provided by reason, not through blind obedience to frustrating precepts but by channeling their own dynamism toward the object that is shown in the light of universal values. Moderation in eating and drinking does not mean negating the pleasure of eating and drinking. It means situating this pleasure within the context of greater goods, such as health, respect for others, and appreciation for the qualities of good cooking. If the natural expression of emotions is denied, and if there is a tendency in the psyche to treat the reflex of emotions as reprehensible, this will result in a neurotic expansion of the emotions rather than their channeling by the light of reason. One will not acquire the virtue of chastity by denying sexuality but by directing it toward the good that is love, the transmission of life, and respect for others. Emotions give dynamism and color to stirrings and, as such, have their place in the psyche. Joy, sadness, indignation at evil, enthusiasm, fascination, and fear are all normal, healthy human reactions. Kant was wrong when he held that only actions performed out of duty would be valuable. Actions that spring from fascination, the desire for happiness, and delight are good, if the input of reason and will in them is accepted. And if, in this choice of good, there is also openness to a friendship with God and a joyful response to the Holy Spirit's encouragement, the action will ultimately be not only good but also marked by divine power.

In the Church, another interpretation is also known, tied with St. Bonaventure, who located the virtues of temperance and fortitude not in the emotions but in the will. It suggests that the dynamics of the emotions are an unruly force that the will is only supposed to subdue. Placing a strong emphasis on the will, which is in constant conflict with emotions, brings with it a permanent state of tension. Most often, such an understanding of the psychology of virtues leads to a confusion between the will, which is a spiritual power, and the emotions of the irascible appetite, and especially those of energy — that is, of ambition and courage. Using these emotions to control other emotions leads to neurosis and to practical Pelagianism, in which one attempts to control emotional sensations without grace. Aquinas, following the teachings of Aristotle, knew that virtue is not meant to drive the dynamics of emotions out of consciousness but is supposed to cooperate with the sensitive movements, directing them toward goals that had been illuminated by reason. Emotions are neither to be enslaved nor are they to be unleashed in an animalistic and irrational manner. Rather, virtue is to be compared to the evangelical leaven that enhances the dynamic and gives life.

This does not mean that the channeling of emotions by reason is simple and automatic. Reason has a political rather than despotic power over the emotions. Knowing oneself and one's limitations requires a certain "playing" with oneself, so as not to land in a situation in which the emotions completely take over the initiative. The consequences of Original Sin generate disorder and disruption between the emotional and spiritual realms. But faith in Christ and His gift of the Holy Spirit bring peace. The Holy Spirit, as the Paraclete, defends against the hidden accuser, who, drawing on the experience of failures, keeps sowing discouragement, suggesting self-recrimination and a fixation on mistakes and shortcomings. It is the father of lies who suggests that evil is so powerful that one must constantly think about it. Opening up to the Holy Spirit involves paying attention not to the sharp stones or the mud in the stream but to the living water. Whoever follows the call of grace does not need to worry too much about falling occasionally. In time, the living water will blunt the sharpness of the stones and rinse away the mud. Confidence in grace motivates for the good and restores the natural harmony between emotions and the reason and the will.

Is there also room for virtue in the will? The will is a spiritual power that spontaneously tends toward the good shown to it by reason. In its basic impulse toward the good and toward happiness, it needs no particular virtue. This does not mean, however, that we are to entertain a romantic conviction about the absolute nobility of the will, supposedly incapable of evil, although sins out of deliberate bad will are rare. It is more common to fall into sin out of weakness or out of insensitivity rather than out of thoughtful malice — *ex industria*. But tending toward the good of other people, the will needs to be directed by the virtue of justice so as to learn sensitivity toward their rights; and tending toward God and people for God's sake, the will needs to be fortified by the virtue of charity. The education of the will, therefore, consists in taking up, by free choice, the good toward which God inclines, and also the cultivation of the virtues that are in the emotional sphere, because senses that are not in harmony with free choice screen the spiritual impulse of the will. Faithfulness in eliciting good actions uniquely for the sake of God disposes toward the reception of successive graces and enables perseverance in them.

The traditional classification of virtues distinguishes the theological virtues and the cardinal virtues. The virtues of faith, hope, and charity are given by God to allow contact with Him. Their object is God Himself. That is why they should be given primacy. First, it is necessary to build a bond of friendship and trust with God, and only then comes the application of the received charity into the various aspects of life — that is, the fortification of the moral virtues. It is a mistaken spiritual pedagogy to emphasize the moral virtues first. It happens sometimes that faith in God is declared, but since moral shortcomings are painfully present, the entire attention is focused on sins that one wishes to overcome. Since faith is only declared but does not provoke a friendship with God and it is not extended to all dimensions of life, the whole effort is centered on struggling against evil and building the moral virtues. This, however, is attempted only by natural power and turns out to be ineffective, fueling further discouragement or even more concentration on one's vices. First, therefore, it is necessary to nurture a friendship with God through the practice of contemplative prayer, in which trust in God and awareness of being His child are deepened. A concomitant generosity that needs to be cultivated for the sake of others, which, in the initial stage, may even be tainted by a certain pride, in time will be purified, and the trusting communion with God will spill out into solid responsibility in the moral sphere, in which divine love, freely received, will be communicated. When the friendly relationship with God crashes as a result of mortal sin, God leaves the unformed, weak, but nevertheless true virtues of faith and hope, which allow paths toward Him to be rebuilt again. Those who do not live according to charity are still Christians, but they are dwarfed because they are not living out the fullness of divine love. The important thing then is to return to trusting God. Thus, it is good to remind oneself frequently of God's mercy or to read texts that lead to this trust.[170]

From an analysis of the basic faculties, Greek philosophy identified the main moral virtues, which St. Ambrose later named the cardinal virtues. We find an echo of Plato's philosophy in the Old Testament, where the following statement appears: "Or if it be virtue you love, why, virtues are the fruit of her labours, since it is she who teaches temperance and prudence, justice and

---

[170] Bl. Michael Sopoćko, St. Faustina's confessor, translated the phrase "Jesus, I trust in You!" into Latin as *Jesu, in Te confido*, and not, as it is sometimes rendered, as *Jesu, confido Tibi*. This means that the emphasis is on Christ, who is the source of trust, and not on the trust itself. It is not so much a psychological attitude as a Christological one.

fortitude; nothing in life is more serviceable to men than these" (Wisd. 8:7, Jerusalem Bible). St. Ambrose called these virtues *cardinal* (meaning "hinge") because on them, as if on hinges, hangs the entire moral life, although he held that they are present in all virtues, as a general condition of the soul. Aquinas, following Aristotle's philosophy, pointed out that they have their proper subject and their proper object toward which they aim. Prudence basically is located in the practical reason, although it also exerts an influence on the will and ensures that, in eliciting an act, there is indeed a creative transition from intention through possible deliberation and then decision to execution. As a general virtue, prudence has its place in every virtue at the natural level. In the context of grace, charity, which builds friendship with God, is transferred to the whole ethos. Thus, it becomes a supernatural general virtue that does not supplant prudence but points to a higher perspective, having friendship with God as the main engine. Justice fundamentally is in the will. Temperance is in the emotions of the pleasure appetite, and fortitude in the emotions of the irascible appetite. Since it is the basic faculties that are the subject of the cardinal virtues, the fecundity of grace is observed by Aquinas in all dimensions of the personality. His further reflection tries to describe more precisely the spreading out of grace in various dimensions of the moral ethos.

In part IIa-IIae of the *Summa*, Aquinas discusses more than fifty moral virtues that manifest the panorama of divine action in man. For an in-depth grasp of their specifics, the location of the individual virtues in the psyche and their dependence on the basic springs of good action must be recognized. Thus, not only is that which Aquinas writes about each virtue important, but its connection with other virtues is also significant as it relates to its place in the description of the whole ethos. Of course, a classification of virtues may be made according to other criteria. Today, new different terms are emerging that express moral sensitivity. Accordingly, there is a desire to classify them differently. Aquinas's method of classification distinguishes the *integral* parts of the cardinal virtues — that is, those virtues without which the fundamental cardinal virtue would be impossible. And so, patience and perseverance are classified as integral parts of fortitude, since fortitude is impossible without them. Similarly, striving for good and avoiding evil are integral parts of the virtue of justice. Next, Aquinas distinguishes the *subjective* parts of the virtue — that is, the particular species of a given virtue. Thus, moderation in drinking and chastity are the subjective parts of temperance, and social justice and distributive and commutative justice are the subjective parts of justice. Finally, the *potential* parts of virtues refer to allied virtues — that is, virtues that have something of the dynamics of the basic virtue, but they differ from it. The virtue of humility is allied to temperance, as it restrains ambition. Magnanimity is allied to fortitude because it grants a natural hope (the strength for action) when faced with difficult tasks. But the ability to apply oneself to work — *studiositas* — is related to temperance, not to fortitude, for it is not about inciting enthusiasm, but about limiting distractions while the object of the activity itself engages attention.

Moral virtues, which belong to the order of grace and are therefore bound together by the virtue of charity, differ from the intellectual habits, which, although they provide intellectual, technical, or artistic prowess, do not confer ethical righteousness. Among these, Aquinas mentions first the habit of the first principles of theoretical reason, empowering the intellect to grasp intuitively self-evident truths. Then he lists wisdom, which empowers the mind to get to know the whole of reality from the level of the highest principles. A wise person is able to grasp the connection of things to the first cause. Thus, wisdom encompasses also knowledge learned through other sciences. There are three types of wisdom: (1) philosophical wisdom, based on natural reflection; (2) theological wisdom, based on revelation; and (3) the wisdom that is the gift of the Holy Spirit. It is better to know even a little regarding the highest truths, having the ability to relate everything to God and striving to view everything with the eyes of God, than to know a great deal about a narrow field. (Someone who has a detailed knowledge about the construction of an atomic bomb but has no basic knowledge about man, his dignity, and ethical values is dangerous.) The next intellectual habit is knowledge or — if structured — science, which allows one to know a specific temporal reality. While wisdom is essentially one, as it captures everything from the highest point of view, there are many sciences, as there are many fields that can be studied. The next intellectual habit is synderesis, which is an innate habit of the first principles of practical reason. Expressing, as it were, a fusion of the reason and the will, it urges one to pursue good and avoid evil. As a basic habit of the mind, it lies at the basis of conscience. Then there is art, which enables one to perform technical, artistic, or educational and political tasks appropriately. The ability to lead others or to coordinate information and decisions so as to achieve political goals is an art. In the arts, it is the result that is cherished, regardless of the personal morality of the artist. The last intellectual habit is the virtue of prudence, which was mentioned earlier because it is also a cardinal virtue. Due to its subject, it is listed along with intellectual habits; due to its role of governing the moral life, it is included among the moral virtues.

The extensive description of the virtues provided by Aquinas is meant to indicate the growing capacity to respond to the call of the Holy Spirit. Trying to capture divine fecundity within human life, Aquinas looks at those qualities that shape a sanctified man. The in-depth psychological analysis that seeks to locate a particular virtue appropriately in specific faculties and to describe the principles of its functioning is a theological discourse meant to help us perceive how grace permeates the psyche of the acting person. It thus pertains to the new law as its second element. (The first element of the law of the New Covenant is the grace of the Holy Spirit given to those who believe in Christ. The second element is instruction transmitted by word and writing that disposes to the grace of the Holy Spirit and shows how to use it in practice.) Aquinas's theological intent explains why his description is so general. There is no casuistry in Aquinas. When it is said that fortitude finds the right measure between courage, bravado, perseverance, and withdrawal, or when it is said that chastity means determining the proper place for the sexual drive, Aquinas's discourse does not give a practical answer as to how one should behave in a particular situation. This paucity of Aquinas's exposition grants a perennial relevance to his teaching. His pedagogical wisdom respects the reason of each individual, who, living in union with God, must discern for himself what is right in a given situation. Aquinas's discourse, which combines a discussion of the virtues with a reference to the gifts of the Holy Spirit, followed by a description of the toxic opposites of a given virtue and concluding with a brief reference to a commandment, presupposes that the human mind, formed by faith and open to the intuitions of the Holy Spirit, may be educated in such a way that, on its own, it will become capable of grasping what course of action is right, and, together with the will, it will become capable of guiding action on its own authority, in such a way that, in the end, the action will be creative and performed easily, quickly, and with spiritual joy. This manifests an incredible trust in the reason and the will of the individual, which at times may be shocking to the modern mentality.

Modern moral theology, centered on casuistry and attempting to derive the correct answer to every imaginable moral query from the divine and ecclesial commandments, and furthermore tainted by Pelagianism, which failed to realize the possibility of allowing grace into the dynamics of moral agency, was characterized by a certain distrust of the moral reason of the individual. On the one hand, this theology attributed incredible authority to the practical resolutions it proposed, and on the other hand, it instilled distrust in the independent moral search of individuals. Confessors admittedly studied moral theology in order to help people educate their conscience so that it would make confident judgments, but the way in which casuistry addressed detailed moral problems suggested that there was the need to appeal to the professional opinion of a moral expert. By questioning the right to determine independently the moral object of the act,[171] did not this theology contribute to the undermining of the conviction about the cognitive capacity of reason that we perceive and deplore today?[172]

Aquinas's aretaics should be read in conjunction with the long study that he conducted on the transcendentals in public debates. We have extant scholarly records of the *quaestiones disputatae*, compiled and published by Aquinas himself. In them, he examines the cognitive capacities of reason

---

[171] Let me quote the novel words of St. John Paul II's encyclical *Veritatis splendor*, which are in keeping with the medieval rather than the modern perspective: "In order to be able to grasp the object of an act which specifies that act morally, it is therefore necessary to place oneself *in the perspective of the acting person*" (78).

[172] St. John Paul II, encyclical *Fides et ratio* (September 14, 1998): "But this does not mean that the link between faith and reason as it now stands does not need to be carefully examined, because each without the other is impoverished and enfeebled.... It is an illusion to think that faith, tied to weak reasoning, might be more penetrating" (48). "I cannot but encourage philosophers ... to trust in the power of human reason" (56).

and the properties of functioning of the will. In *De veritate*, a work that also includes a sequel under one title (which probably should have been published separately with the title *De bono*), we get a thorough study of the nature of the spiritual powers, their capacities, and their enrichment by grace. *De veritate* opens with an examination of truth itself; then it proceeds to the study of truth in God, and so we have questions about divine knowledge, ideas in God, the Word in God, providence and predestination, and the book of life. Aquinas then proceeds to study the cognition and knowledge of angels. He next looks at the human mind, which is an image of the Trinity. Then he investigates the pedagogical role of the teacher, prophetic cognition, rapture, the virtue of faith in reason, higher reason and lower reason, synderesis, and conscience. Curiosity about man's cognitive capacities drives him to consider the cognition of the first man in his state of original innocence and the cognition of the soul after death. The search for truth ends with a reflection on Christ's knowledge.

After such an in-depth study of the mind's adherence to truth, Aquinas continues with a study of the good. After considering the good in itself, he examines the spiritual desire for the good — that is, the will. He then studies free choice, in which reason and will function together. In subsequent questions, he examines factors that externally influence the will's drive toward the good, and so he studies concupiscence, emotions, and grace. The work concludes with a reflection on the justification of the wicked and grace in the life of Christ. Confidence in the cognitive capacities of reason, as well as in the will's tending toward the good, while recognizing factors external to the spiritual faculties, such as the movements of senses and the contribution of grace, provides the context for Aquinas's aretaics. Since the spiritual faculties, wounded but not thoroughly destroyed by Original Sin and enriched by grace, are properly equipped, they have the capacity to grasp the appropriate true good, the *verum bonum*, in action. In morally good action, in which the fecundity of grace manifests itself, the supernatural virtues, anchored in the human faculties, enable the creative recognition of specific moral challenges and responses to them.

The moral theology of Aquinas, which shows how grace may be used, pointing to the numerous virtues that are located on the grid of the human psyche, does not relieve one from thinking, from recognizing where true good lies in the midst of various unforeseen human situations. Refraining from handing out a definitive answer to many practical human situations — as if on a platter — may appear to be a weakness of Aquinas's moral theology. Many theologians over the centuries held that they had to take the matter further, and through deduction, derived usually from the divine commandments, sought to present solutions to almost every imaginable situation. Even if they employed the category of virtue, although modern moral theology favored tying everything to the commandments, they often interpreted virtue as a duty and an exemplar, and in this way they moralized grace. Aquinas's reticence in this matter is therefore a sign not of his weakness, but precisely of his greatness.

Aquinas's study of the mind's orientation toward truth and the will's movement toward the good, given the confidence he puts in the individual seeking the verum bonum in the context of virtuous action, points to a completely different understanding of truth from that which has prevailed in European culture in modern times. The Enlightenment introduced a disengaged, precise understanding of scientific truth. Armed with his microscope and examining measurable facts, the modern scientist aims at precise and certain cognition. The starting point of modern cognition is suspicion, averse to dogmatic judgments not supported by verifiable facts and averse to subjective conditionings of cognition, whatever their origin.

The Middle Ages, while, on the one hand, recognizing that just as the fish is made for water so human reason is made for truth and the will is made for goodness, and, on the other hand, analyzing external factors such as grace or sensuality that affect the functioning of the spiritual faculties, did not grant the verum bonum sought in virtuous action that kind of immutable, cold, colorless, or even "dry, yeastless factuality" that the Enlightenment mentality suggests.[173] This verum bonum, seized in response to a personally perceived moral dilemma, defies the strict distinction between ontological and logical truth. Moral truth is not so much the conformity of words to thought as the conformity of a creative, responsible, and variegated response to a perceived good, which has the right to be multihued, and therefore also has the right to

---

[173] See Timothy Radcliffe, O.P., "Crisis of Truth in Our Society," lecture given at the Angelicum in Rome, November 15, 2004, on the occasion of receiving an honorary doctorate.

be perceived in different ways by different people. Stimulated by the gifts of the Holy Spirit, the grasping of the true good permits the tying of that good to the salvific truths about creation and salvation. Since this apprehension of the moral verum bonum is personal, it also permits pondering, searching, and even falling in error. The truth of creation means that God now generously sustains everything in existence and grants potentiality to everything, so we can look at ourselves and others not only as having a specific, exact factuality but also from the perspective of what we may all become. And we are all on our way to salvation. Thus, the contemplative gaze does not confine oneself and others in an eternal frame, but hoping in the fecundity of grace sees a future saint even in a criminal (this is how Christ looked at the thief hanging on the cross!).

The verum bonum, as the object of virtue, is linked to charity, infused in the soul by the Holy Spirit Himself. The pursuit of truth, which underlies the virtues, is rooted in merciful love and not in mathematical precision. Respect for the personal recognition of moral dilemmas and for one's own creative undertaking of acts of virtue generates a culture in which there is room for personal inventiveness, for searching, for testing new ideas, a culture in which the right to make mistakes is respected. Precisely because we profess the same Faith, because we attribute a prominent role to the gifts of the Holy Spirit, we have the right to have different opinions about what should be done and about what we consider a pressing matter. The modern assumption that conclusions pertaining to all imaginable moral cases, elaborated by moral theologians who claim to be specialists, are accurate in their precision and immutable, together with a concomitant distrust of the spiritual endowment of the individual who seeks the verum bonum, has led to a breakdown of trust in every moral teaching, with all its tragic consequences. Aquinas's sensible restraint here shows a way out.

Since the theological description of the virtues given by Aquinas is general, pedagogical, and not casuistic, it is clear that he recognizes that there are also other external, social factors at play in the personalistic formation of ethical sensitivity. The Scottish American philosopher Alasdair MacIntyre made an attempt to search for the essential foundation of virtue.[174] In

---

[174] Alasdair MacIntyre, *After Virtue: A Study in Moral Theory* (Notre Dame: University of Notre Dame Press, 2007).

interpreting his famous book, it is necessary to take into account the slip of thought that has occurred over the centuries, into which MacIntyre also lapsed. While in Aquinas, the word *virtue* refers primarily to the psychological and pedagogical quality resulting from grace, in modern understanding, the word has become tainted by the obligation-centered mentality. When the word *virtue* is associated with a quality defining moral action to which one must necessarily conform, an important question arises — that of the legitimacy of such or of another course of action. MacIntyre, interested primarily in the content of ethical requirements — grasped admittedly through the category of virtue rather than the category of commandment but still understood in terms of obligation — surveyed the history of ethical thought and literature, and he noted that what people consider to be virtuous behavior is marked by tradition and the prevailing views in a given society. And these change over time. Virtue was understood differently by Homer, for whom it was a manifestation of heroism, and differently by the English novelist Jane Austen, for whom a virtuous man acted in the way that was proper for an English naval officer to behave in the eighteenth century. The case-study attempt to give a definitive and immutable description of how one should behave virtuously turns out to be unsuccessful, because ethical requirements formulated in different eras and contexts prove to be different.

For someone trained in the moral theology of Aquinas, this is not so surprising a discovery. Man's spiritual faculties are capable of grasping what the verum bonum will be in a particular situation, but this verum bonum will always be marked by ideas that are typical for a given society and will depend on the situation and circumstances that are changeable by nature. And there is nothing surprising about this. The Word of God and the teachings of the Church will refine ethical sensitivity, freeing it from selfishness, from hidden motivations that are not fully realized, and from social oversimplifications, but grasping and persisting in the verum bonum will always be a personal work. Also, some people will be more sensitive to some issues while others will be more sensitive to different ones. Certain issues will receive more attention in one country or era, while something else will receive more attention in another era or country.

The fact that, over the course of history, there have been different notions of what passes for virtuous conduct points to the contextualization of virtues. Of course, the basic values and commandments are immutable, but what is considered serious sin and what is easily downplayed depends on social opinion. Years back, the Polish statesman Roman Dmowski pointed out that, in Protestantism, small sins cause outrage while a blind eye is turned to crimes, whereas in Catholicism, the opposite is true.[175] In American thinking, where the influence of Protestant Puritanism has infiltrated Catholic society, there is more emphasis placed on private morality than on public morality. When President Bill Clinton lied about his affair, the American public was outraged, both by the fact that he had committed sexual sins and even more by the fact that he had lied about them. The president was almost impeached and removed from office. When President George W. Bush explicitly spoke out against abortion, which essentially is a matter of private morality, he garnered massive public support. In contrast, the fact that he lied about Iraq's alleged weapons of mass destruction in order to justify the invasion of that country did not bother many people, and Bush was reelected president, even though at least a hundred thousand people died as a result of the invasion and the ensuing chaos.

In Europe, ethical sensibilities are different. Moving on to smaller matters, which are also indicative of a personal ethos, cheating on exams is acceptable in Poland, whereas it is absolutely unacceptable in Anglo-Saxon countries. In Anglo-Saxon countries, sexual abuse, especially committed by the clergy, causes outrage, but even more outrage is caused by the covering up of such matters by their superiors. In Latin countries, if such cases occur, they are not discussed because honor and covering up the cases are prized more highly than a fair and honest resolution of the matter.

The respect that Aquinas has for personal spiritual faculties when they undertake virtuous action turns out to be especially noteworthy when the ethos proposed by Aquinas is compared with Muslim ethics. The social influence on the action of the reason and the will constitutes the context in which man creatively undertakes virtuous action, but in Aquinas's understanding

---

[175] I heard this from my father, who knew Dmowski personally.

of the virtues, it is not the decisive factor. The capacity to grasp truth for its own sake by an independent individual is the measure of ethical maturity. A virtuous person is sometimes able to resist social pressure heroically because he perceives the verum bonum with the clarity of a cultivated conscience and he stands for it. In Muslim ethics, the education of the spiritual faculties so that they can advocate a given course of action on their own authority is much weaker than in Christian ethics. The personal education of the conscience and the cultivation of the virtues do not play a significant role in Islam. There are no autobiographies in Islamic literature. Also, there is little theology in Islamic religious thought. It primarily consists in the application of the law derived from the Quran.

In Christianity, we believe that the Word of God became flesh, whereas the text of the Scriptures is secondary in respect to the Person of Christ. Therefore, Christianity allows biblical exegesis and thinking within the Faith. In Islam, the word of God has become the Quran. Thus, there is no question of being able to undertake a literary critique of the Quran; there is no room for independent theological thinking and for nurturing personal moral invention. At the center of Muslim morality is what religious observances are in Christian religious life. Externally imposed rules regarding dress, food, and all behavior are the central axis of the Muslim moral education. Since the inner life is uneducated, the only defense against evil is external pressure. In order for a man to be free from sexual temptations and view a woman as a person and not as an object of desire, she must be covered from head to toe. In order for thieves not to steal, they must know that they risk having their hand amputated as a punishment. Such an externally imposed vision of conduct leaves no room for creative individual moral responsibility. It is primarily collective. As a result, it gives rise to a narrow-minded personality, incapable of taking an independent broader view. This is why it is so difficult for someone to break out of this armor. Everything is decided by the social model of behavior, with the tight repression of one's own dynamism and invention, and this results in a focus on sexuality and produces anger when a block is removed from the hermetically constructed facade. Islam today is faced with the difficult challenge of adapting to the modern world, and it is defenseless in this dilemma because it lacks a personalistic anthropology and ethics that would respect self-reliance, personal invention, and the dignity of a person's own discernment of the verum bonum. The lack of personalism also explains the inability of Muslim civilization to embrace democracy.

It is important, therefore, for the social climate to foster an independent formation of personal virtues and for the maturity of individuals to be valued. A common characteristic of all dictatorships is the negation of individual self-reliance. A crowd that is passive, intimidated, and incapable of responding personally to values can be manipulated more easily, but ultimately human energy is wasted and social stagnation ensues. Independence in thinking, creativity in personal responsibility, and resourcefulness in economic, social, and political life ultimately benefit everyone. The collapse of communism began where Catholic and Protestant personalism prevailed (and where food production was fragmented). When minds and free choice are paralyzed, social change comes about more slowly. But if the social climate carries no values, it will not contribute to the development of personal virtues. When tolerance changes into ethical nihilism that denies the possibility of knowing the basic truths about the human person, it results in helplessness and in succumbing to the manipulative influence of others. In such a climate, some fall into hedonism, culminating in despair, while others seek security in sects or in Islam, which offer solutions that may be bizarre but are simple and absolve people from thinking.

That is why the processes of liberal neoconservative capitalism, in which everything is beginning to be decided solely by market criteria, have to be watched with concern. When schools and universities, film production, museums, health care, and educational institutions are measured only by purely economic criteria, the ethos of social and professional groups that used to transmit values and defend the capacity for virtuous creativity in the name of a personally recognized verum bonum, and not just for the sake of multiplying capital, is lost along the way. The reduction of human beings to only two functions, to making money and spending it quickly, results in a psychic hollowness in which there is no room or will for the gift of self.

The classic catalog of virtues that Aquinas offered is by no means exhaustive. Aquinas knew Greek terms for virtues that "evaporated" somewhere over time, and they never had a Latin version (e.g., the virtues of *eubulia, synesis, gnome*, and *eutrapelia*).[176] Today, new terms are being coined to express modern moral sensibilities that were unknown to medieval aretaics. We speak now of *solidarity, tolerance, openness, reliability, simplicity,* and *free generosity.* New ethical terms are emerging, such as *transparency* — that is, reliability in providing information (e.g., regarding finances); *inclusiveness*, which is openness to people who are different and is the opposite of an exclusive attitude; *ecological respect* for nature's riches; or *homeliness* — that is, creating an atmosphere of a welcoming domesticity. Not all of these new sensibilities are a mere sign of fashionable and fleeting or ideologized political correctness. These terms echo a real sense of moral responsibility. The emergence of these new ethical sensibilities should not come as a surprise, even though we do not know how to locate them accurately within the psyche in the manner of Aquinas's classification of virtues. Like the classical virtues, this new aretaics needs to be supported by trust in the cognitive faculties of the mind. If these new virtues are accompanied by a postmodern epistemological nihilism that denies the possibility of knowing human nature, its finality, and man's spiritual and corporeal structure, and if they lack reference to dogmas (consciously or unconsciously embraced), then very soon these new, groundless, semi-religious expressions of ethical sensibility will "evaporate" like a temporary intellectual fad or like empty, meaningless platitudes. Where philosophical and theological certitudes are missing, the new aretaics will devolve into political or cultural manipulation or will stop at the level of an insignificant subjective description of impressions.[177] Tolerance combined with intellectual skepticism and nihilism means an escape from taking a stand, rather than a conscious openness to cognitive intuitions coming from a previously unknown direction. For ethical sensitivities to remain, it is necessary that

---

[176] *Eubulia* empowers one to follow advice properly and to apply the right means to action; *synesis* means having a good sense of what is to be done according to the law; *gnome* means the ability to see situations in which an exception to the law must be made; *eutrapelia* means the virtue of having good fun.

[177] St. John Paul II, *Fides et ratio* 83: "A theology without a metaphysical horizon could not move beyond an analysis of religious experience, nor would it allow the *intellectus fidei* to give a coherent account of the universal and transcendent value of revealed truth."

carriers of values — that is, people who live according to these values and defend them — be present in society. Likewise, if the new ethical sensibilities are not accompanied by belief in the power of grace and initiation into its application to life, then very soon these new terms, spoken in an obligatory tone so as to denounce evil, will sink to the level of intolerable contextual moralizing and will generate boredom.

A growing receptivity to the guidance of the Holy Spirit

Understanding virtue in a Kantian way as the conformity of the will to obligation led to a frustrating self-centeredness and the separation of normative ethics from dogmatics. The erroneous claim that the acquisition of moral virtues is a prerequisite for receiving grace led to the marginalization of the spiritual life and eventually to discouragement with the idea of virtue. Biblical teaching and ancient synods that rejected the heresy of semi-Pelagianism speak of something different. The supernatural life is a gift, freely given by God. One enters into communion with God through the theological virtues, which are received rather than earned through one's own efforts. A personal contribution is needed only to sustain the received gift, to apply it to life, but there is no transition from disbelief to faith as a result of natural effort. A dead person cannot resurrect himself. He can only receive the gift of supernatural life from God. This life confers inner freedom and generates the ability creatively to undertake the good, which is accomplished easily, quickly, and with delight. Aquinas, when he studied sorrow and acedia, saw sin in the lack of joy in the fact of being saved. Practicing the virtues produces joy.

Since the Holy Spirit does not wait for the moment of our moral perfection to guide us, attention should be directed to Jesus and the promptings of His Spirit. If we allow the Holy Spirit to guide us according to His schedule, charity will grow, and over time, we will overcome weakness. And in the process, the awareness of being a child in God's hands will grow. "All who are led by the Spirit of God are sons of God" (Rom. 8:14). Jesus is not looking for our perfection; He expects our trust and our love. A cultivated attitude of being a child of God allows us to trust in His power. St. Thérèse of Lisieux explains that there is no need "to be discouraged by one's faults, because children often fall, but they are too small to do themselves much harm."[178] In the examination of conscience, it is not so much a case of weeping over sins but of using the experience of one's limitations to deepen one's trust in divine mercy and to invite God's grace into those particular wounds that need healing. This is also what is to take place in the reception of the Sacrament of Reconciliation. An examination of conscience makes sense only if it is not just a depressing self-analysis but a springboard that launches one into the embrace of divine mercy. We need to view our own sinfulness from the perspective of the divine heart and not merely from that of our own wounded soul or psyche, let alone from the perspective of a broken order that would require readjustment. God is a Father, and precisely because He is the Father, we need not fear His justice. A trustful faith in God's presence in one's own soul provides light that shapes the spiritual intuition, sharpens the perception, and allows one to view oneself and others from the perspective of divine mercy. The greater the gift, the more fragile and delicate it is. The gift of grace is the greatest gift, and that is why it seems to be so fleeting and elusive. It therefore requires special care.

What is crucial is trust in God and striving to surrender to Him completely. He Himself will take care of the rest. God is not looking for immediate results. Measuring effectiveness belongs to economics or technology. In the spiritual life, the fecundity of grace is more important. It will reveal itself in a life of trustful communion with God and total giving of oneself to Him. A wonderful text by St. Thérèse of Lisieux gives us a description of growing in infused virtues. Thérèse said this to a disheartened novice:

> You make me think of a little child that is learning to stand but does not yet know how to walk. In his desire to reach the top of the stairs to find his mother, he lifts his little foot to climb the first step. It is all in vain, and at each renewed effort he falls. Well, be like that little child. Always keep lifting up your foot to climb the ladder of holiness, and do not imagine that you can mount even the first step. All

---

[178] Yellow Notebook, CJ August 6, 1897, no. 8, Archives du Carmel de Lisieux, https://archives.carmeldelisieux.fr/en/archive/cj-aout-1897/#le-6-aout.

God asks of you is good will. From the top of the ladder He looks lovingly upon you, and soon, touched by your fruitless efforts, He will Himself come down, and, taking you in His arms, will carry you to His kingdom never again to leave Him.[179]

Spiritual and moral growth is based, therefore, on two fundamental dispositions that need to be simultaneous: total reliance on God in trust and receptivity to the stirrings of the Holy Spirit — that is, responding generously to His gentle whispers. God expects signs of our love, offered daily in small, ordinary things. Overcoming a moment of laziness, doing work for God's sake as an added motivation, responding to a recognized situation that requires our prompt and authentic response — these are ways through which signals of love are communicated to God. Each of these in themselves seems as simple as the lifting of a leg by the child. Grace is to be lived out immediately. It cannot be stockpiled. Spiritual and moral reserves cannot be accumulated. But the way of faithfulness to the merciful God is not simple or painless. A true responsiveness to God requires authenticity and integrity in every moment. Trustful reliance on Him is to be tied with the gift of self, offered out of love, and this sometimes requires renunciation. It is not so much the renunciation itself that matters, but the good that one undertakes out of love for God, but *all of which*, as St. Thérèse specifies, *is done in peace*. The attention of a virtuous man is directed to people, to their needs, and not to himself and his growth in virtue. A virtuous man is not concerned with himself. He remembers others and serves them and does not spend time analyzing his own state. Was Mary conscious of her grace and holiness? Probably not, because her gaze was simple, focused on God.

Blessed are those ...

Having discussed the operation of grace in man through the gifts of the Holy Spirit and virtues that transform the personality, finally it is possible to return to the starting point, which is the desire for happiness. Jesus addresses this

---

[179] Quoted in P. Marie-Eugène, O.C.D., *I Am a Daughter of the Church: A Practical Synthesis of Carmelite Spirituality*, vol. 2 (Chicago: Fides, 1955), 406.

desire in the Sermon on the Mount, in which He offers us the Beatitudes. In a life of practical faith, in which there is a generous self-giving, God responds by bestowing His happiness. Jesus says, "It is more blessed to give than to receive" (Acts 20:35). He is speaking about Himself, about the happiness of the Blessed Trinity, which finds joy when it can give itself because it encounters a soul receptive to the divine gift. But He is also speaking about us, because the gift of self, generously given, based on prior trust, bestows an inner spiritual joy. Even a small child may experience this joy that comes from a freely given generosity.

Theological reflection, in an attempt to name the different elements of divine fecundity in human action, while distinguishing the virtues and the gifts of the Holy Spirit, ponders also the Beatitudes mentioned by Jesus. Are they yet another kind of habitus, shaping the personality — different from the virtues and gifts? St. Albert the Great and St. Bonaventure both thought so. Or maybe the Beatitudes are an extra precept, expressing an additional religious duty under the guise of eudaemonistic language? The encyclical *Veritatis splendor* seems to recognize their normative aspect, although admittedly in a subtle way:

> The Beatitudes are not specifically concerned with certain particular rules of behavior. Rather, they speak of basic attitudes and dispositions in life and therefore they do not coincide exactly with the commandments. On the other hand, there is no separation or opposition between the Beatitudes and the commandments: both refer to the good, to eternal life. The Sermon on the Mount begins with the proclamation of the Beatitudes, but also refers to the commandments (cf. Mt 5:20–48). At the same time, the Sermon on the Mount demonstrates the openness of the commandments and their orientation towards the horizon of the perfection proper to the Beatitudes. These latter are above all promises, from which there also indirectly flow normative indications for the moral life. In their originality and profundity they are a sort of self-portrait of Christ, and for this very reason are invitations to discipleship and to communion of life with Christ. (16)

The perspective outlined in the Beatitudes is captivating, and as such, it obliges, but it is only their beauty that attracts and so is binding.

Aquinas held that it is not necessary to multiply the kinds of habitus that God produces in us by grace. The infused virtues and the gifts of the Holy Spirit that stimulate them are sufficient to describe the dynamics of the divine presence within human action. The Beatitudes, like the fruits of the Holy Spirit listed by St. Paul, are acts arising from grace (Gal. 5:22–23). Actually, there is no significant difference between the joy-giving fruits and the Beatitudes, except that the Beatitudes describe more perfect acts, bestowing eternal beatitude. All the Beatitudes are fruits, but not all fruits of the Holy Spirit are characterized by the fact that they bestow spiritual happiness. There is a profound truth in this insight. Happiness comes through action. Sometimes it seems to us that eternal life in Heaven will be soporific, that Martha had to elbow the dreamy Lazarus, who had returned from the other world. The prayer "Eternal rest grant unto them, O Lord!" — which, incidentally, is based only on apocrypha and not on any biblical text — does not capture eternal bliss accurately. We do not go to Heaven in order to rest after the hardships of life but in order to love more. Those who live by charity here on earth already have one foot in Heaven because charity is the only reality of Heaven that we can savor while we are here on earth. Saints are not sluggish dreamers but people of action. The Beatitudes mentioned in the Sermon on the Mount are actions that flow from the stirrings of grace, and, as such, they bestow happiness. Those who do good purely out of love for God experience happiness. This happiness is not the first goal of action. It is a side effect of an action that has its primary object, undertaken for the sake of God, Who is beloved.

We have a wonderful text by St. Augustine, which can be found in the retreat on the Sermon on the Mount he preached in his youth. In short sentences, St. Augustine compiles the seven Beatitudes (the eighth is a repetition of the others), seven gifts of the Holy Spirit, and seven petitions from the Lord's Prayer. The text is intelligible only if it is read in faith, silently expressing the petitions contained in the Our Father, and if the gifts of the Holy Spirit are not substituted by the notion of virtue (whether taken as a psychic quality or, even worse, understood as an expression of obligation).

The gifts of the Holy Spirit have to be understood as "spiritual antennae" that open to the direct stirrings of God.

> For if it is the fear of God through which the poor in spirit are blessed,... let us ask that the name of God may be hallowed among men through that "fear which is clean, enduring for ever."
>
> If it is piety through which the meek are blessed,... let us ask that His kingdom may come,... that we may become meek, and not resist Him.
>
> If it is knowledge through which those who mourn are blessed,... let us pray that His will may be done ... because ... then we shall not mourn.
>
> If it is fortitude through which those are blessed who hunger and thirst after righteousness,... let us pray that our daily bread may be given to us today.
>
> If it is counsel through which the merciful are blessed,... let us forgive their debts to our debtors, and let us pray that ours may be forgiven to us.
>
> If it is understanding through which the pure in heart are blessed,... let us pray not to be led into temptation, lest we should have a double heart,... pursuing things temporal and earthly.
>
> If it is wisdom through which the peacemakers are blessed, inasmuch as they shall be called the children of God; let us pray that we may be freed from evil, for that very freedom will make us free, i.e., sons of God.[180]

---

[180] *De Serm. Dom. in Monte*, bk. 2, chap. 11, PL 34, 1285. Cf. St. Thomas Aquinas, *ST*, IIa-IIae, q. 83, art. 9, ad 3.

10

Tire Valve, Template, or Yeast?[181]

I DO NOT REMEMBER ANY MORE SINS, I am sorry for all my sins, and I firmly intend to sin no more.
Are you sure that you will sin no more?
I cannot be sure, but I really want to change my life. I can no longer live like that; I have to change, and I promise that I will amend my life.

Many times the confessional lattice bars have heard such fervent assurances, undoubtedly spoken sincerely and with conviction, stemming from the hope that things will finally change this time. One does not have to be a seasoned expert on souls to know how often these assurances end in frustration. For what could be a more hopeless matter than trying to achieve moral perfection by the power of one's own efforts? Even when the intention to amend one's life, spoken with such emphasis, is made while kneeling before a priest, it remains ineffective if it stems from a pagan perspective. A sacrament that, in the psychological perception of the penitent, is limited to a thorough examination of conscience and a firm resolve to amend one's life has little effect. For the sacrament to be fruitful, reconciliation has to take place, an encounter of human wretchedness with a merciful, forgiving, and giving God. The Sacrament of Reconciliation, first and foremost, is like a dialogue — an encounter between two persons — the divine and the human.

---

[181] This chapter was originally published in the Polish monthly *W drodze* 175–176, nos. 3–4 (1988): 88–89.

Our mass practice of auricular confession is overshadowed by the thorn of the heresy of Pelagianism. And that is why these confessions are so often barren. There is in them no encounter or trust in God; instead, there is a continuous reliance on oneself and one's own perfection.

For some, religion is reduced to avoiding sins, to living in keeping with the commandments; consequently, the most important thing is to know exactly what is allowed and what is not. In such a perspective, one must basically know the law, know how to follow it, apply the general prohibitions and precepts of the Decalogue to specific situations, and then mobilize the will to protect effectively against sin. The shrewder a person, the better he will know how to interpret the law, so that compliance with the rules is preserved, and at the same time there is room for freedom. We know the famous questions in the series: "Is it a sin to . . . ?" — indicating a sincere desire to avoid sin and a lack of interest in the positive development of the divine leaven.

Others ask themselves a deeper question. For them, religion is not a negative avoidance of evil. They want a positive perspective. They know that virtues need to be cultivated. Hence, they seek to force themselves to exercise gentleness, kindness, patience, and purity. They are convinced that, in order to attain sanctity, all one needs to do is to develop perfection — that is, cultivate moral virtues that are supposed to guarantee holiness.

Both of these options, which have behind them the authority of traditional manuals of moral theology with which clergy used to be educated (Noldin, Prümmer), lose sight of that which is fundamental somewhere along the way. The personal relationship with God and entering the current of His life are lost in them. They assume that virtue is a necessary ornament allowing one to approach God. Meanwhile, the Gospel shows us the first canonized person, in whom the eminent cardinals of the Congregation for the Causes of Saints would not have found a single heroic virtue. He was hanging on a cross and convinced that his suffering was only a prelude to even harsher punishments that awaited him on the other side. He had nothing to offer God while his worthless life was trickling away. Even Christ's radical exhortation "Sell all that you have and . . . come, follow me" (Luke 18:22) no longer made sense to the dying thief. In the final humiliation of the criminal, the unexpected encounter with Christ on the Cross turned out to be fruitful.

The recognized depth of wretchedness became the proper disposition for invoking and receiving the depths of mercy.

The awareness of our weakness opens us to Him Who is the source of sanctity. This is the meaning of the penitential act at the beginning of the Mass. It is not clear why the call to apologize to God, along with the suggestion that, through this apology, we become worthy to participate in the Holy Sacrifice, have slipped into the Polish liturgical texts. Supposedly it is sufficient to say that we are sorry, and then we become worthy! Can we ever be worthy — so perfect that God is owed to us? Neither the Confiteor of the Tridentine liturgy nor the current Latin text has such overtones. The *Ordo Missae* says something different. Let us recognize our sinfulness — *agnoscámus peccáta nostra*, so that we may be properly disposed to celebrate the sacred mysteries — *ut apti simus ad sacra mystéria celebránda*. Realizing our own sinfulness is the right disposition for the celebration of divine love. It is not a matter of forcing perfection or endowing ourselves with dignity but of recognizing the hunger for grace so as to immerse in it all the more eagerly. The penitential act is only a prelude to the Mass, and then sins have to be forgotten in order to savor God's goodness. The liturgy will remind us again of sin and of our radical lack of dignity when we receive Holy Communion, to show us the One Who takes away our sin and Whose blood is shed for the remission of sins.

The religious life of many Christians is burdened by an overly materialistic demand for the formation of moral virtues. Virtue is traditionally understood as a lasting disposition that channels the psychic forces, so that one may act well, easily, quickly, and with pleasure. Virtue is not a passive custom or a mindless, mechanical habit. In a virtuous act, reason is at work establishing the proper measure of the act. Fr. Jacek Woroniecki gives the example of a man who, as part of his job, has to take money to the bank. If, during the whole way to the bank, he keeps thinking about whether to steal the money, he is not yet an honest man; and this is true even if he ends up not stealing the money. An honest man is one who never thinks of stealing. The former has a more difficult path: he has to confront an inner temptation, but he has not yet acquired virtue — because, for him, a virtuous life does not come about either easily, quickly, or with pleasure.

This traditional understanding of virtue as a spiritual and moral improvement meets today with much reluctance. Max Scheler wrote that he associated virtue with "an old, toothless, and grouchy aunt." For many, reflection on virtue is redolent of perfectionism. It suggests that one should cultivate one's spiritual garden and submit to moralizing because this is a prerequisite for all religious life. Such a feeling has its historical justification. The transfer of the treatise on grace from the domain of moral theology to dogmatic theology, which took place in seminary teaching during the post-Tridentine period, crippled Catholic moral reflection. From a consideration of the way one may participate in the divine life, moral theology became ethics, the study of the commandments, obligations and edifying role models, and the analysis of case studies. Instead of being presented as a manifestation of God's action in the moral life, virtue became a noble but essentially difficult and dull theoretical model of conduct. Theology continued to distinguish between the acquired virtue, worked out by human effort, and the infused virtue, bestowed by grace, but this distinction was discussed only within the framework of general moral theology. In the more detailed consideration of morality, the infused virtue was forgotten. Cooperation with grace was replaced by practical Pelagianism. Thus, Scheler's aversion to virtue conceived in this way is understandable.

Incidentally, Scheler was not the only one who could not come to terms with such an understanding of moral virtue. St. Thérèse of Lisieux said of herself: *Je n'ai pas de vertus!*[182] "I have no virtues!" When the whole spiritual climate of nineteenth-century France seemed to cry out that a young nun should practice the virtues, Thérèse rejected such requirements. With childlike confidence, she preferred to immerse herself in God's love, building a personal relationship with Jesus and believing that He, in an excess of grace, will compensate for her deficiencies.

An all-too-human understanding of virtue results from the overemphasis on the firm purpose of amendment in the existential experience of the Sacrament of Reconciliation in many of the faithful. The penitent mentioned at the beginning is not looking for God; he is striving only to amend his life

---

[182] Poem 53.

by his own effort, forcing the construction of the edifice of his virtue. He considers that this is what religion obligates him to do. When he lacks strong willpower, supported by emotional fervor, he does not feel worthy to receive absolution. He cannot — like St. Peter — believe that Christ enters our filth and helplessness so as to freely wash our feet.

The term *virtue* should not disappear from our religious language, as it is disappearing from our pulpits. In rehabilitating the concept of virtue, it has to be cleansed of foreign, non-Christian impurities. I suggest the consideration of three models of virtue that function in our religious perception. A calm and infrequent reflection about virtue is one thing, and an automatic, thoughtless reflex, generated by subconsciousness, emotional inhibitions or upbringing, is another.

The first model is virtue conceived as a tire valve that is lodged in the inner tube of a bicycle and does not allow the air to escape. Virtue considered in this way is meant to extinguish the movements of the emotions, keep them in check, and prevent them from directing themselves to their object. This model stems from a distrust of the emotions. At its core lies a judgment, most often an emotional one, that the feelings are dangerous, and it is better to repress them within oneself. There are different ways the emotions may be denied. Their analysis falls more within the domain of psychiatry than moral theology. When a neurotic feels the movement of certain emotions, immediately an instinctive, sensory, negative evaluation of the stirring is triggered. So instantly, with the help of another emotion, he strives to extinguish the unwanted emotion. When the smothering emotion is fear, this gives rise to scrupulosity. The scrupulous person panics about the emotions and deems any stirring of them sinful. His sole defense is in the fear, which is the only thing he trusts.

In another type of neurotic reaction, a resolute person attempts to eradicate the undesirable emotion through his own energy, by force. This generates a rigid, closed, inhumane attitude. This may then be described in the language of psychiatry as energy neurosis or as Pelagianism in the language of theology. Fundamentally it is the conviction that man can work out perfection in himself by his own energy — precluding the freedom afforded by relying on grace. This invariably amounts to a certain hubris and the development not of true virtue but of a rigid, laboriously achieved mask. Chesterton was right when he wrote that a madman is not one who has lost his reason. A madman is one who has retained his reason but lost everything else. If reason will not be supported by the wealth of the emotions, it will itself begin to malfunction.

Moral virtue in the traditional view of St. Thomas Aquinas is not a tire valve; it is a gentle cooperation of the reason and the will with the emotions, and, in the case of justice and charity, virtue resides in the will. Reason recognizes the fundamental goodness of the emotions and directs them. Virtue is capable of using the energy of the emotions. Not all of theological tradition agrees with this view. According to some theologians, virtue is found only in the reason and the will. St. Bonaventure could not comprehend that fortitude and temperance have their subject, or seat, in the emotions. He held that the task of these virtues consisted in harnessing the emotions. But such a position is, in fact, a baptized stoicism, which appears in many authors of devotional books. Aquinas approached human corporeality with much greater confidence. In his view, moral virtue takes place within the stirrings of the emotions. A synchronization of the rational and corporeal levels is both possible and necessary. Reason accepts the good of the emotional stirring and determines how it is to be expressed externally, given the proper good of the object. When the sight a beautiful woman gives rise to a pleasurable sensation, it is, for the time being, a premoral ground for an act of virtue or sin, or no act at all. The mere fact of experiencing pleasure is not an evil. So reason in the act of virtue, considering the objective order of things, determines what is truly good for this woman and for me and determines how to direct the emotion. Only those desires that exceed the measure set by mature reason and to which the will voluntarily assents, as well as those that do not adhere to that measure, are harmful. So, considering the concrete, actual good, true virtue allows the emotions to come into play. The value of emotions in virtue consists in the fact that they provide a momentum that is directed to a concrete good. Christ, under the inspiration of piety, taking into account the real good, which is respect for the temple, used all the riches of His emotional reaction, took a whip in His hand, and overturned tables and seats, most likely raising His voice in the process. He was angry, but in a virtuous and not in a sinful way. Emotions participate in virtue not by being subjected to frustrating precepts but by expressing themselves in harmony with the virtue, as, following the guidance of reason, they move toward their proper objects. The full development of personality, and so also the blossoming of sanctity, requires that we use emotions within the virtues. And this is not only because an element of the personality should not be repressed but also because the will, if it is not supported by the momentum of emotions, will never achieve its goal. It will remain cold, slow, and dispirited.

I remember a conversation about charity that I had with a young nun. Everything was prompting her to love, to serve God. But at the same time, she felt repressed and apprehensive because — as she said — she was constantly reminded that love is dangerous, it may knock you over, so it is better not to risk loving. I had to explain to her that religious life without charity is meaningless. The living out of the evangelical counsels is worthwhile only if it develops charity. We need to trust our ability to love, just as we trust other capacities. The emotional apparatus of love has to be functional. Love requires the using of one's whole self. Only when it embraces the whole wealth of our being does it beget happiness.

Trusting Christ and relying on His power liberates charity from constraining fears. "Bring me out of prison" (Ps. 142:7), we cry out to Christ, because He wants us to have life and have it to the full (John 10:10). A person who distrusts his emotions has an incomplete, mutilated life. To open ourselves to this full, flourishing life, we need to believe that our sins are truly forgiven, that we can trust the fundamental goodness of our own nature. But this sometimes can come with great difficulty, because although we believe that God has forgiven us, we do not want to forgive ourselves. Sin can be so frightening that it holds us captive. Fear of repeating it prevents the emotions from blossoming and love from growing. It prompts to repress the emotions with the tire valve of a quasi-virtue.

The woman in the Pharisee's house sensed Christ's forgiveness even before He said, "Your sins are forgiven." Jesus' heartfelt kindness convinced her that there was plenty of goodness in her, shattered her disgust with herself, and allowed her to trust herself. Since she discovered such great value in herself that Christ loved her, she herself showed great love (Luke 7:47).

Virtue, therefore, should not be equated with a tire valve that prevents unexpected outbursts of emotions. Emotions, by their very nature, reach out into the unknown, and they do so by the will of their Creator. Virtue does not merely perform a negative function with respect to the emotions. It affirms their essential goodness and drives them like a good superior who enjoys the initiative of his subordinates, giving them general guidance. He allows them to show initiative, even if the subordinates sometimes do things that he does not anticipate, or even if they do something wrong. A mistake that has been committed is by no means a rationale for taking away the right to independent, private initiative. True virtue does not enslave the emotions in an atmosphere of blind obedience.

A virtuous man may have true joy because he is guided by reason, which affirms the value of emotions. When, by reason, he decides to watch a game on TV, he does not wonder all the time whether he should not get up and do something else. He does not allow remorse over time wasted to take away the pleasure of watching the game. He does not regard entertainment as a waste of time, and therefore enjoys mental relaxation to the full. The conscience, formed by the virtues, does not tolerate an unwarranted feeling of guilt. It provides a healthy self-confidence and triggers an appetite for life.

An emotional reaction is always unique and new because it is singular and directed to the concrete. Virtue that uses an emotion is not therefore a template, not a single pattern of behavior, always reproduced in the same way. God does not want us all to act in an identical way. He has an individualized measure for each one of us. In doing so, He does not indicate His will for every circumstance. God's law is external. By excluding specific evil acts, it shows a general direction. Only the law of the Spirit is individualized. The virtues described in manuals of theology present the framework of goodness inherent in specific spiritual and psychic faculties only in a general way, whereas each individual has to determine the course of his actions on his own in a creative way. In the operation of virtue, one needs to use reason and reflect on how to act. Thus, there are no unconscious acts of virtue. The act of virtue is always an original reiteration of God's creative work. Every individual has some personal talents or abilities that may serve others. Virtue uses them in innovative ways. It profits from the entire wealth of the personality. Therefore, in considering the cultivation of virtues, one should not start by thinking about vices and ways to combat them. For the growth of the virtues, one should also do a positive examination of conscience, analogous to the traditional one. One should ask: What are my pros? What good can I do? What talents do I have? When was the last time I used them for the good of others? Sometimes it is easier to identify our cons than our pros. We can immediately answer the question "What are my flaws?," listing a whole litany of our shortcomings. There will be no mature moral life in us unless we can answer a similar question: What gifts has nature bestowed on me? And to what extent am I using them?

These questions are much more pressing on strictly Christian grounds. The order of grace elevates us to the level of the supernatural. The judgment of reason in the act of Christian virtue is subject to additional impulses flowing from charity implanted in the depths of the soul by God, Who dwells there. Therefore, the Christian asks himself further questions: What is a concrete way to communicate the charity that I have received? To what extent do I, through my actions, enable the Mystical Body of Christ, His love, and His Church to reach this place where I am now? Since Christ has placed the distribution of grace in human hands, to what extent am I consciously participating in the common priesthood, handing out the gift that I have freely received? Christian virtue is more than mere efficiency in acting according to reason in the moral realm. Divine power and charity are channeled through free, rational human decisions, and bearers are needed to carry this love wherever it is needed most. This divine pleading for the help of human hands and hearts is gentle, yet persistent. Christ is standing at the door, knocking (Rev. 3:20). Moreover, divine love is not a dead weight to be carried; it shapes and transforms the carrier. The Lord does not want bearers of His charity made out of marble; He seeks living hearts that find their joy and happiness in giving what they have received.

The twentieth-century reading of St. Thomas Aquinas's *Summa theologiae* casts a shadow over the popular interpretation of the role of virtues in the moral life. This classic work gives the most complete description of the virtues, encapsulated in a coherent, logical system. Aquinas discusses approximately fifty virtues grouped around the three theological virtues (faith, hope, and charity) and the four cardinal virtues (prudence, justice, fortitude, and temperance). Studying each of the virtues one by one, he also discusses their opposite vices. Everything is framed by a consistent methodology, and the whole is grounded in philosophical anthropology. Aquinas's depiction of the moral life forms an impressive edifice, certainly towering in optimism over the negative moral synthesis compiled on the basis of the Ten Commandments and the precepts of the Church. Numerous twentieth-century investigators of the thought of Aquinas claimed that his intention was to gather the whole moral content of Christianity and frame it within the scientific conceptual apparatus provided by the newly discovered Aristotle. According to this view, the entire moral section of the *Summa theologiae* is, in fact, a philosophical work that seeks to reconcile the evangelical message of faith with rational, philosophical knowledge. Christ's moral teachings are thus jammed into a rigorous philosophical framework, taken from Aristotle, which delights with its logical, scientific order. With such a reading of the *Summa*, there is not much difference between a specifically Christian and a pagan moral virtue. Both are habits of good action that are to be worked out within oneself.

In the last decades of the twentieth century, readers of Aquinas (Jean-Pierre Torrell, Servais Pinckaers, Albert Patfoort, Gilles Emery, Dalmazio Mongillo) saw in him primarily a theologian who pondered the Word of God and a continuator of the perspective of the Church Fathers, and not just a philosopher enamored of Aristotle. The theological perspective sensitive to the role of grace in life allowed for a fresh reading of Aquinas's moral theology. The Italian theologian Giuseppe Abbà made a detailed comparison of the *Summa theologiae* with the earlier works of Aquinas.[183] He demonstrated significant differences and an evolution of his thought, which allows for a fully theological interpretation of the *Summa*.

Throughout his work, Aquinas constantly poses one question: Who is God? He seeks to learn more about God. He uses the conceptual and methodological apparatus of the time, enriched by Aristotle, but he does

---

[183] *Lex et virtus: Studi sull'evoluzione della dottrina morale di san Tommaso d'Aquino* (Rome: LAS, 1983).

not lose sight of the question, which is a theological question per se. He therefore derives the answer to this question from revelation. Philosophy remains the handmaiden of theology, and theology the handmaiden of faith. Theological reflection is to serve the faith, to bolster it, never to replace it. In part I, Aquinas answers the basic question by looking at God as the Creator. In part III, he shows God as the Savior, the giver of the sacraments. The whole second part, which spans half of the *Summa*, also addresses the question "Who is God?" But the field of observation is the moral life of man. Aquinas wonders how divine action manifests itself in man's moral life. There is a different way of God's being in Himself and in creation that is dependent on the Creator; there is a different way of God's being in man who is sanctified by grace; and there is a different way of God's being in Christ and in the sacraments.

Thus, Aquinas's moral theology reflects upon what new things we can say about God through the observation of the *motus rationalis creaturae in Deum*, the movement of the rational creature toward God. Aquinas observes the *motus* — the movement, and not the *motio* — the moving of man toward God. Man is moved by God, but in such a way that he also moves himself. God treats man as a free cause. He creates meritorious acts in man and endows him with His power in such a way that man voluntarily chooses the good. Only God can move the human will from within while preserving human freedom. When man invites God into his life, God moves him — but He never hurls him. In this perspective, Christian virtue takes on a completely different meaning. It is a manifestation of divine creativity within man. When Aquinas discusses the moral virtues one by one, he thereby presents new aspects of the divinity — he exposes a particular character of God's fecundity — one that is different from the work of creation and different from the work of redemption. The scientific, theological description of this divine fecundity is, of course, general, but it aims to cover the whole range of human situations in which this fecundity manifests itself; thus, it is not a completed edifice. Much may be added — pointing to virtues that Aquinas does not discuss because their observation or formulation is modern. Aquinas does not speak of sincerity or solidarity because these are new concepts. They fit into his scheme, however, since, by all means, they attest to divine fecundity.

Aquinas's answer to the question "Who is God in man's moral activity?" is psychological. One by one, he shows how, through the virtues, divine action reaches all the nooks and crannies of the human psyche in all theoretically conceivable situations.

One could also pose an existential question, describing specific instances of divine goodness that have been observed in life. This would not be a scientific, theological reflection, but it would also speak of God. Has it not happened to us that, seeing the good deeds of our neighbors, we praised not our neighbors but our Heavenly Father?

This new perspective that St. Thomas Aquinas employed when he was writing the *Summa theologiae* explains the different treatment of virtue as contrasted with his earlier works. In his *Commentary on the Sentences*, which he wrote as a young man, Aquinas saw virtue as having a negative function. It serves to apply the general moral law to the concrete. The task of virtue is to calm the emotions so that reason may freely read the norm. The same is also true in the *Summa contra gentiles*. God is shown there as the paragon of righteousness Who gives the eternal and universal law. Man has the possibility of free choice and may submit to this law or not. But actually he has no alternative — he is under the regime of the law and is required to make the effort to conform to the exemplary idea that is in the mind of God. In the *Summa theologiae*, Aquinas treats this issue quite differently. Compared with the *Summa contra gentiles*, the law is here dethroned. The written law is only a servant, an aid in the moral life. For Christians, the most important and ultimate norm is the law of the Spirit, the law of love, which is unwritten. It manifests itself in the individual inspirations of the Holy Spirit. In virtue, therefore, reason is not merely a spokesperson of an external law. Between the law and virtue, there is no relationship of command and execution. Virtues are needed not so much for the maintenance of the moral law as for its realization — that is, the effective choosing and, indeed, loving of the highest good, about which the moral law instructs only in a general way. Through virtue, man surpasses the limits of the law and goes beyond its letter. In virtue, reason must make a personal discernment that transcends obedience to the precept. Hence, virtue does not impose a template on us but develops our creativity.

In this context, it is worth noting the change in the psychological climate that took place after the Second Vatican Council or is taking place in religious communities. Old constitutions and religious customs regulated common life down to the smallest detail. It was held that fidelity to God requires blind obedience to the rule and the superiors. In the liturgy, it was held that it was enough to recite all the prescribed prayers — even if hurriedly, without understanding, or not at the proper time. A priest who expected a busy day would recite the entire breviary in the morning, including Evening Prayer and Compline, and felt no remorse, because, after all, he had fulfilled the prescribed obligation. The vow of poverty was sometimes reduced to the necessity of obtaining the *placet* of the superior; when a superior allowed the possession of an item, it was deemed that poverty was not violated. Today — probably rightly so — there is a move away from a legalistic consciousness. Obedience to the law does not seem to be a guarantee of salvation.

Young people entering religious life today are much more sensitive to the love of neighbor, seeking an authentic community life, which they measure more by mutual respect, listening, and caring than by fidelity to monastic practices. They are more concerned that prayer will be deep, enriching, and conducive to contemplation rather than being merely an obligation to be fulfilled. If love of one's neighbor requires that some prescribed prayer be dropped, they have no difficulty in doing so. Charity is more important. A certain relaxation of the old strict, external customs is creative, but by no means is it easier. It was much easier merely to fulfill the prescribed duty. When you have to think for yourself, to consider what is more important at a given moment, you have to make a choice, and having made that choice, you have to have confidence in the judgment of your conscience. A true virtue is always creative, innovative; it is a marriage with value, and like any successful marriage, it has to be constantly renewed and deepened, seeking new ways to express the cultivated charity. To be authentic and not become just a template, virtue requires courage, a climate of trust, and a protective cloister that does not infantilize but develops independent creativity.

Whoever backs away from a good deed when he hears the objection "This was never done before!" will not acquire virtue. Yielding to such objections restrains magnanimity and prevents growth. One must dare to initiate new actions, even if they are incomprehensible to others.

An independent, courageous virtue observed in one's neighbor notedly points to God. It speaks of divine wisdom in a different way than moral law. It shows God's fecundity and is proof of His action. For God so moves man that he becomes capable of governing himself, of transmitting creatively the divine wisdom that he has received.

That is why neither the tire vent model nor the template model is suitable for virtue; the best model is that of yeast. Virtue is the evangelical leaven; it is movement, not stagnation. The mustard seed grew and became a huge tree. The talent was not to be buried but put into economic circulation. It had to be imbued with an intelligent, independent initiative. St. Augustine says of Christian virtue that it is the order of love planted by God in the soul that manifests itself in every dimension of life. The development of a virtuous life requires, therefore, a climate of freedom, room for initiative, and trust in the emotions, together with a consciously cultivated sensitivity to the inspirations and stirrings of the Holy Spirit.

The primacy in the construction of a righteous moral life belongs to its main author — God, Whose action is worth recognizing. The Church instructs us:

> The fullness of divine gifts is in many ways a consequence of the indwelling of the Holy [Spirit] in the souls of the just.... Among these gifts are those secret warnings and invitations, which from time to time are excited in our minds and hearts by the inspiration of the Holy [Spirit]. Without these there is no beginning of a good life, no progress, no arriving at eternal salvation.[184]

A community most fully deserves to be called Christian when it values these impulses and allows its members to respond to them. This matter was well understood by St. Mother Teresa of Calcutta, who wrote in the constitutions of her Congregation of the Missionaries of Charity:

---

[184] Pope Leo XIII, encyclical *Divinus illud munus* (May 9, 1897), no. 9.

Formation is basically grounded in the Holy Spirit, who invites with power and gentleness, but He leaves in this complete freedom for the response. This freedom has to be respected and developed in each sister.[185]

True Christian virtue could be called the folly of the Holy Spirit, Who conquers the soul step by step, grace by grace. His gentle invitation reaches further than the rich young man, who knew the commandments and knew how to give a calculated response to them but lacked the imagination and courage to follow Christ's call. In the vision of this way of life, room must be made for grace to bring about a transformation in the moral order and unleash a generous creativity in the personal and social life, capable of gratuitous initiatives undertaken without waiting for others, without an attitude of entitlement and a constant complaint addressed to the world, the state, or the Church, and at the same an initiative that is ready, if necessary, for the folly of the Cross. Sanctity is not righteousness, but charity that dazzles the reason and submits it to the light and guidance of the Holy Spirit. The experience of divine love does not at all require the edifice of moral virtues as a necessary foundation. On the contrary, the patient bearing of one's infirmities may accompany graces. Recognizing weakness predisposes one to receive God and sensitizes one to His action. A saint is not one who is perfect in every way but one who recognizes divine inspirations and follows them — and thus walks moved by God. When St. Paul addressed his letters to the saints in Achaia, Ephesus, or Philippi, he was not writing to people who were morally perfect. He was writing to those who, through faith in the living Person of Jesus Christ, allowed themselves to be led by God. The fruits of such divine-human cooperation are the virtues, but they are more likely to be recognized by outsiders. The virtuous man himself experiences the feeling of being only a useless servant, a vehicle for love, which he did not create. He still retains an awareness of his weakness. The interconnectedness of the virtues makes them grow all together, but they are not all equally perfect. Similarly, difficulties arising from the temperament and the psychophysical

---

[185] *Constitution of the Missionaries of Charity*, 189 (my translation).

constitution, different in each individual, remain even when the character is highly formed and spiritualized.

In Christian life, charity is more important than painstakingly acquired moral perfection. The catalogue of virtues is not a program to be worked out one by one, although in ethical formation, of course, it is good to reflect upon them, bearing in mind, however, that ethical knowledge in itself is fruitless. We should not think what useful things we can offer to God. We can add no goodness to God. He does not need our forced kindness or our haughty offerings. He is hungry only for our love, our trusting hearts. He desires to give Himself to us and to bestow grace. And for this, it is enough initially to take advantage of the humiliations that accompany sins. The realization of our weakness and the discovery of our helplessness allow us to throw ourselves into the arms of the merciful One and open the path of contemplation.

A personal relationship with Christ, built on a thirst for grace, is the prerequisite for all moral growth. This living relationship allows us to hear God's gentle plea for our participation in His manifestation of love. Cooperation with grace consists in flexibility, a conscious, creative availability to God, so that our neighbors will recognize in our virtue something of the reality and warmth of charity. Christian "work on oneself" covers two moments: surrender to God and availability toward the One on Whose benevolent influence we are relying. It is more of a flight toward Christ and His Spirit than a perfectionist struggle with oneself.

Traditionally, it is said that three means are viewed as necessary for the growth of virtues: the sacraments, prayer, and meritorious deeds. Through the Sacrament of Baptism, God dwells in the soul; the sacraments that follow restore this divine presence, disrupted by sin. Marriage and priesthood dedicate a person to a specific form of transmitting the received grace. The sacramental life gives virtue an objective, divine foundation. Prayer builds friendship with God, forms intimate trust, and develops a reflex of relying upon God. Through the prayerful attitude, we may hear God's invitations, whereas meritorious deeds are our cooperation with the One we love. They are our deeds but are imbued with the willing, power, and love of God Himself. The surrender to Jesus by the reason is the acceptance, in an act of faith, of the conviction that without Him we can do nothing (John 15:5). Emotional reliance on Him is a psychic prelude to contemplation, a confidence that rises from the depths of carnality and disposes to adoration, granting inner peace. Reliance on Christ in deeds is the using of one's heart, will, initiative, and creativity to give oneself to Him, Who appears imperceptibly, like a small amount of yeast, so as to make out of our lives and our communities a nourishing bread, the Mystical Body, the visible fount of Love in the world.

About the Author

FR. WOJCIECH GIERTYCH is a Polish Dominican, born in 1951 in London. Since 2005, he has been the Theologian of the Papal Household. He is also a consultor in the Dicastery for the Doctrine of the Faith and in the Dicastery for the Causes of Saints. Since 1994, he has been a professor of the Pontifical University of St. Thomas, the Angelicum, in Rome. He lives in the Vatican.